Psychology Revivals

Current Issues in Rational-Emotive Therapy

In his earlier book *Rational-Emotive Therapy: Fundamentals and Innovations* Dr Dryden outlined the central features of Rational-Emotive Therapy (RET) as it had developed in and from the work of Albert Ellis. He then proceeded to discuss innovations within the theory, several of which had been instigated by the author.

Originally published in 1987, this book builds upon these latter elements. It discusses the theoretical basis of RET, arguing that it can be accurately described as theoretically consistent eclectic therapy, and analyses the problems encountered in, and the benefits derived from, its practice. At the time this book provided a state of the art discussion of RET and will still be of interest for those involved in counselling, psychotherapy, clinical psychology, psychiatry and social work.

Current Issues in Rational-Emotive Therapy

Windy Dryden

Routledge
Taylor & Francis Group
LONDON AND NEW YORK

First published in 1987
by Croom Helm Ltd

This edition first published in 2014 by Routledge
27 Church Road, Hove BN3 2FA

and by Routledge
711 Third Avenue, New York, NY 10017

Routledge is an imprint of the Taylor & Francis Group, an informa business

Publisher's Note
The publisher has gone to great lengths to ensure the quality of this reprint but points out that some imperfections in the original copies may be apparent.

Disclaimer
The publisher has made every effort to trace copyright holders and welcomes correspondence from those they have been unable to contact.

A Library of Congress record exists under ISBN: 0709945574

ISBN: 978-1-138-79129-9 (hbk)
ISBN: 978-1-315-76291-3 (ebk)
ISBN: 978-1-138-79130-5 (pbk)

Current Issues in Rational-Emotive Therapy

WINDY DRYDEN

CROOM HELM
London • New York • Sydney

Croom Helm Ltd, Provident House, Burrell Row,
Beckenham, Kent, BR3 1AT
Croom Helm Australia, 44-50 Waterloo Road,
North Ryde, 2113, New South Wales

Published in the USA by
Croom Helm
in association with Methuen, Inc.
29 West 35th Street,
New York, NY 10001

British Library Cataloguing in Publication Data

Dryden, Windy
Current issues in rational-emotive
therapy.
1. Rational-emotive psychotherapy
I. Title
616.89'14 RC489.R3

ISBN 0-7099-4557-4

Library of Congress Cataloging-in-Publication Data

Dryden, Windy.
Current issues in rational-emotive therapy.

Bibliography: p.
Includes index.
1. Rational-emotive psychotherapy. I. Title.
[DNLM: 1. Psychotherapy. WM 420 D799ca]
RC489.R3D784 1987 616.89'14 87-15610
ISBN 0-7099-4557-4

Printed and bound in Great Britain by
Biddles Ltd, Guildford and King's Lynn

CONTENTS

Preface

1. RATIONAL-EMOTIVE THERAPY: AN UPDATE (with Albert Ellis) 1

2. LANGUAGE AND MEANING IN RATIONAL-EMOTIVE THERAPY 46

3. THE THERAPEUTIC ALLIANCE IN RATIONAL-EMOTIVE INDIVIDUAL THERAPY 59

4. COMPROMISES IN RATIONAL-EMOTIVE THERAPY 72

5. RET AS A THEORETICALLY CONSISTENT FORM OF ECLECTIC THERAPY 88

6. RATIONAL-EMOTIVE COUPLES THERAPY 113

7. RATIONAL-EMOTIVE CONCILIATION COUNSELLING (with David McLoughlin) 140

8. PROBLEMS IN LIVING: THE FRIDAY NIGHT WORKSHOP (with Wouter Backx) 154

9. USING RET IN THE SUPERVISION OF COUNSELLORS 171

10. WHERE IS THE EVIDENCE? PROMOTING QUALITY RET RESEARCH 192

References 202

Index 214

To Ruth Wessler, a fine rational-emotive therapist, trainer and supervisor

PREFACE

This book follows my previous book for Croom Helm (Rational-Emotive Therapy: Fundamentals and Innovations) in providing discussions of current issues in rational-emotive therapy (RET). After presenting an update of the current theory and practice of RET in chapter 1, I expand my thinking on RET and therapeutic alliance theory (chapters 2 and 3), discuss the concept of making compromises in RET (chapter 4) and place RET in the broader zeitgeist of eclecticism and psychotherapy integration (chapter 5). In chapters 6 - 9, I show how RET can be applied in a variety of different helping modalities and in conclusion I briefly discuss the rather poor state of the art of RET research (chapter 10).

I wish to thank the following who agreed to allow me to include our co-authored work in this book: Albert Ellis (chapter 1); David McLoughlin (chapter 7); and Wouter Backx (chapter 8).

I wish to thank the following for granting me permission to reprint material in original or modified form: British Journal of Cognitive Psychotherapy; Brunner/Mazel; Carfax and ASMT; The Counsellor; Guilford Press; Harper & Row and Human Sciences Press.

Finally, I would like to thank Mrs. Sue Weston for her excellent work in preparing the camera-ready manuscript.

Windy Dryden London

Chapter One

RATIONAL-EMOTIVE THERAPY: AN UPDATE

WINDY DRYDEN & ALBERT ELLIS

HISTORICAL DEVELOPMENT OF RET

Rational-emotive therapy (RET) was founded in 1955 by Albert Ellis, a New York clinical psychologist who began his career in the helping professions in the early 1940s. As a result of research he was doing at that time for a massive work to be entitled The Case for Sexual Liberty, Ellis gained a local reputation for being an authority on sexual and marital relationships. He was consulted by his friends on their sexual and relationship problems and discovered that he could be successful in helping them with these problems in a short period of time. He decided to pursue formal training in clinical psychology after discovering that there were no formal training possibilities then offered in sexual and marital counselling. After getting a PhD degree in clinical psychology, he chose to be trained in psychoanalysis, believing then that it was the deepest and most effective form of psychotherapy available. He decided on this course of action because his experiences as an informal sex-marital counsellor had taught him that disturbed relationships were really a product of disturbed persons, 'and that if people were truly to be helped to live happily with each other they first had better be shown how they could live peacefully with themselves' (Ellis, 1962, p.3).

Ellis initially enjoyed working as a psychoanalyst partly because it allowed him to express both his helping and problem-solving interests. However, he became increasingly dissatisfied with psychoanalysis as an effective and efficient form of treatment. In the early 1950s, Ellis began to experiment with different forms of therapy, including psychoanalytic-orientated psychotherapy and eclectic-analytic therapy. But although he became more effective with his clients, he remained dissatisfied with the efficiency of these methods. During this period of experimentation, Ellis returned to his lifelong hobby of reading philosophy to help him with his search for an effective and efficient form of therapy. One of the major influences on his thought at that time was the work of the Greek and Roman Stoic philosophers (e.g. Epictetus and Marcus Aurelius). They emphasised the primacy of philosophic causation of psychological disturbances - a viewpoint which was not popular in America in the 1950s - and de-emphasised the part played by psychoanalytic psychodynamic factors. In essence, the Stoic viewpoint which stated that people are disturbed not by things but by their view of things, became the foundation of RET, in particular, and this perspective (following Ellis's pioneering formulations) remains at the heart of present-day cognitive-behavioural approaches to psychotherapy.

Major Philosophical Influences

Apart from Stoicism, present-day RET owes a philosophical debt to a number of other sources that have influenced its development: (a) Immanuel Kant's writings on the power (and limitations) of cognition and ideation strongly impressed Ellis(1981a) and the work of Spinoza and Schopenhauer was also important in this respect. (b) Philosophers of science, such as Popper (1959, 1963), Reichenbach (1953), and Russell (1965), were influential in helping Ellis see that all humans develop hypotheses about the nature of the world. Moreover, these philosophers stressed the importance of testing out the validity of such hypotheses rather than assuming that they are necessarily correct. Ellis has frequently argued that the practice of RET is synonymous, in many respects, with the logico-empirical methods of science (Ellis, 1962, 1979a). Ellis (1983a, 1985a) also stresses the flexibility and antidogmatism of the scientific method and holds that RET opposes all dogmas, just as science does, and that rigid absolutism is the very core of human disturbance (Ellis, 1986). (c) Although the philosophy of RET, as found in Ellis's writings, is at variance with devout religiosity, in one respect Christian philosophy has been most influential. RET's theory of human value (which will be discussed later) is similar to the Christian viewpoint of condemning the sin, but forgiving the sinner (Ellis, 1983a; Hauck,

1972; Powell, 1976). (d) Due to its stand on self-acceptance and its bias against all forms of human rating, RET allies itself with the philosophy of ethical humanism (Russell 1950, 1965) which opposes the deification and devil-ification of humans. Since RET considers that humans are at the centre of their universe (but not of _the_ universe) and have the power of choice (but not of unlimited choice) with regard to their emotional realm, it has its roots in the existential philosophies of Heidegger (1949) and Tillich (1977). Indeed, Ellis (1973) often portrays RET as having a pronounced humanistic-existential outlook. (e) Ellis was influenced, particularly in the 1960s, by the work of the general semanticists (e.g. Korzybski, 1933). These theorists outlined the powerful effect that language has on thought and the fact that our emotional processes are heavily dependent on the way we, as humans, structure our thoughts by the language we employ.

Major Psychological Influences

Ellis, in developing RET, has similarly been influenced by the work of a number of psychologists. (a) Ellis, himself, received a training analysis from an analyst of the Karen Horney school and Horney's (1950) concept of the 'tyranny of the shoulds' was certainly an early influence on his emphasis on the primacy of absolute, dogmatic evaluative thought in the development and maintenance of much psychological disturbance. (b) The work of Adler was important to the development of RET in several respects.

> Adler (1927) was the first great therapist to really emphasize inferiority feelings - while RET similarly stresses self-rating and the ego anxiety to which it leads. Like Adler and his Individual Psychology, RET also emphasizes people's goals, purposes, values and meanings. RET also follows Adler in regard to the use of active-directive teaching, the stress placed on social interest, the use of a holistic and humanistic outlook, and the employment of a highly cognitive-persuasive form of psychological treatment. (Ellis, 1981b).

(c) Although RET was originally termed 'Rational Psychotherapy', it has always advocated the use of behavioural methods as well as cognitive and emotive techniques in the practice of therapy. Indeed, Ellis utilized some of the methods advocated by some of the earliest pioneers in behaviour therapy (Dunlap, 1932; Jones, 1924; Watson & Rayner, 1920), first in overcoming his own early fears of speaking in public and of approaching women, and second in the active-directive form of sex therapy which he practised in the early 1950s. This behavioural active-directive emphasis remains prominent in present-day RET.

In its thirty years' existence, RET has been practised in various therapeutic modalities (individual, group, marital and family), by many kinds of helping professionals (e.g. psychologists, psychiatrists, social workers) with a variety of client populations (e.g. adults, children, the elderly) suffering from a wide range of psychological problems and disorders. Apart from its use in counselling and psychotherapy, rational-emotive principles have been applied in educational, industrial, and commercial settings. A very recent development has been the application of RET to public education in the form of nine-hour intensive workshops. In this respect, it is playing a significant role in the field of preventative psychology. RET is practised throughout the world and there are RET Institutes in the United States, Italy, West Germany, Holland, Australia, England and Mexico. It is thus a well-established form of cognitive-behaviour therapy.

BASIC THEORY

In this section we will begin by considering what image of the person is put forward by rational-emotive theory. We will then outline the theory's perspective on the nature of psychological health and disturbance, the acquisition and perpetuation of psychological disturbance, and conclude the section by examining RET's theory of therapeutic change.

Image of the Person

Rational-emotive theory conceives of the person as a complex, bio-social organism with a strong tendency to establish and pursue a wide variety of goals and purposes. While people differ enormously in *what* will bring them happiness, the fact that they *do* construct and pursue personally valued goals shows that they strive to bring a sense of meaning to their lives. Humans are thus seen as hedonistic in that their major goals appear to be to stay alive and to pursue happiness. In this respect they are further seen as having the related tasks of satisfying both their self interests and their social interests. It is noted that humans normally do better at satisfying these twin interests by active rather than by passive pursuit.

The concept of rationality is central to an understanding of the rational-emotive image of the person. Here 'rational' means that which aids and abets people to achieve their basic goals and purposes. Although humans are motivated by hedonistic concerns, they often experience a clash between short-range and long-range goals. RET theory holds that while humans had better satisfy some of their short-range goals, if they are to achieve their basic goals and purposes then it would be wise for them to adopt a philosophy of long-range hedonism. Irrational, then, means that which hinders and obstructs people from achieving their basic (long-range) goals and purposes. It is thus apparent that rationality is not defined in any absolute sense in RET theory.

While RET theory does stress the role played by cognitive factors in human functioning, Ellis has from the inception of RET, claimed that cognition, emotion and behaviour are not to be viewed as separate pyschological processes but rather as processes which are highly interdependent and interactive. Thus, the statement 'cognition leads to emotion' tends to accentuate a false picture of psychological separatism. In the famous ABCs of RET, 'A' has traditionally stood for an Activating event - or strictly speaking, from a phenomenological point of view - the perception of the event; 'B' for the way that perceived event is evaluated (i.e. the person's Beliefs); and 'C' for the emotional and behavioural Consequences that stem from 'B'. As stated however, this model does not emphasize the interactive nature of the psychological processes contained within it (Ellis, 1985b). And yet, when humans adhere to a particular set of evaluative Beliefs at 'B', this tends very much to influence the perceptions they make and environments they seek out at 'A'. While Beliefs do affect emotion and behaviour, it is equally true that the way we feel and act has a profound effect on our Beliefs. Our emotional and behavioural reactions help to create environments and skew our perceptions of these environments which in turn have a constraining effect on our emotional and behavioural repertoires (as in the 'self-fulfilling prophecy' effect). Thus, it should preferably be underscored that RET theory sees the person as having overlapping intrapsychic processes and as being in constant interaction with his or her social and material environment.

However, a model which emphasizes the interactive and interdependent nature of intrapsychic and interpersonal processes does not have to take the position that all have equal explanatory variance in accounting for human psychological disturbance. Indeed, RET has become renowned for the central role it has given to cognition in general and to evaluative Beliefs in particular in its theory and practice.

When cognitive factors are considered from the vantage point of the rational-emotive view of the person, Ellis (1976a, 1979a) has stressed that humans have two major biological tendencies. First, humans have a strong tendency to think irrationally. They appear, in particular, according to RET theory, to show great ease in converting their strong preferences into devout absolutistic demands. While Ellis (1984a) has acknowledged that there are social influences operating here, he has also noted '.... even if everybody had had the most rational upbringing, virtually all humans would often irrationally escalate their individual and social preferences into absolutistic demands on (a) themselves, (b) other people, and (c) the universe around them' (p. 20).

Ellis (1976a, 1979a) has argued that the following constitutes evidence in favour of his hypothesis of the biological basis of human irrationality:

(a) Virtually all humans including bright and competent people show evidence of major human irrationalities.
(b) Virtually all the disturbance-creating irrationalities (absolutistic shoulds and musts) that are found in our society are also found in just about all social and cultural groups that have been studied historically and anthropologically.
(c) Many of the irrational behaviours that we engage in, such as procrastination and lack of self-discipline, go counter to the teachings of parents, peers, and the mass media.
(d) Humans - even bright and intelligent

people - often adopt other irrationalities after giving up former ones.

(e) People who vigorously oppose various kinds of irrational behaviours often fall prey to these very irrationalities. Atheists and agnostics exhibit zealous and absolutistic philosophies and highly religious individuals act immorally.

(f) Insight into irrational thoughts and behaviours helps only partially to change them. For example, people can acknowledge that drinking alcohol in large quantities is harmful yet this knowledge does not necessarily help them abstain from heavy drinking.

(g) Humans often return to irrational habits and behavioural patterns even though they have often worked hard to overcome them.

(h) People often find it easier to learn self-defeating than self-enhancing behaviours. Thus, people very easily overeat but have great trouble following a sensible diet.

(i) Psychotherapists who presumably should preferably be good role models of rationality often act irrationally in their personal and professional lives.

(j) People frequently delude themselves into believing that certain bad experiences (e.g. divorce, stress, and other misfortunes) will not happen to them.

However, lest this evidence gives the impression that RET has a gloomy image of the person, it is important to state that RET theory stresses the existence of a second basic biological tendency. Here humans are seen as having both the ability to think about their thinking and the ability to exercise their power to choose to work towards changing their irrational thinking. Thus, people are by no means powerless slaves to their tendency towards irrational thinking and they can transcend (although not fully) its effects by deciding to actively and continually work towards changing this thinking by employing cognitive, emotive and behavioural challenging or Disputational methods. In the final analysis, then, in this respect, the RET image of the person is quite an optimistic one.

Finally, RET emphasizes that the person is by nature fallible and most probably not perfectible. Humans 'naturally' make errors and, as described above, easily seem to defeat and obstruct themselves in the pursuit of their long-range goals. Therapeutically, they are thus encouraged to accept themselves as fallible human beings and to challenge their self-created demands for perfection and the self-damnation that virtually always accompanies such demands (particularly when these are not met). RET emphasizes that the person is also an incredibly complex organism and one who is constantly in flux. As such, RET theory considers that humans have great potential to utilise the many opportunities they encounter to effect changes in the ways in which they think, feel and act.

The Nature of Psychological Disturbance and Health.
Psychological disturbance. Rational-emotive theory posits that at the heart of psychological disturbance lies the tendency of humans to make devout, absolutistic evaluations of the perceived events in their lives. These evaluations are couched in the form of dogmatic 'musts', 'shoulds', 'have to's' and 'oughts'. Ellis (1983a) has argued that these absolutistic cognitions are at the core of a philosophy of religiosity which he claims to be the central feature of human emotional and behavioural disturbance. These Beliefs are deemed to be irrational in RET theory in that they usually (but not invariably) impede and obstruct people in the pursuit of their basic goals and purposes. Absolute musts do not invariably lead to psychological disturbance because it is possible for a person to devoutly believe 'I must succeed at all important projects', have confidence that he or she will be successful in these respects and actually succeed in them and thereby not experience psychological disturbance. However, the person remains vulnerable in this case because there is always the possibility that he or she may fail in the future. So while on probabilistic grounds RET theory argues that an absolutistic philosophy will frequently lead to such disturbance it does not claim that this is invariably the case. Thus, even with respect to its view of the nature of human disturbance RET adopts an anti-absolutistic position.

RET theory goes on to posit that if humans adhere to a philosophy of 'musturbation', they will strongly tend to make a number of irrational conclusions which are deemed to be derivatives of these 'musts'. These derivatives are viewed as irrational because they too tend to sabotage a person's basic goals and purposes.

The first derivative is known as '**awfulizing**'. This occurs when a perceived event is rated as being more than 100% bad - a truly exaggerated and magical conclusion which stems from the Belief: 'This must not be as bad as it is'.

The second derivative is known as '**I-can't-stand-it-itis'**. This means believing that one cannot experience virtually any happiness at all, under any conditions, if an event which 'must' not happen actually occurs or threatens to occur.

The third derivative, known as '**damnation**' represents the tendency for humans to rate themselves and other people as 'sub-human' or 'undeserving' if self or other does something that they 'must' not do or fail to do something which they 'must' do. 'Damnation' can also be applied to the world or life conditions which are rated as being 'rotten', for failing to give the person what he or she must have.

While Ellis (1984a) has argued that 'awfulizing', 'I-can't-stand-it-itis' and 'damnation' are secondary irrational processes in that they stem from the philosophy of 'musts', these processes can sometimes be primary. Indeed, Wessler (1984) has argued that they are more likely to be primary and that 'musts' are derived from them. However, the philosophy of 'musts', on the one hand, and those of 'awfulizing', 'I-can't-stand-it-itis' and 'damnation' on the other, are, in all probability, interdependent processes and often seem to be different sides of the same 'cognitive' coin.

It is possible to discern two major categories of human psychological disturbance in RET theory: **ego disturbance** and **discomfort disturbance** (Ellis, 1979b, 1980a). In ego disturbance the person damns herself as a result of making musturbatory demands on self, others, and the world. In discomfort disturbance, the person again makes demands on self, others and the world but these demands reflect the Belief that comfort and comfortable life conditions must exist.

Ellis (1984a, 1985b) notes that humans also make numerous kinds of illogicalities when they are disturbed. In this respect RET agrees with cognitive therapists (Beck, et al 1979; Burns, 1980) that such cognitive distortions are a feature of psychological disturbance. However, RET theory holds that such distortions almost always stem from the 'musts'. Some of the most frequent of them are:

(1) <u>All-or-none thinking</u>: 'If I fail at any important task, as I <u>must</u> not, I'm a <u>total</u> failure and <u>completely</u> unlovable!'
(2) <u>Jumping to conclusions and negative non sequiturs</u>: 'Since they have seen me dismally fail, as I <u>should</u> not have done, they will view me as an incompetent worm'.
(3) <u>Fortune telling</u>: 'Because they are laughing at me for failing, they know that I <u>should</u> have succeeded, and they will despise me forever'.
(4) <u>Focusing on the negative</u>: 'Because I <u>can't stand</u> things going wrong, as they <u>must</u> not, I can't see any good that is happening in my life'.
(5) <u>Disqualifying the positive</u>: 'When they compliment me on the good things I have done, they are only being kind to me and forgetting the foolish things that I <u>should</u> not have done'.
(6) <u>Allness and neverness</u>: 'Because conditions of living <u>ought</u> to be good and actually are so bad and so intolerable, they'll <u>always</u> be this way and I'll never have any happiness'.
(7) <u>Minimization</u>: 'My good shots in this game were lucky and unimportant. But my bad shots, which I <u>should</u> never have made, were as bad as could be and were totally unforgivable'.
(8) <u>Emotional reasoning</u> 'Because I have performed so poorly, as I <u>should</u> not have done, I feel like a total nincompoop, and my strong feeling proves that I <u>am</u> no damned good'.
(9) <u>Labelling and overgeneralization</u>: 'Because I <u>must</u> not fail at important work and have done so, I am a complete loser and failure!'
(10) <u>Personalizing</u>: 'Since I am acting far worse than I <u>should</u> act and they are laughing, I am sure they are only laughing at me; and that is <u>awful!</u>'
(11) <u>Phonyism</u>: 'When I don't do as well as I <u>ought</u> to do and they still praise and accept me, I am a real phony and will soon fall on my face and show them how despicable I truly am!'
(12) <u>Perfectionism</u>: 'I realize that I did fairly well, but I <u>should</u> have done perfectly well on a task like this, and am therefore really an incompetent!'

Although RET clinicians at times discover all the illogicalities just listed - and a number of others that are less frequently found with clients - they particularly focus on the unconditional shoulds, oughts and musts that seem to constitute the philosophic core of irrational Beliefs which lead to emotional disturbance. For they hold that if they do not get to and help clients surrender these core Beliefs, the clients will most probably keep holding them and create new irrational derivatives from them.

RET practitioners also particularly look for 'awfulizing', for 'I-can't-stand-it-itis' and for 'damnation', and they show clients how these almost invariably stem from their musts and can be surrendered if they give up their absolutistic demands on themselves, or other people, and on the universe. At the same time, rational-emotive therapists usually encourage their clients to 'have strong and persistent desires, wishes, and preferences, and to avoid feelings of detachment, withdrawal, and lack of involvement'(Ellis, 1973, 1984b).

More importantly, RET holds that unrealistic and illogical cognitions do not in themselves create emotional disturbance. Why? Because it is quite possible for people to unrealistically think 'Because I frequently fail, I always do' and it is possible for them also to think illogically, 'Because I have frequently failed, I always will'. But they can, in both these instances, rationally conclude, 'Too bad!' Even though I always fail, there is no reason why I must succeed. I would prefer to but I never have to do well. So I'll manage to be as happy as I can be even with my constantly failing'. They would then rarely be emotionally disturbed.

To reiterate, the essence of human emotional disturbance, according to RET, consists of the absolutistic musts and must nots that people think about their failure, about their rejections, about their poor treatment by others, and about life's frustrations and losses. RET therefore differs from other cognitive-behaviour therapies - such as those of Beck (1976), Bandura (1977), Goldfried & Davison (1976), Janis (1983), A. Lazarus (1981), Maultsby (1984), and Meichenbaum (1977) - in that it particularly stresses therapists looking for clients' dogmatic, unconditional musts, differentiating these from their preferences, and teaching them how to surrender the former and retain the latter (Bard, 1980; Ellis, 1962, 1984b, 1985b; Ellis & Becker,

1982; Ellis & Harper, 1975; Grieger & Boyd, 1980; Grieger & Grieger, 1982; Walen, DiGiuseppe & Wessler, 1980; Wessler & Wessler, 1980).

Psychological health. If the philosophy of musturbation is at the core of much psychological disturbance then what philosophy is characteristic of psychological health? RET theory argues that a philosophy of relativism or 'desiring' is a central feature of psychologically healthy humans. This philosophy acknowledges that humans have a large variety of desires, wishes, wants, preferences, etc., but if they refuse to escalate these non-absolute values into grandiose dogmas and demands they will not become psychologically disturbed. They will, however, experience appropriate negative emotions (e.g. sadness, regret, disappointment, annoyance) whenever their desires are not fulfilled. These emotions are considered to have constructive motivational properties in that they both help people to remove obstacles to goal attainment and aid them to make constructive adjustments when their desires cannot be met. Hence they can also be termed 'rational' negative emotions.

Three major derivatives of the philosophy of desiring are postulated by rational-emotive theory. They are deemed to be rational in that they tend to help people reach their goals or formulate new goals if their old ones cannot be realised.

The first derivative is known as 'rating or evaluating badness'. Here, if a person does not get what she wants she acknowledges that this is bad. However, because she does not believe 'I have to get what I want' she contains her evaluation along a 0-100 continuum of badness and does not therefore rate this situation as 'awful' - a magical rating which is placed on a nonsensical '101% - infinity' continuum. In general, when the person adheres to the desiring philosophy, the stronger her desire the greater her rating of badness will be when she does not get what she wants.

The second derivative is known as 'tolerance' and is the rational alternative to 'I-can't-stand-it-itis'. Here the person (a) acknowledges that an undesirable event has happened (or may happen); (b) believes that the event should empirically occur if it does; (c) rates the event along the badness continuum; (d) attempts to change the undesired event or accepts the 'grim' reality if it cannot be modified, and (e) actively pursues other goals even though the situation cannot be altered.

The third derivative known as '<u>acceptance</u>' is the rational alternative to 'damnation'. Here the person accepts herself and others as fallible human beings who do not have to act other than they do and as too complex and fluid to be given any legitimate or global rating. In addition, life conditions are accepted as they exist. People who have the philosophy of acceptance fully acknowledge that the world is highly complex and exists according to laws which are often outside their personal control. However, it is important to emphasize here that acceptance does not imply resignation. A rational philosophy of acceptance means that the person acknowledges that whatever exists empirically should exist but does not have to absolutistically exist forever. This prompts the person to make active attempts to change reality. The person who is resigned to a situation usually does not attempt to modify it.

Rational-emotive theory argues that people can hold rational and irrational Beliefs at the same time. Indeed, Ellis often refers to people escalating their desires into demands. Thus I may rationally believe 'I want you to love me' and simultaneously believe that: 'Since I want you to love me, you must do so'.

<u>Two types of negative emotions</u>. Rational-emotive theory also makes unique distinctions between appropriate (rational) and inappropriate (irrational) negative emotions. Appropriate (rational) negative emotions are deemed to be associated with rational Beliefs and inappropriate (irrational) negative emotions with irrational Beliefs. In the following the appropriate (rational) negative emotion is listed first:

(1) **<u>Concern vs Anxiety</u>**. Concern is an emotion which is associated with the belief: 'I hope that this threat does not happen but if it does, it would be unfortunate'. Anxiety occurs when the person believes: 'This threat must not happen and it would be awful if it does'.

(2) **<u>Sadness vs Depression</u>**. Sadness is deemed to occur when the person believes: 'It is very unfortunate that I have experienced this loss but there is no reason why it should not have happened'. Depression, on the other hand, is associated with the Belief: 'This loss should not have occurr-

ed and it is terrible that it did'. Here, when the person feels responsible for the loss, he or she will tend to damn themselves: '*I* am no good', whereas if the loss is outside the person's control he or she will tend to damn the world/life conditions: '*It* is terrible'. As shown earlier, RET theory holds that it is the philosophy of musturbation implicit in such evaluations that leads the person to consider that they will *never* get what they want - an inference which leads to feelings of hopelessness (e.g.: 'Because I must always get the things I really want and did not get it this time, I'll never get it at all. It's hopeless!')

(3) *Regret vs Guilt*. Feelings of regret or remorse occur when a person acknowledges that he has done something bad in public or private but accepts himself as a fallible human person for doing so. The person feels badly about the act or deed but not about himself because he holds the Belief: 'I prefer not to act badly, but if I do, it's unfortunate'. Guilt occurs when the person damns himself as bad, wicked or rotten for acting badly. Here, the person feels badly both about the act and about his 'self' because he holds the Belief:'I must not act badly and if I do it's *awful* and I am a *rotten* person!'

(4) *Disappointment vs Shame/Embarrassment.* Feelings of disappointment occur when a person acts 'stupidly' in public, acknowledges the stupid act but accepts herself in the process. The person feels disappointed about her action but not with herself because she prefers but does not demand that she act well. Shame and embarrassment occur when the person again recognizes that she has acted 'stupidly' in public and then condemns herself for acting in a way that she should not have done. People who experience shame and embarrassment often predict that the watching audience will think badly of them, in which case they tend to agree with these perceived judgments. Thus, they often believe that they absolutely need the approval of these others. Shame can sometimes be distinguished from embarrassment in that the

public 'pratfall' is regarded by the person as more serious in shame. However, both emotions involve self-denigration.

(5) **Annoyance vs Anger**. Annoyance occurs when another person disregards an individual's rule of living. The annoyed person does not like what the other has done but does not damn him or her for doing it. Such a person tends to believe. 'I wish the other person did not do that and I don't like what he/she did but it does not follow that he/she must not break my rule'. In anger, however, the person does believe that the other absolutely must not break the rule and thus damns the other for doing so. Annoyance is sometimes referred to as 'non-damning' anger while anger is distinguished from annoyance in this way by being referred to as 'damning' anger.

It should be noted that rational-emotive therapists do not target appropriate negative emotions for change during therapy since they are deemed to be Consequences of rational thinking.

If ego disturbance and discomfort disturbance are cornerstones of the rational-emotive view of human psychological problems, self-acceptance and a high level of discomfort tolerance are the two cornerstones of psychological health and are implicit in a philosophy of non-devout desire. Ellis (1979a) has outlined nine other criteria of positive mental health: 1) enlightened self-interest; 2) social interest; 3) self-direction; 4) acceptance of ambiguity and uncertainty; 5) scientific thinking; 6) commitment and being vitally absorbed in important projects; 7) flexibility; 8) calculated risk-taking and 9) acceptance of reality.

Acquisition and Perpetuation of Psychological Disturbance

Acquisition of psychological disturbance. Rational-emotive theory does not put forward an elaborate view concerning the acquisition of psychological disturbance. This partly follows from Ellis's (1976a) hypothesis that humans have a distinct **biological** tendency to think and act irrationally, but it also reflects the RET viewpoint that theories of acquisition do not necessarily suggest therapeutic interventions. While Ellis argues that humans' tendencies towards irrational thinking are biologically rooted, he does acknowledge that environmental variables do <u>contribute</u> to psychological disturbance and thus encourage people to make their biologically-based demands (Ellis, 1979a). Thus, Ellis (1984b) has said 'parents and culture usually teach children <u>which</u> superstitions, taboos and prejudices to abide by, but they do not originate their basic tendency to superstitiousness, ritualism and bigotry' (p. 209).

Rational-emotive theory also posits that humans vary in their disturbability. Some people emerge relatively unscathed psychologically from being raised by uncaring or overprotective parents, while others emerge emotionally damaged from more 'healthy' childrearing regimes (Werner & Smith, 1982). In this respect, Ellis (1984b) claims that 'individuals with serious aberrations are more innately predisposed to have rigid and crooked thinking than those with lesser aberrations, and that consequently they are likely to make lesser advances' (p. 223). Thus, the RET theory of acquisition can be summed up in the view that as humans we are not made disturbed simply by our experiences; rather we bring our ability to disturb ourselves to our experiences.

<u>Perpetuation of psychological disturbance</u>. While rational-emotive theory does not posit an elaborate view to explain the acquisition of psychological disturbance, it does deal more extensively with how such disturbance is perpetuated. First, people tend to maintain their psychological problems by their own 'naive' theories concerning the nature of these problems and to what they can be attributed. They lack what Ellis (1979a) calls 'RET Insight No. 1': that psychological disturbance is primarily determined by the absolutistic Beliefs that people hold about negative life events ('B' determines 'C'). Rather they consider that their disturbances are 'caused' by these situations ('A' causes 'C'). Since people make incorrect hypotheses about the major determinants of their problems, they consequently attempt to change 'A' rather than 'B'. Second, people may have Insight No. 1 but lack 'RET Insight No. 2': that people remain disturbed by re-indoctrinating themselves <u>in the present</u> with their absolutistic Beliefs. While they may see that their problems are determined by their Beliefs they may distract themselves and thus perpetuate their problems by searching for the historical antecedents of these Beliefs instead of directing themselves to change them as currently held. Third, people may

have Insights No. 1 and No. 2 but still sustain their disturbance because they lack 'RET Insight No. 3': that only if people diligently work and practise in the present as well as in the future to think, feel and act against their irrational Beliefs are they likely to change them and make themselves significantly less disturbed. People who have all three insights clearly see that they had better persistently and strongly challenge their Beliefs cognitively, emotively and behaviourally to break the perpetuation of disturbance cycle. Merely acknowledging that a Belief is irrational is usually insufficient to effect change.

Ellis (1979a) has argued that the major reason why people perpetuate their psychological problems is because they adhere to a **philosophy of low frustration tolerance (LFT)**. Such people believe that they must be comfortable, and thus do not work to effect change because such work involves experiencing discomfort. They are short-range hedonists in that they are motivated to avoid short-term discomfort even though accepting and working against their temporary uncomfortable feelings would probably help them to reach their long-range goals. Such people rate cognitive and behavioural therapeutic tasks as 'too painful', and even more painful than the psychological disturbance to which they have achieved some measure of habituation. They prefer to remain with their 'comfortable' discomfort rather than face the 'change-related' discomfort which they believe they must not experience. Maultsby (1975) has argued that people often back away from change because they are afraid that they will not feel right about it. He calls this the 'neurotic fear of feeling a phony' and actively shows clients that these feelings of 'unnaturalness' are natural concomitants of relearning. Another prevalent form of LFT is 'anxiety about anxiety'. Here, individuals believe that they must not be anxious and thus do not expose themselves to anxiety-provoking situations because they might become anxious if they did so - an experience they would rate as 'awful'. As such, they perpetuate their problems and overly restrict their lives to avoid experiencing anxiety.

'Anxiety about anxiety' constitutes an example of the clinical fact that people often make themselves **disturbed about their disturbances**. Having created secondary (and sometimes tertiary) disturbances about their original disturbance, they become pre-occupied with these 'problems about problems' and thus find it difficult to get back to solving the original problem. Humans are often very inventive in this respect. They can make themselves depressed about their depression, guilty about being angry (as well as anxious about their anxiety), etc. Consequently, people often are advised to tackle their disturbances about their disturbances before they can successfully solve their original problems.

RET theory endorses the Freudian view of human defensiveness in explaining how people perpetuate their psychological problem (Freud, 1937). Thus, people maintain their problems by employing various defence mechanisms (e.g. rationalization, avoidance) which are designed to help deny the existence of these problems or to minimize their severity. The RET view is that these defences are used to ward off self-damnation tendencies and that under such circumstances, if these people were to honestly take responsibility for their problems they would severely denigrate themselves for having them. In addition, these defence mechanisms are also employed to ward off discomfort anxiety; since if, again, such people admitted their problems they would rate them as 'too hard to bear' or 'too difficult to overcome'.

Ellis (1979a) has noted that people sometimes experience a form of perceived _pay off_ for their psychological problems other than avoidance of discomfort. The existence of these payoffs serves to perpetuate these problems. Thus, a woman who claims to want to overcome her procrastination may avoid tackling the problem because she is afraid that should she become successful she might then be criticized by others as being 'too masculine', a situation she would evaluate as 'awful'. Her procrastination serves to protect her (in her mind) from this 'terrible' state of affairs. Dryden (1984a) has noted that 'rational-emotive therapists stress the phenomenological nature of these payoffs, i.e. it is the person's view of the payoff that it is important in determining its impact, not the events delineated in the person's description' (p. 244).

Finally, the well documented 'self-fulfilling prophecy' phenomenon also helps to explain why people perpetuate their psychological problems (Jones, 1977; Wachtel, 1977). Here, people act according to their evaluations and consequent predictions and thus often elicit from themselves or from others responses which they then interpret in a manner which confirms their initial hypotheses. Thus, a socially anxious man may believe that other people would not want to get to know 'a worthless individual such as I truly am'. He then attends a social function and acts as if he were worthless, avoiding eye contact and keeping away from others. Unsurprisingly, such social behaviour does not invite approaches from others, a lack of response which he interprets thus: 'You see, I was right, other people don't want to know me. I really am no good'.

In conclusion, RET theory holds that people 'naturally tend to perpetuate their problems and have a strong innate tendency to cling to self-defeating, habitual patterns and thereby resist basic change. Helping clients change, then, poses quite a challenge for RET practitioners' (Dryden, 1984a, pp. 244-245).

Theory of Therapeutic Change

In the section, 'Image of the Person', we argued that the rational-emotive view of the person is basically an optimistic one, since although it posits that humans have a distinct biological tendency to think irrationally, it also holds that they have the capacity to <u>choose</u> to work towards changing this irrational thinking and its self-defeating effects.

There are various different levels of change. Rational-emotive theory holds that the most elegant and longlasting changes that humans can effect are ones that involve philosophic restructuring of irrational Beliefs. Change at this level can be specific or general. Specific philosophic change means that individuals change their irrational absolutistic demands (musts, shoulds) about <u>given</u> situations to rational relative preferences. General philosophic change involves people adopting a non-devout attitude towards life events in general. Ellis has distinguished between super-elegant and semi-elegant philosophic change at the general level. Discussing these changes Ellis has said:

> 'By superelegant I mean that practically under all conditions for the rest of their life they would not upset themselves about anything. Very few will ever do this because it is against the human condition and people fall back to <u>must</u>urbating and thereby disturbing themselves. Some will effect a semi-elegant solution, meaning that in most

> instances they will call up a new rational-emotive philosophy that will enable them to feel sad or annoyed but not anxious, depressed, or angry when poor conditions occur'.
> (in Weinrach, 1980, p.156).

To effect a philosophic change at either the specific or general level, people had better:

(1) First, realize that they create, to a large degree, their own psychological disturbances and that while environmental conditions can contribute to their problems they are in general of secondary consideration in the change process.
(2) Fully recognise that they do have the ability to change these disturbances significantly.
(3) Understand that emotional and behavioural disturbances stem largely from irrational, absolutistic dogmatic Beliefs.
(4) Detect their irrational Beliefs and discriminate them from their rational alternatives.
(5) Dispute these irrational Beliefs using the logico-empirical methods of science.
(6) Work towards the internalization of their new rational Beliefs by employing cognitive, emotive and behavioural methods of change.
(7) Continue this process of challenging irrational Beliefs and using multimodal methods of change for the rest of their lives.

When people effect a philosophic change at 'B' in the ABC model they often are able to correct spontaneously their distorted inferences of reality (overgeneralizations, faulty attributions, etc.) - which can be viewed as 'A' cognitions (Wessler & Wessler, 1980). However, they often had better challenge these distorted inferences more directly, as RET has always emphasized (Ellis, 1962) and as Beck (Beck et al., 1979) has also stressed.

PRACTICAL APPLICATIONS

The Therapeutic Relationship

RET is an active-directive form of psychotherapy in that RET therapists are active in directing their clients to identify the philosophical source of their psychological problems, and in showing them that they can challenge and change their irrational, absolute evaluations. As such RET is an educational form of therapy. Ellis (1979c, 1984b) has sometimes conceptualized the role of the effective RET therapist as that of an authoritative (but not authoritarian!) and encouraging teacher who strives to teach his or her clients how to be their own therapist once formal therapy sessions have ended.

Therapeutic conditions. Given the above role, RET therapists strive to accept unconditionally their clients as fallible human beings who often act self-defeatingly, but who are never essentially bad (or good). No matter how badly clients behave in therapy, the RET therapist attempts to accept them as people but will frequently, if appropriate, let them know his or her reactions to the client's negative behaviour (Ellis, 1973).

Ellis (1977a), writing about his approach to the therapeutic relationship, says that he strives to be as open as therapeutically feasible and will not hestitate to give highly personal information about himself should his clients ask for it, except when he judges that clients would use such information against themselves. RET therapists often disclose examples from their own lives concerning how they experienced similar problems and more importantly how they have gone about solving these problems. Thus, they strive to be therapeutically genuine in conducting sessions.

RET therapists tend to be appropriately humorous with most of their clients since they think that much emotional disturbance stems from the fact that clients take themselves and their problems, other people, and the world too seriously and thus strive to model for their clients the therapeutic advantages of taking a serious but humorously ironic attitude to life. They endeavour, however, not to poke fun at clients themselves but rather at the clients' self-defeating thoughts, feelings and actions (Ellis, 1977b, 1977c, 1981c). In the same vein and for similar purposes, RET therapists tend to be informal and easygoing with most of their clients. However, RET opposes therapists' unethically indulging themselves in order to enjoy therapy sessions at their clients' expense (Ellis, 1983b).

RET therapists show their clients a special kind of empathy. They not only offer them 'affective' empathy (i.e. communicating that they understand how their clients feel), but also offer them 'philosophic' empathy (i.e. showing them that they understand the philosophies that underlie these feelings).

Thus, with certain modifications, they agree with Rogers's (1961) views concerning therapist empathy, genuineness and unconditional positive regard. However, rational-emotive therapists are very wary of showing the vast majority of their clients undue warmth. Ellis (1977a, 1982a) has argued that if RET therapists get really close to their clients and give them considerable warmth, attention, caring and support, as well as unconditional acceptance, then these therapists run two major risks.

The first major risk is that therapists may unwittingly reinforce their clients' dire needs for love and approval - two irrational demands which are at the core of much human disturbance. When this happens, clients appear to improve because their therapists are indeed giving them what they believe they must have. They begin to 'feel better' but do not necessarily 'get better' (Ellis, 1972). Their 'improvement' is illusory because their irrational philosophies are being reinforced. Since they seem to improve, their therapists have restricted opportunities to identify these ideas, show them how they relate to their problems, and help them challenge and change them. Consequently, while such clients are helped by their therapists, they are not shown how they can help themselves and are thus vulnerable to future upset.

The second major risk concerns therapists unwittingly reinforcing their clients' philosophies of low frustration tolerance (LFT) - a major form of discomfort disturbance. Clients with LFT problems:

> 'almost always try to seek interminable help from others instead of coping with life's difficulties themselves. Any kind of therapy that does not specifically persuade them to stop their puerile whining and to accept responsibility for their own happiness tends to confirm their Belief that others must help them. Close relationship therapy is frequently the worst offender in this respect and thereby does considerable harm' (Ellis, 1977a, p.15).

However, since RET is relative in nature and is against the formulation of absolute, dogmatic therapeutic rules, it does recognize that under certain conditions (e.g. where a client is extremely depressed, accompanied by powerful suicidal ideation), distinct therapist warmth may be positively indicated for a restricted period of time.

Therapeutic style. While Ellis (1979d) recommends that RET therapists adopt an active-directive style with most clients and a particularly forceful version of that style with some very disturbed and resistant clients, not all RET therapists concur with this view. Some recommend a more passive, gentle approach under specific, or even most, conditions with clients (e.g. Garcia, 1977; Young, 1977). Eschenroeder (1979) notes that it is important to ask in RET 'which therapeutic style is most effective with which kind of client?' (p. 5). In the same vein, recent proponents of eclectic forms of therapy argue that the style of therapeutic interaction needs to be varied to meet the special situation of individual clients (Beutler, 1983; Lazarus, 1981). While this is a scantily researched area in RET, it may be best for RET therapists to avoid (a) an overly friendly, emotionally charged style of interaction with 'hysterical' clients, (b) an overly intellectual style with 'obsessive-compulsive' clients, (c) an overly directive style with clients whose sense of autonomy is easily threatened (Beutler, 1983), and (d) an overly active style with clients who easily retreat into passivity. This line of reasoning fits well with the notion of flexibility which rational-emotive therapists advocate as a desirable therapeutic quality. Varying one's therapeutic style in RET does not mean departing from the theoretical principles on which the content of therapy is based. As Eschenroeder (1979) points out, in RET 'there is no one-to-one relationship between theory and practice' (p. 3).

Strategies of Treatment

Ellis (1979e, 1980b) has pointed out that there are two forms of RET - preferential and general.[1] He says that general RET is synonymous with cognitive-behavioural therapy (CBT) while preferential RET is unique in a number of important respects. Since a major aim of the chapters in this book is to present the distinctive features of RET, the emphasis here will be on preferential RET (although it should be noted that RET therapists routinely use strategies derived from both forms of RET). The major goal of preferential RET is an ambitious one: to encourage clients to make profound philosophic change in the two main areas of ego disturbance and discomfort disturbance. This involves helping clients, as far as humanly possible, to give up their irrational musturbatory thinking processes and to replace them with rational nonabsolute thinking.

In preferential RET, the major goals are to help clients pursue their long-range basic goals and purposes and to help them do so as effectively as possibly by fully accepting themselves and tolerating unchangeable uncomfortable life conditions. Practitioners of preferential RET further strive to help clients obtain the skills which they can use to prevent the development of future disturbance. In encouraging clients to achieve and maintain this profound philosophic change, rational-emotive therapists implement the following strategies. They help their clients see that:

(a) Emotional and behavioural disturbance have cognitive antecedents and these conditions normally take the form of absolutistic devout evaluations. RET practitioners train their clients to observe their own psychological disturbances and to trace these back to their ideological roots.

(b) People have a distinct measure of self-determination and can thus *choose* to work at undisturbing themselves. Thus, clients are shown that they are not slaves to their biologically based irrational thinking processes.

(c) People can implement their choices and maximize their freedom by actively working at changing their irrational musturbatory Beliefs. This is best achieved by employing cognitive, emotive and behavioural methods - often in quite a forceful and vigorous manner (Ellis, 1979d).

Therapeutic strategies in a 'typical' RET session. What therapeutic strategies do rational-emotive therapists employ in a 'typical' session of preferential RET? The following is meant to be a flexible guide rather than a rigid framework:

1. *Check on any homework assignments that the client agreed to do since the previous session (if relevant).*
   (a) If these assignments have been executed successfully, enquire what the client gained from doing them.

(b) Troubleshoot any problems that emerged as a result, particularly if the assignment was not attempted. Assess the possible existence of irrational Beliefs that prevented the client from doing the homework assignment. Dispute these Beliefs and reassign the task (if appropriate).

2. *Ask for the client's most pressing primary problem.*

(a) Assess this problem using the ABC framework.

(b) Identify the most relevant inference that provided the context for the emotional and/or behavioural problem.

(c) Assume that the inference is correct for the moment and urge the client to do the same.

(d) Check whether the client has a secondary problem (e.g. depression about feeling depressed). If so, do an ABC analysis of this problem and proceed as below, having explained to the client the advisability of working on the secondary problem first and getting the client's agreement to do so. This step can also occur before 2(a) above.

3. *Help the client see the relationship between (a) musturbatory irrational Beliefs and their absolute evaluative derivatives and (b) the emotional and/or behavioural problem, and how the former tend to 'create' or 'cause' the latter.*

Show the client the desirability of disputing irrational Beliefs in order to promote constructive and desired emotional and behavioural changes.

4. *Dispute the client's irrational musturbatory Beliefs and/or their absolute evaluative derivatives by asking for any evidence that truly supports them.*

(a) Show the client that any evidence provided is usually in support of 'rational' Beliefs but not of 'irrational' Beliefs - e.g. there is evidence that it is preferable for clients to perform well and be approved but not that they therefore must succeed.

(b) Repeat 4(a) until the client acknowledges that the evidence justifies the existence of the 'rational' Beliefs but not that of the 'irrational' Beliefs.

(c) Help the client see the relationship between the rational Beliefs and the constructive and desired emotional and behavioural changes.

5. *Help the client see the advisability of continuing to Dispute the irrational Beliefs in this and other relevant situations.*

6. *Negotiate a homework assignment which will give the client an opportunity to Dispute the irrational Beliefs and act on the new rational Beliefs.*

(a) Troubleshoot possible obstacles to the successful completion of the assignment in advance.

(b) Conduct in-session practice in which the client can rehearse the assignment using imagery or simulated exercises (if relevant).

7. *Identify and correct any distorted inferences which were assumed to be true in 2(c) (if time allows).*

The above framework indicates clearly that the 'typical' RET session is sequentially structured. It is highly desirable if the client can make sense of and agrees to his or her active participation in this structure (as will be discussed further in Chapter 3).

Major Treatment Techniques

RET represents a major form of eclecticism known as 'theoretically consistent eclecticism' (Dryden, 1984b) in that techniques are liberally borrowed from other therapeutic systems, but employed for purposes usually consistent with RET's underlying theory. In particular, RET therapists are mindful of the short-term and long-term effects of particular therapeutic techniques and will rarely employ a technique that has beneficial immediate, but harmful long-range, Consequences. While rational-emotive therapists employ a large number of cognitive, emotive, and behavioural techniques, only the major ones will be discussed here. It should be noted at the outset that probably all the following techniques have cognitive, emotive, and behavioural elements to them and that 'pure' techniques (e.g. purely cognitive) probably do not exist. Techniques are grouped below to show which psychological process predominates.

Cognitive techniques. Probably the most common technique employed by RET therapists with the majority of their clients is the Disputing of irrational Beliefs. There are four sub-categories of Disputing (Ellis, 1977d). DETECTING consists of looking for irrational Beliefs - particularly musts, shoulds, oughts, and have to's - which lead to self-defeating emotions and behaviours. DEBATING consists of the therapist asking a number of questions which are designed to help the client give up irrational Beliefs. Questions such as 'Where is the evidence ...?' 'In what way does this Belief have truth or falseness?' and 'What makes it so?' are frequently employed. The therapist proceeds with such questioning until the client acknowledges the falseness of his or her irrational Belief and, in addition, acknowledges the truth of its rational alternative. DISCRIMINATING involves the therapist helping the client to distinguish clearly between his or her nonabsolute values (wants, preferences, likes and desires) and his or her absolutistic values (needs, demands and imperatives). DEFINING involves the therapist helping the client to make increasingly accurate definitions in the language that he or she employs when referring to his or her Beliefs (Dryden, 1984c). Rational-emotive therapists are often very creative in their use of Disputing sequences (e.g. Young, 1984a, 1984b, 1984c) and sometimes employ such methods in a highly dramatic fashion (Dryden, 1984c). A formal version of Disputing that includes some of its main components is known as DIBS (Disputing irrational Beliefs). Ellis (1979c) outlines its form thus:

Question 1: What irrational Belief do I want to dispute and surrender?
Answer: I must be as effective and sexually fulfilled as most other women.

Question 2: Can I rationally support this Belief?
Answer: ....

Question 3: What evidence exists of the truth of this Belief?

Answer: ....

Question 4: What evidence exists of the falseness of my Belief that I must be as orgasmic as other women are?

Answer: ....

Question 5: What are the worst possible things that could actually happen to me if I never achieved the orgasm that I think I must achieve?

Answer: ....

Question 6: What good things could happen or could I make happen if I never achieved the heights of orgasm that I think I must achieve?

Answer: ....

(Ellis, 1979c, pp. 79-80)

DIBS is one example of cognitive homework that is frequently given to clients to do between sessions after the client has been trained to use them. Other examples appear in Figures 1 and 2. The purpose of these forms is to provide a clear framework for clients to learn to do Disputing for themselves.

Clients can also use audio-cassettes as an aid to the Disputing process. They can listen to audio-tapes of therapy sessions and also Dispute their own irrational Beliefs on tape (Disputing on tape). Here they initiate and sustain a dialogue between the rational and irrational parts of themselves with the goal of strengthening the rational part and weakening the irrational part (Ellis, 1985a).

Clients who do not have the intellectual skills necessary to perform cognitive Disputing are usually helped to develop rational self-statements which they can memorize or write out on 3 x 5 cards and repeat at various times between sessions. An example developed by one of us (WD) with a client was 'Just because my being overweight is bad, doesn't mean that I am bad. My overeating makes me too heavy and is therefore wrong but I can correct it and get better results'. Three cognitive methods which are often employed by RET therapists to help clients reinforce their new rational philosophy are (a) bibliotherapy where clients are assigned self-help books to read (e.g. Ellis & Becker, 1982; Ellis & Harper, 1975; Young,

1974); (b) _the use of RET with others_ - a technique which gives clients an opportunity to practise thinking through rational arguments with their friends and relatives and (c) listening to _audio cassettes of RET lectures_ on various themes (e.g. Ellis, 1971, 1976b).

A number of semantic methods are also employed in RET, the purpose of which is to help clients use language in a less self-defeating manner. Thus instead of 'I can't ...' clients are urged to use: 'I haven't yet ...'. In particular, _referenting_ techniques are often employed (Danysh, 1974). Here, clients are encouraged to list both the negative and positive referents of a particular concept such as 'smoking'. This method is employed to counteract clients' tendencies to focus on the positive aspects of a harmful habit and to neglect its negative aspects.

RET therapists also employ a number of imagery techniques. Thus, _rational-emotive imagery_ (Ellis, 1979c; Maultsby & Ellis, 1974) is often employed. Here, clients gain practice at changing their inappropriate negative emotions to appropriate ones ('C') while maintaining a vivid image of the negative event at 'A'. Here they are in fact learning to change their self-defeating emotions by changing their underlying Beliefs at 'B'. _Time projection_ imagery methods are also employed in RET (Lazarus, 1984). Thus, a client may say that a particular event would be 'awful' if it occurred. Rather than directly challenging this irrational Belief at this stage, the therapist may temporarily go along with this but help the client to picture what life might be like at regular intervals after the 'awful' event has occurred. In this way clients are indirectly helped to change their irrational Belief because they come to 'see' that life goes on after the 'awful' event, that they will usually recover from it, and that they can continue to pursue their original goals or develop new ones. Such realisations encourage the person to re-evaluate their irrational Belief. Finally, a number of therapists have successfully employed RET in a _hypnosis_ paradigm (e.g. Boutin & Tosi, 1983; Golden, 1983).

Emotive techniques. RET, as a therapeutic system, has often been falsely accused of being too intellectual and insufficiently emotive. However, this is far from being true, and rational-emotive therapy sessions are frequently charged with emotion. The practice of effective RET is based upon the therap-

Figure 1

A guide for solving your emotional and behavioural problems by re-examining your self-defeating thoughts and Beliefs (Dryden 1982)

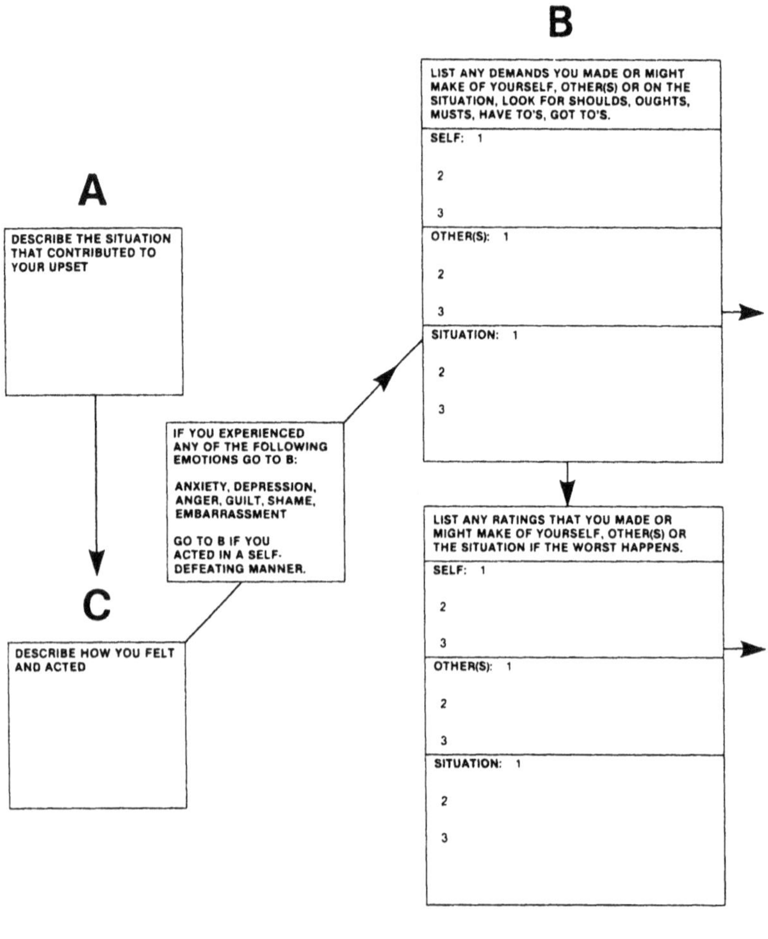

Figure 1 (cont.)

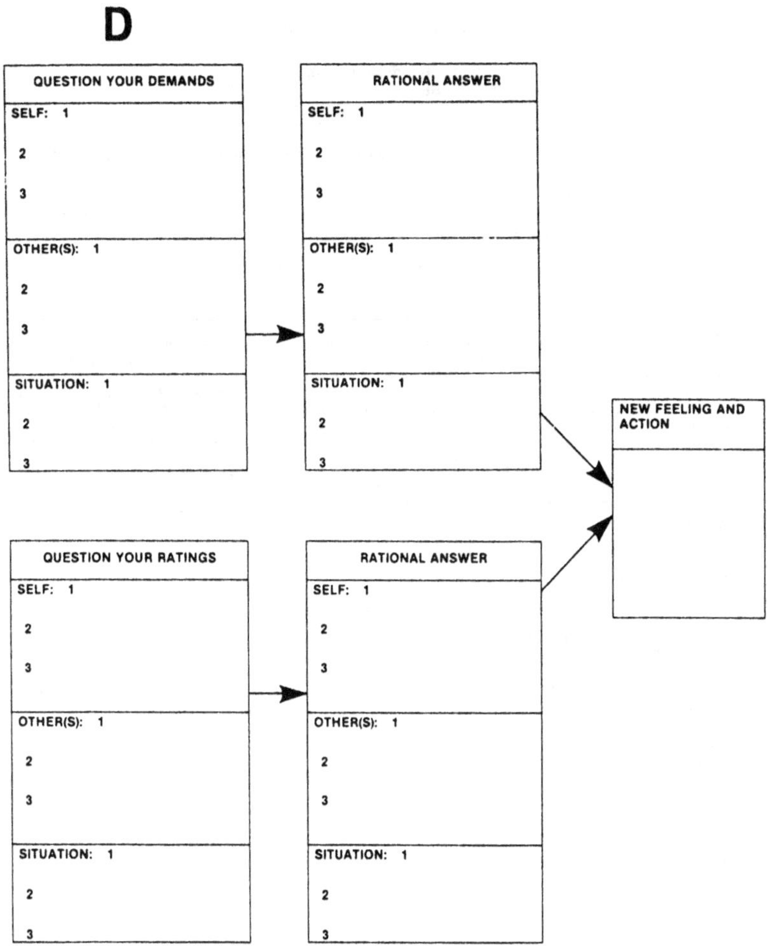

Figure 2

RET self-help form (Sichel and Ellis 1984)

RET SELF-HELP FORM

Institute for Rational-Emotive Therapy
45 East 65th Street, New York, N.Y. 10021
(212) 535-0822

(A) ACTIVATING EVENTS, thoughts, or feelings that happened just before I felt emotionally disturbed or acted self-defeatingly: ______________________________

____

(C) CONSEQUENCE or CONDITION—disturbed feeling or self-defeating behaviour—that I produced and would like to change: ______________________________

____

(B) BELIEFS—Irrational BELIEFS (IBs) leading to my CONSEQUENCE (emotional disturbance or self-defeating behaviour). Circle all that apply to these ACTIVATING EVENTS **(A).**	**(D) DISPUTES** for each circled IRRATIONAL BELIEF. Examples: "Why MUST I do very well?" "Where is it written that I am a BAD PERSON?" "Where is the evidence that I MUST be approved or accepted?"	(E) EFFECTIVE RATIONAL BELIEFS (RBs) to replace my IRRATIONAL BELIEFS (IBs). *Examples: "I'd PREFER to do very well but I don't* HAVE TO." "I am a PERSON WHO *acted badly, not a BAD PERSON." "There is no evidence that I* HAVE TO *be approved, though I would* LIKE *to be."*
1. I MUST do well or very well!		
2. I am a BAD OR WORTHLESS PERSON when I act weakly or stupidly.		
3. I MUST be approved or accepted by people I find important!		
4. I am a BAD, UNLOVABLE PERSON if I get rejected.		
5. People MUST treat me fairly and give me what I NEED!		
6. People who act immorally are undeserving, ROTTEN PEOPLE!		
7. People MUST live up to my expectations or it is TERRIBLE!		
8. My life MUST have few major hassles or troubles.		
9. I CAN'T STAND really bad things or very difficult people!		
10. It's AWFUL or HORRIBLE when major things don't go my way!		

Figure 2 (cont.

11. I CAN'T STAND IT when life is really unfair!		
12. I NEED to be loved by someone who matters to me a lot!		
13. I NEED a good deal of immediate gratification and HAVE TO feel miserable when I don't get it!		
Additional Irrational Beliefs:		
14.		
15.		
16.		
17.		
18.		

(F) FEELINGS and BEHAVIOURS I experienced after arriving at my EFFECTIVE RATIONAL BELIEFS: ____________

I WILL WORK HARD TO REPEAT MY EFFECTIVE RATIONAL BELIEFS FORCEFULLY TO MYSELF ON MANY OCCASIONS SO THAT I CAN MAKE MYSELF LESS DISTURBED NOW AND ACT LESS SELF-DEFEATINGLY IN THE FUTURE.

Joyce Sichel, Ph.D. and Albert Ellis, Ph.D.

ist offering the client the emotional attitude of unconditional acceptance (as discussed in the section on the therapeutic relationship). From this foundation, RET therapists frequently and judiciously employ humorous techniques to reduce the client's irrational Beliefs to absurd, amusing conclusions; the use of rational humorous songs (Ellis, 1977b, 1977c, 1981c); and amusing anecdotes, all of which are designed to encourage the client to think rationally by not taking him or herself, others and the world *too* seriously.

Moreover, RET therapists strive to serve as good rational role models both in their interactions with their clients and in their disclosures concerning how they handle their own psychological problems. In doing so, they employ a good measure of therapist self-disclosure. They encourage the use of role-playing and, in particular, rational role reversal where the therapist may adopt the irrational side of the client and encourage the client to Dispute irrational Beliefs from his or her rational side - a technique which is particularly employed with clients who have gained some mastery of the ABC framework and Disputing methods.

In an important paper, Ellis (1979d) has advocated the use of force and energy in the practice of psychotherapy. RET is unique among the cognitive behavioural therapies in emphasizing the employment of such interventions that fully involve clients' emotions. Thus, RET therapists suggest that clients can help themselves go from intellectual to emotional insight by vigorously Disputing their irrational Beliefs. Vigour is often employed by clients in rational role reversal where they forcefully and dramatically adopt the role of their rational 'self' whose goal is to successfully Dispute self-defeating Beliefs as articulated by their irrational 'self'. Force and energy also play a significant part in RET's now famous shame-attacking exercises (Ellis & Becker, 1982). Here clients deliberately seek to act 'shamefully' in public in order to accept themselves and to tolerate the ensuing discomfort. Since clients had better neither harm themselves nor other people, minor infractions of social rules often serve as appropriate shame-attacking exercises (e.g. calling out the time in a crowded department store, wearing bizarre clothes designed to attract public attention and going into a hardware store and asking if they sell tobacco). Risk-taking exercises come into the same category. Here clients deliberately force themselves to take calculated risks in areas where they wish to make changes. While disputing relevant irrational Beliefs I (A.E.) overcame my anxiety about approaching women by deliberately forcing myself to speak to 100 women in the Bronx Botanical Gardens. I (W.D.) pushed myself to speak on national and local radio as part of a campaign to overcome my public-speaking anxiety. Both of us took these risks while showing ourselves that nothing 'awful' would result from such experiences. Repeating *rational self-statements in a passionate and forceful manner* is also often used in conjunction with such exercises (Ellis, 1985a).

Behavioural techniques. The use of a wide variety of behavioural techniques is advocated wherever possible since it is realized that cognitive change is very often facilitated by behavioural change (Ellis, 1979c; Emmelkamp, Kuipers & Eggeraat, 1978). However, some behavioural techniques are favoured over others. Thus *in vivo* rather than imaginal techniques are preferred because 'live' exposure presents clients with more opportunities for philosophic change than 'imagined' exposure (Ellis, 1983c). For the same reason RET therapists often encourage their clients *to expose themselves fully* to, say, feared events, although in practice compromises often have to be reached concerning how fully clients are prepared to expose themselves (Dryden, 1985 and Chapter 4).

Other behavioural methods often used in RET include: (a) *'stay-in-there' activities* (Grieger & Boyd, 1980) which give clients an opportunity to raise their level of frustration tolerance by encouraging them to remain in uncomfortable (but not harmful or traumatic) situations for a period of time while tolerating their feelings of chronic discomfort; (b) *anti-procrastination exercises* where clients are encouraged to push themselves to start tasks earlier rather than later, thus Disputing their dire need for comfort-of-the moment (Ellis & Knaus, 1977); (c) various *skill training methods* which equip clients with key skills in which they are deficient (e.g. assertion and social skills training), and which are usually employed after cognitive Disputing methods have been used and and some philosophic change has been encouraged (Ellis, 1977e); (d) the use of *rewards and penalties* which are used to encourage clients to implement self-change programmes and (e) Kelly's (1955) *fixed role therapy* is sometimes employed in

RET - here clients are encouraged to act 'as if' they already think rationally, to enable them to get the experience that change is possible.

<u>Techniques that are avoided or used sparingly in RET</u>. By now it should be clear that RET is a multimodal form of therapy that advocates the employment of techniques in the cognitive, emotive, and behavioural modalities. However, because the choice of therapeutic techniques is inspired by RET theory, the following available therapeutic techniques are avoided or used sparingly in the practice of RET (Ellis, 1979c, 1984b):

(1) Techniques that help people become more dependent (e.g. undue therapist warmth as a strong reinforcement and the creation and analysis of a transference neurosis).

(2) Techniques that encourage people to become more gullible and suggestible (e.g. unrealistic positive thinking).

(3) Techniques that are long-winded and inefficient (e.g. psychoanalytic methods in general and free association in particular; encouraging clients to give lengthy descriptions of Activating experiences at 'A').

(4) Methods that help people feel better in the short-term rather than get better in the long-term (Ellis, 1972) (e.g. some experiential techniques like fully expressing one's feelings in a dramatic, cathartic, and abreactive manner - i.e. some gestalt methods and primal techniques. The danger here is that such methods may encourage people to practise irrational philosophies underlying such emotions as anger).

(5) Techniques that distract clients from working on their irrational philosophies (e.g. relaxation methods, Yoga and other cognitive distraction methods). These methods may be employed, however, <u>along with</u> cognitive Disputing designed to yield some philosophic change.

(6) Methods that may unwittingly reinforce clients' philosophy of low frustration tolerance (e.g. gradual desensitization).

(7) Techniques that include an anti-scientific philosophy (e.g. faith healing and mysticism).

(8) Techniques that attempt to change Activating events ('A') before or without showing clients how to change their irrational Beliefs ('B') (e.g. some strategic family systems techniques).
(9) Techniques that have dubious validity (e.g. neurolinguistic programming).

Finally, to reiterate, RET therapists do not dogmatically avoid using the above methods. They may on certain occasions, with certain clients, utilise such techniques particularly for pragmatic purposes. For example, if faith healing is the only method that will prevent some clients from harming themselves then RET therapists would probably either employ it themselves or, more probably, refer such clients to a faith healer (Ellis, 1985a).

Overcoming Obstacles to Client Progress

When RET is practised efficiently and effectively and when clients understand and are prepared continually to implement its basic concepts, then it can achieve remarkable results. However, frequently (and perhaps more frequently than most therapists are prepared to admit!), various obstacles to client progress are encountered in the practice of RET (and indeed all other forms of therapy). Three major forms of obstacles are deemed to occur in RET: (a) relationship obstacles; (b) therapist obstacles; and (c) client obstacles (Ellis, 1985a).

'Relationship' obstacles to client progress. These can be first attributed to poor therapist-client matching. Such mismatching may occur for many reasons. Thus, clients 'may have a therapist who, according to their idiosyncratic tastes or preferences, is too young or too old, too liberal or too conservative, too active or too passive' (Ellis, 1983d, p. 29). If these 'relationship match' obstacles persist, then it is preferable for that client to be transferred to a therapist with more suitable traits. Other relationship obstacles may occur because the therapist and client may get on 'too well' and get distracted from the more mundane tasks of therapy. In such cases, the paradox is that if the client improves, the 'life' of the satisfactory relationship is threatened. As a result, collusion may occur between therapist and client to avoid making therapy as effective an endeavour as it might otherwise be. This problem can be largely overcome if the therapist helps first himself or herself and then the client to overcome the philosophy of low frustration tolerance implicit in this collusive short-range hedonism.

<u>Therapist obstacles to client progress</u>. There are two major types of therapist obstacles: skill-orientated obstacles and disturbance-orientated obstacles. When obstacles to client progress can be mainly attributed to therapist skill deficits, these may appear in a variety of forms but most commonly therapists may impede client progress by:

(a) Improperly inducting clients into therapy and failing to correct unrealistic expectations such as 'my therapist will solve my problems for me'.

(b) Incorrectly assessing clients' problems and thus working on 'problems' that clients do not have.

(c) Failing to show clients that their problems have ideological roots and that 'C' is largely (but not exclusively) determined by 'B' and not by 'A' - inexpert therapists often fail to persist with this strategy or persist with an ineffective strategy.

(d) Failing to show clients that the ideological roots of their problems are most frequently expressed in the form of devout, absolutistic 'musts' or one of the three main derivatives of 'musturbation'. Instead, inexpert RET therapists frequently dwell too long on their clients' anti-empirical or inferentially distorted thinking.

(e) Assuming that clients will automatically change their absolute thinking once they have identified it. Inexpert RET therapists either fail to Dispute such thinking at all or use Disputing methods sparingly and/or with insufficient vigour. In addition, inexpert therapists routinely fail to: give their clients homework assignments which provide them with opportunities to practise Disputing their irrational Beliefs; check on their clients' progress on these assignments; and help their clients to identify and change their philosophic obstacles to working continually at self-change.

(f) Failing to realize that clients often have problems about their problems and thus working only on a primary problem when the client is preoccupied with a secondary problem.

(g) Frequently switching from ego to discomfort disturbance issues within a given session so that clients get confused and thus distracted from working on either issue.

(h) Working at a pace and a level inappropriate to the learning abilities of clients so that these clients are insufficiently involved in the therapeutic process due to confusion or boredom.

For these reasons it is highly desirable for RET therapists to strive continually to improve their skills by involving themselves in ongoing supervision and training activities (Dryden, 1983; Wessler & Ellis, 1980, 1983).

Client progress can also be hindered because therapists may bring their own disturbance to the therapeutic process. Ellis (1983b) has outlined five major irrational Beliefs that lead to therapeutic inefficiency.

(a) 'I _have_ to be successful with all my clients practically all of the time'.

(b) 'I _must_ be an outstanding therapist, clearly better than other therapists I know or hear about'.

(c) 'I _have to_ be greatly respected and loved by all my clients'.

(d) 'Since I am doing my best and working so hard as a therapist, my clients _should_ be equally hard working and responsible, _should_ listen to me carefully and _should_ always push themselves to change'.

(e) 'Because I am a person in my own right, I _must_ be able to enjoy myself during therapy sessions and to use these sessions to solve my personal problems as much as to help clients with their difficulties'.

In such cases, it is recommended that RET therapists apply RET principles and methods to search for and Dispute their own self- and client-defeating Beliefs which may (a) impede them from confronting their clients; (b) distract them and their clients from getting the therapeutic job done; (c) foster undue therapist anxiety and anger; and (d) encourage inappropriate behaviour antithetical to the practice of effective and ethical therapy.

Client obstacles to client progress. As noted earlier, in order really to benefit from RET, clients had better achieve three forms of insight, namely: (a) Psychological disturbance is mainly determined by the absolutistic Beliefs that they hold about themselves, others, and the world. (b) Even when people acquired and created their irrational Beliefs in their early lives, they perpetuate their disturbance by re-indoctrinating themselves in the present with these Beliefs. (c) Only if they constantly work and practise in the present and future to think, feel and act against these irrational Beliefs are clients likely to surrender their irrationalities and make themselves significantly less disturbed.

In a study by Ellis (1983e) on the characteristics of clients who 'failed' in RET, the following categories of 'failure' client emerged: (a) Clients who did poorly in RET failed to do consistent *cognitive* self-Disputation. They were characterized amongst other factors by extreme disturbance, by grandiosity, by lack of organization, and by plain refusal to do these cognitive assignments. (b) Clients who refused to accept responsibility for their 'inappropriate' emotions and refused to change forcefully and *emotively* their Beliefs and actions, were more clingy, more severely depressed and inactive, more often grandiose and more frequently stubbornly rebellious than clients who benefited from RET. (c) Clients who did poorly in the *behavioural* aspects of RET showed 'abysmally low frustration tolerance, had serious behavioural addictions, led disorganized lives, refrained from doing their activity homework assignments, were more frequently psychotic and generally refused to work at therapy' (Ellis, 1983e, p. 165).

Thus, clients' own extreme level of disturbance is a significant obstacle to their own progress. While a full discussion of what 'special' therapeutic methods and techniques the therapist should employ with such clients is outside the scope of this chapter (see Ellis, 1985a), therapists can adopt a number of strategies to enhance therapeutic effectiveness with these DCs ('difficult customers'). Amongst other tactics, therapists had better, first, be consistently and forcefully encouraging in their therapeutic interactions with these clients, showing them that they can do better if they try. Second, therapists would be wise to keep vigorously showing these resistant clients that they (the therapists) do, in fact, unconditionally accept them with all their psychological difficulties and that they can indeed accept themselves in the same way. Third, therapists can often be successful with such clients by consistently showing them that their refusal to work on their problems will generally lead to bad consequences and needless suffering. Fourth, therapists had better be flexible in experimenting with a wide range of therapeutic techniques (including some unusual ones!) in their persistent efforts to help their 'difficult' clients. Above all, rational-emotive therapists had better be good representatives of their therapeutic system and accept themselves and tolerate the discomfort of working with difficult clients while sticking to the therapeutic task!

TWO TYPICAL CASE EXAMPLES OF RET

A Case of Anxiety

Freda was a 40 year old divorced woman with grown-up children, both of whom lived with her. She consulted me (WD) because she suffered from severe anxiety about driving. She was involved in a car accident eighteen months previously in which she was a passenger. While not seriously hurt, she experienced anxiety when driving ever since that time. Freda's anxiety was experienced on two levels. First, she became anxious whenever a large truck approached her from the rear. Second, she became enormously anxious about her anxiety and felt real panic. I first worked on her secondary level anxiety. Her irrational Belief here was: 'I must not be anxious and it is horrible when I am'. I Disputed this Belief and helped her to see that 'anxiety is uncomfortable, but not dangerous' (Low, 1952). Her primary anxiety problem was tackled next. I used 'inference chaining' (Moore, 1983) to reveal that she was terrified about (a) dying 'before her time' and (b) what would happen to her two sons after her death. First, I helped her see that there was no law of the universe that declared that she must not die in a car crash and that she must live longer than she does. Second, I asked her what was the worst fate she could imagine for her sons. This revealed that she was particularly anxious about her elder son, who seemed somewhat vulnerable. She was anxious that he might not cope on his own and might become a vagrant which she evaluated as 'terrible'. I Disputed this irrational Belief and helped her to see that if he did become a vagrant that would be very bad or tragic but hardly terrible - there being no law of the universe that said that he must not become a vagrant. And even if he became a vagrant, he might still have some happiness. Behaviourally, I first encouraged her to drive anxiously while tolerating this experience as 'bad' but not 'awful'. After this brought some improvement, I urged her to actively seek out big trucks and tolerate the discomfort of being 'hemmed in'.

The disclosure of this theme of being 'hemmed in' revealed further problems. She was at that same time being romantically pursued by a man in whom she showed no interest. She felt trapped in that he was not discouraged by her polite requests for him to leave her alone. I asked her what would stop her from being firm and back this assertion up with a refusal to talk to him. She considered that this approach would discourage him but said that she would feel guilty if he was hurt by such a direct approach. I helped her to see that her guilt stemmed from the Belief: 'I would be a bad person for causing him pain'. First I Disputed this Belief and showed her that even if she did directly cause the man pain, she could accept herself as a fallible human being for acting badly. I then helped her see that she would be responsible for _depriving_ him rather than for cruelly _hurting_ him. For if he felt hurt or denigrated by her rejections, he would create these feelings by irrationally downing himself. In the next session, she claimed success at asserting herself with the man and reported further alleviation of her driving anxiety. She spontaneously reported that feeling less 'hemmed in' in her personal relationships helped her feel less 'hemmed in' while driving.

In subsequent sessions, Freda discussed further problems concerning lack of assertion, guilt, and embarrassment. I helped her to see that there were links between these problems and she became increasingly proficient at detecting and Disputing her irrational Beliefs. Most noteworthy was the way she counteracted some of her irrational philosophies through dramatic action. I explained to her the concept of shame-attacking exercises and in the next session she reported undertaking one. For years she had been anxious about bringing men home to meet her two sons. On this occasion she met a much younger man at a dance and took him home that night. She did so to Dispute her shame inducing Belief: 'My sons would look down on me as a cradle-snatcher and that would prove that I would be a shit'. She felt this was very beneficial. Her sons did make several negative comments which she did not like but she reported that she told them that she was going to live her way and that she would like their approval but if they chose to regard her as 'a desperate old woman' that was unfortunate but hardly the end of the world.

At the end of twelve weekly sessions, Freda had made significant progress in Disputing her dire needs for approval and comfort. More importantly she had learned to internalize the scientific method of Disputing and saw clearly the benefits of actively working to counteract her irrational philosophies.

A six-month follow-up revealed that she had maintained her progress. She was able to drive quite comfortably although she still did not like big trucks behind her. However, she was no longer anxious about encountering this situation. Interpersonally, she felt much freer to speak her mind and to act more in her own interests even though others might view her in a negative light. She reported that her sons had changed their attitude towards her. 'They seem to respect the "new me" more than the old one'.

A Case of Depression

Bob, a 50 year old man, was severely depressed after losing his job and experienced resultant sex problems. He was referred to me (WD) after his G.P. had discovered that he was feeling suicidal. In our first session I learned that he was feeling hopeless about his future because he considered that he was 'finished as a man'. I very persistently showed him that he could accept himself as a man who had temporary lost employment and erectile sufficiency rather than damn himself as being less of a man for these two losses. His mood lifted appreciably by the end of the session but I told him that he could telephone me between sessions if he became suicidal again.

In our second session I discovered he was also ashamed about being depressed and about seeking psychotherapeutic help. Again I helped him to Dispute his irrational Belief: 'I must be able to solve my problems on my own' and also encouraged him to counteract his shame by telling his best friend about his problems.

He reported feeling much better in our third session. He did not feel ashamed about telling his friend about his problems and had received a sympathetic response from the friend who in turn confided that he had similar problems the previous year.

This actually had a profound effect on my client because he began to see that he could gain happiness by changing some of his priorities. He began to see that friendship was as important as achievement and that it was possible for him to re-define what it meant to be a man.

In our fourth session I Disputed his anxiety-creating Belief about his sexual performance: 'I must get it up to be a man'. Even by the fourth session it was apparent that Bob clearly understood the difference between rational and irrational Beliefs. He went home and enjoyed several sexual experiences with his wife when he resolved to act on the Belief that 'an erection and orgasm would be nice but sex can be enjoyed without them'. Additionally, Bob decided to do some voluntary work in a local hospital and enjoyed it even though he predicted he would gain no satisfaction from doing so.

He began to show increasing interest in the area of gender identity and read several books on the pressures of being a male in today's society. He began taking a more active role doing domestic chores and by the seventh session no longer regarded it as 'women's work'. In the eighth session he relapsed and reported feeling depressed again. Interestingly, when this was explored it transpired that he was condemning himself for being 'an erstwhile male chauvinist'. I showed him again that he was a fallible human being and that he could accept himself as such even if he had adhered to a male chauvinistic philosophy in the past and even if he still retained some of this philosophy today. We had a full discussion of the concept of unconditional self-acceptance and he resolved to act on this philosophy.

In our final two sessions we discussed several career-related issues. He decided as a result of this discussion to attend a university and study for a degree in social work. At our final session, he considered that he had changed some fundamental attitudes: 'Looking back, I can realise that I had believed in the concept of two-dimensional man. I was O.K. as long as I was in a good job and my cock functioned well. Now I can see that there is much more to being a man than that. I feel you have helped me widen my horizons and I now view myself as being considerably more complex than before. I have increased enjoyment of friendship now and sex with my wife is incredibly more enriching'.

A six-month follow-up revealed Bob enjoying his university course and free from depression. At his first therapy session his Beck Depression Inventory score was in the severe range (42). At his tenth and final session of regular therapy his score had gone down to 3 and at 6 months follow up it was 1.

Note

1. While in this section, I (WD) go along with the terms 'preferential' and 'general' RET, I shall argue against their usage in Chapter 4.

Chapter Two

LANGUAGE AND MEANING IN RATIONAL-EMOTIVE THERAPY

WINDY DRYDEN

INTRODUCTION

In this chapter the issue of language and meaning in rational-emotive therapy will be discussed - a topic which has received scant attention in the RET literature. For example, two of the major texts in rational-emotive therapy, (Walen, DiGiuseppe & Wessler, 1980; Wessler & Wessler, 1980) devote a little over a page to this issue. Wessler & Wessler (1980) make the important point which encapsulates the argument that will be made in this chapter: 'Since all words are abstractions and subject to varying denotations and connotations, it is important that we use a shared vocabulary with a client - specifically, that we define our terms and check out the meanings of the client's terms - and try to keep the dialogue as concrete as possible' (p. 179). In addition to understanding the client's language, it is equally important that the therapist ensures that the client understands the therapist's use of language. Since therapist language can be best construed as 'A' in the ABC framework, it is likely then to be interpreted idiosyncratically by the client who will then proceed to make evaluations about such interpretations at 'B'. Thus, the possibilities for misunderstanding are legion. RET is often also misconstrued by fellow professionals given the different meanings that can be attributed to the term 'rational'. Young (1975) has argued that people often construe rational to mean cold, logical and unemotional whereas in RET rational is defined as 'that which aids and abets our clients' basic goals and purposes'. However, this use of the word 'rational' is not commonly held and if unexplained will often lead to wrong impressions being created in the minds of both non RET therapists and clients.

THE LANGUAGE OF FEELING

RET theory states that when people do not get what they want and do not dogmatically insist that they get what they want, then they are still liable to experience negative emotions. To the extent that these emotions stem from rational Beliefs and are deemed to motivate people to recover and to set new goals for themselves or to pursue old ones that are blocked, these emotions are deemed to be constructive. In RET terminology specific words exist for these constructive emotions and these are contrasted with emotions that are deemed to be destructive, not only because they stem from absolutistic musturbatory evaluations (musts, shoulds, oughts, have to's, etc.) but also because most of the time they inhibit clients from achieving their basic goals and purposes. Thus in RET 'anxiety' is considered to be destructive and 'concern' is deemed to be constructive. However, when listening to clients' accounts of their own problems, it is important that RET therapists remember that the ways in which clients spontaneously (i.e. before RET) use language particularly with regard to feeling words may suggest different meanings to that denoted by RET language.

Thus opportunities for confusion and misunderstanding that arise when we consider the ways in which feeling words are used by clients and RET therapists are many. Consider the term 'anxiety'. Anxiety in RET terminology is deemed to result when there exists a threat to the client's personal domain, a threat which is absolutistically evaluated as 'terrible' or 'awful' and which absolutely <u>must</u> not occur. Concern is deemed to result when the client does not evaluate this perceived threat in an absolutistic manner, but instead believes: 'I really don't want this threat to occur but if it does, it does'. Such a Belief will result in the person concluding that if the threat does occur it would be unfortunate and bad rather than (absolutistically) awful and terrible. However, clients do not make this distinction spontaneously. They may, for example, report feeling 'concern' when a cognitive analysis reveals that they are, in RET terms, 'anxious'. Conversely other clients will report feeling 'anxious' when they are, according to RET theory, experiencing strong 'concern' since they are not making absolutistic irrational evaluations. For example, one of my clients consistently used the term 'anxiety' to refer to keenness. Had I assumed that his use of the term 'anxiety' was in fact synonymous with the RET use of the term 'anxiety' I would have wasted a lot of therapeutic time by seeking to find irrational evaluations which did not exist. I might have also assumed that the client was a D.C.(difficult customer) because he would not admit to such irrational evaluations.

An additional issue needs to be considered when the term 'anxiety' is subjected to an analysis of its meaning. Although a client may agree that his or her feelings of anxiety stem from the irrational Belief: 'This perceived threat must not occur', the client may not agree with the therapist's position that such feelings are destructive. Indeed, many clients consider that anxiety (in the RET sense) will in fact motivate them to carry out a given task. Whether anxiety will motivate them to better performances is, of course, the issue which needs to be addressed. However, for RET therapists to assume that once anxiety has been elicited the client will necessarily wish to change feelings of anxiety to those of concern overlooks an important fact - namely that clients make inferences and evaluations about their feelings. As DiGiuseppe (1984) has shown, some people consider that good things might happen or bad things might not happen as a result of experiencing (in RET terms) destructive negative feelings. This is one good reason why it is often helpful to discuss with clients their goals for change (Wessler & Wessler, 1980). To assume that the client wishes to change a destructive negative emotion without checking that this is the case may be a recipe for therapeutic failure.

Depression, according to RET theory, is a destructive negative emotion which occurs when clients evaluate some loss to their personal domain as absolutistically awful or terrible, conclusions which stem from the Belief: 'This loss must not occur or must not be as bad as it is'. It is contrasted with the constructive negative emotion, sadness, which occurs when such losses are evaluated as bad but without the concomitant 'must'. Again, clients regularly refer to their own feelings of 'sadness' when they are really, in RET terms, 'depressed' and vice versa! Continuing the analysis outlined above covering the implications of destructive negative feelings, some depressed clients construe this painful emotion as a sign of acute sensitivity (in a productive sense) and may view a therapist's attempts to help them to give up their depression as an attempt to make them less sensitive - efforts they would stubbornly resist. Thus, again, it is important for rational-emotive therapists to be aware that some clients create private meanings about their feelings of depression which may refer to positive implications of this emotion rather than the negative implications held by their RET therapists.

Guilt, according to RET theory, occurs when clients break their moral or ethical codes and absolutistically insist that this must not have occurred. Such individuals damn themselves as 'bad' individuals for committing such a 'bad' act. The rational alternative to guilt is often expressed in the RET literature as remorse, regret, or sorrow. These emotions are deemed to occur when the bad act is viewed as bad but when the person concerned does not demand: 'I must not have done this bad thing' or conclude: 'I am bad for doing it'. Rather the person accepts him or herself as a fallible human being without (and this is important) excusing him or herself from acting badly. Clients often misconstrue their therapists' interventions when the emotion of guilt is targeted for change, particularly when therapists do not check out with their clients that this is a troublesome emotion for them. Thus, some clients may accuse the RET therapist of encouraging them to do bad things or, less problematically, not discouraging them from doing bad things because they use the term 'guilt' in a different way from their therapists. In addition, clients often believe that guilt, in the RET use of the word, will actually protect them from doing bad things in the future rather than, as is argued in RET theory, encouraging them to do bad things. In this latter analysis once one has damned oneself and regards oneself as bad, this will lead to the person committing more rather than less bad acts. As Ellis puts it: 'How can a shit be deshitified?'

Anger is a particularly troublesome emotion since it often has several meanings. Anger, according to RET theory, is regarded as being a destructive negative emotion which stems from an absolutistic Belief that the other person must not break my rule or must not act as badly as they do, in fact, act. It is contrasted with the appropriate feeling alternative - annoyance which is regarded as being constructive and stems from the Belief: 'I don't like your bad behaviour but there is no reason why you must not act this way and you are not a worm (or any other sub-human term that the client uses) for acting badly'. It is important to realise, as DiGiuseppe (1984) has done, that people often consider that if they are not angry they will, by definition, then allow other people to dominate them. In a sense they believe: 'I have to be angry in order to protect myself from other people's bad influence'. If RET therapists do not first clearly distinguish between the RET meanings of anger and annoyance for their clients then the latter may view therapists' attempts to change their anger to annoyance as (1) advice to act less powerfully in the social arena, or (2) suggestions that they would be wise to experience *less* strong emotions and thus to deny the strength of their rational desires. RET theory holds that annoyance is not necessarily less intense than anger but clients often conclude that it is. This is, of course, not the true intention of RET therapists but without discussing these distinctions *before* implementing Disputing strategies, client 'resistance' is likely to occur, although, of course, it is not resistance but the results of a poorly designed therapeutic intervention.

Ellis (personal communication) has recently advocated that in order to get over these semantic problems with respect to the term 'anger', damning anger (an inappropriate emotion) be distinguished from non-damning anger (an appropriate emotion). Again, if this distinction is not made then the client who positively values 'anger' will be unlikely to give up his or her 'positive' emotion. However, if the therapist can help the person to realise that there are different types of anger and that non-damning anger is in fact productive and damning anger, unproductive, then the client is at least liable to listen to the therapist whereas in the previous scenario the client may well switch off from the therapist who is viewed as a person who is trying to encourage the client to relinquish a 'positive' emotion.

Similar arguments can be used when jealousy is the focus for discussion and the distinction between destructive and constructive jealousy can usefully be introduced to clients who, while experiencing the negative behavioural, emotional and interpersonal consequences of destructive jealousy, nevertheless regard their feelings of jealousy as evidence that they really love their partner. If a therapist encourages such a person to work on giving up feelings of jealousy without making distinctions between its destructive and constructive forms then the person is likely to 'resist' the therapist who in their mind is advocating that they relinquish their feelings of love for their partner.

PREMISE LANGUAGE

Wessler & Wessler (1980) have argued that a person's Beliefs can be put in the form of a syllogism which contains both a premise and a derivative. Thus, 'I must do well' is a premise and 'If I don't do well I would be worthless' would be the derivative from the premise. It is apparent that semantic confusion can often result when RET therapists refer to such terms as musts, shoulds, oughts, have to's, etc. A major problematic area here concerns the conditionality of these terms. Thus, the statement 'I must do well in order to pass my exams' is a conditional phrase and not therefore irrational because the person is outlining the conditions which have to be met in order for an outcome to be achieved. Indeed, novice RET therapists who are only so delighted to have identified a 'must' in the client's thinking wrongly assume that all 'musts' are irrational and therefore to be targeted for change. This is certainly not the case. It is to be understood at this point that rational-emotive therapists are only interested in targeting for change irrational 'musts' (i.e. those that are absolutistic in nature) especially when these are implicated in feelings that the client wishes to change. This latter point is important. I have often heard RET therapists doing sound RET but not therapeutic RET. Here therapists have in fact identified absolutistic musts and are using correct Disputational strategies to help the client to give them up, but the problem is that the client does not want to change his or her destructive negative emotions or dysfunctional behaviour.

The term 'should' is particularly problematic. As Vertes (1971) has shown, the word 'should' has several different semantic meanings. It can mean, of course, I absolutely should. It can also mean, I preferably should. It also has an empirical meaning (e.g. given the conditions that exist in the world at this present time, the sun should come up in the morning). It can also refer to matters of recommendation, (e.g. 'You really should go and see Chariots of Fire). I have on more than one occasion heard novice RET therapists challenge such non-absolutistic 'should': 'Why *must* you see 'Chariots of Fire'?'. 'Because I like it', the client replies. 'But why must you have what you like?' retorts the therapist. This elementary therapeutic error would not occur if therapists learn not to confuse the word with its meaning.

A particular problem is encountered when the word 'right' is used in therapy in sentences such as: 'He has no right to act that way'. I have sometimes heard RET therapists involve themselves in unproductive discussions with their clients concerning the non-absolutistic meaning of the word 'Right'. 'You have the right to do anything; you have the right to rape and murder if that's your inclination' is an example. While this is theoretically correct (this statement really means that there is no law in the universe to suggest that the person must not rape or pillage), the word 'right' is extremely problematic, and in my experience will often be construed by clients as meaning that the therapist is either actively advocating these activities or refusing to condemn their 'badness'. Such is the confusion about the term 'right', that RET therapists might be well advised to drop this from their vocabulary, at least in therapy.

Similar problems can occur when relative or rational Beliefs are considered. Thus RET therapists often teach their clients that the rational form of 'must' is 'I want to' or 'I would prefer to'. While this is correct, it is not the only way of expressing a relative Belief. Thus, the term 'It would be better' is also a rational Belief but one which does not indicate that the person may actually *want* to carry out the activity in question Take, for example, students who believe that they absolutely must pass an exam. A therapist in trying to help such clients discriminate between their preferences and demands correctly helps them see that they *want* to pass the exam but they do not have to. But what if such clients go on to express an irrational Belief about working to pass the exam? The therapist who tries to help them to see that while they don't have to work, they would want to work is likely to be using an unproductive strategy which ignores the notion that a person may not want to do what *would be better*. Rational Beliefs can then take the form of a desire and therefore a client can be encouraged to undertake an activity because of their desire. But a client can also be encouraged to undertake an undesired activity that would be in their best interests because they want the results of doing this activity. Their desire concerns the outcome of the activity and not the process.

DERIVATIVE LANGUAGE

Semantic problems can occur when the language of derivatives is analysed particularly when the terms 'horror', 'awful' and 'terrible' are considered. These terms in RET theory are distinguished from terms such as 'catastrophe' and 'tragedy' (as in the phrase, tragedies are not awful). In RET terminology, a tragedy is something that occurs which is rated as very bad. 'Terrible' and related terms in RET theory add to the notion of tragedy. 'Terrible' relates to the Belief that this tragedy must not occur or must not be as bad as it is. This distinction needs to be carefully made with clients otherwise they may assume that their therapists are being insensitive to their tragedies by trying to show them that such bad events are not _that_ bad. Such clients may ask: 'Are you trying to argue that it wasn't that bad for me to lose all my possessions and my family in that fire?'. Indeed, my experience in working with people who have recently experienced tragedies such as losing a loved one, or being raped, has shown me that endeavours to teach the client the difference between tragedy and horror may themselves be viewed as insensitive interventions by clients who regard their destructive negative emotions as highly appropriate to their situation.

Semantic confusion can often arise when the term 'fallible human being' is being discussed in therapy. First, it is important to ascertain that the client actually understands what the term 'fallible' means. One of the my clients in Birmingham (U.K.) thought that it meant 'obese' and was insulted as I tried to encourage her to accept herself as a fallible human being in such circumstances! In addition, clients may construe therapists' attempts to encourage them to accept themselves as fallible as encouragement for them to condone their bad actions, or as reasons to excuse future bad actions. When clients view the term 'fallible' as having bad connotations it is hardly surprising when they 'resist' their therapists' attempts to encourage them to accept themselves as fallible human beings. Another problem relating to the attitude 'fallible human being' is that it may not accurately reflect the source of the client's irrationality. More than one client has said to me: 'Yes, I can accept myself as a fallible human being' but shortly after implied: '.... who must not act badly'. It is therefore important when planning Disputing strategies to look at <u>both</u> premise <u>and</u> derivative forms of syllogisms to ensure that irrationalities are being challenged at both levels.

The associated term 'self-acceptance' also has its semantic problems. 'Acceptance' is a particularly difficult word because it can often be viewed in clients' minds as meaning 'resignation'. Thus, by encouraging clients to accept themselves, their resistance may indicate that they perceive that they are being asked to resign themselves to being forever the slob that they think they are. Acceptance, when viewed as meaning resignation, also conjures up images of inaction whereas in RET self-acceptance is viewed as encouraging clients towards productive action.

Semantic problems can also arise when issues of self-rating are being discussed with clients. Clients often have their own private ways of rating themselves. It may come as a surprise to most RET therapists that not all clients regard themselves as 'shits'. In supervising a therapy tape, I heard a RET therapist and his client get into a heated argument due to the therapist's insistence that the client was calling himself a 'shit'. The client replied: 'Listen, I have never, ever in my whole life considered myself a shit and I really don't like your attempts to persuade me thus'. Here the client was being more rational than the therapist! Thus the terms shit, bad, worthless, less worthy, undeserving, are not synonymous and in fact I have found it very useful to discover the particular form of negative self-rating that clients use. The resulting shared meaning that I have been able to establish with my clients has been facilitative of both therapeutic communication and the therapeutic change programme.

THE LANGUAGE OF CHANGE

The language which therapists use when they attempt to help clients change can also lead to semantic confusion and constitute obstacles to therapeutic progress. For example, clients may construe the therapist's attempt to have them give up their musts as meaning: 'Give up your desire'. Clients may often assume that the opposite of crucial is indifference. In planning such Disputing strategies and while Disputing irrational musts, therapists are recommended to keep in mind the importance of using the language of desire during this entire process. The term 'homework' can also be extremely problematic because in some clients' minds, certainly in Britain, homework is associated with school and with negative experiences. I often find it helpful to ask the client to give me a word that would capture the notion of the importance of putting into practice between therapy sessions what has been learned in the sessions. Thus, one client came up with the term 'training assignment', while another client came up with the term 'transfer task' to capture the meaning of the phrase usually referred to as homework.

While urging clients to persist at executing assignments, Ellis often exhorts clients to 'work and practise, work and practise'. This is good advice but can be construed as very negative by clients who already have a high degree of low frustration tolerance. Thus, for some clients, words like persistence or repetition may capture similar meanings but be less negative in connotation. In addition, one of the hidden dangers of urging clients to 'work and practise' and to 'push themselves hard in therapy' is that some clients may actually consider that their therapists believe that they _have to_ do the work or that they _have to_ change. In these instances therapists serve as a poor role model in the minds of their clients.

It is important to realise that virtually any word that therapists can use when encouraging people to change may have negative connotations for some clients. It is therefore perhaps a good idea for RET therapists to ask clients at the end of therapy whether in this context they are using any words that the clients are viewing as negative (Beck et al., 1979). If I was a client in RET or cognitive therapy I would view the term 'agenda' negatively. This is because my mother used to ask me at the beginning of every day 'What's on your agenda today, son?' a term which has come to have negative connotations for me.

USING WORDS CLIENTS DO NOT UNDERSTAND

RET is best viewed as an educational therapy. Since good education depends on effective communication, it is important that the therapist uses words that clients can understand. My seven years experience working in a working class community in East Birmingham has taught me to be wary of using a number of words that are in common usage among RET therapists. I have found the following words to be most problematic amongst this population: dysfunction, fallible, evidence, Belief, cognition (to be avoided almost at all costs), rational, etc. Such clients will in fact rarely say to you 'I'm sorry, I don't understand what that means' but will give various non-verbal cues to non-understanding. Thus, I have detected over the years the following patterns of non-understanding: (a) The Glazed Look: here the client displays a glazed expression often accompanied by a fixed smile. (b) The Automatic Head Nod: here the clients nod knowingly as if they understand their therapists' RET terminology. If such nodding goes on for longer than 10 seconds without interruption this is a sign that clients may not understand what is being said. If this is accompanied by the fixed smile then it is almost guaranteed that the client doesn't understand a word the therapist is saying.

TOWARD SHARED MEANING IN RET

In this concluding section ways in which RET therapists can strive towards adopting shared meaning frameworks with their clients will be outlined. One important method of checking whether a client has understood the meaning of a concept which the therapist is using is to ask the client for clarification of the client's understanding. Questions like: 'I am not sure whether I am making myself clear on this point. Can you put into your own words what you think I am saying?', can be used to good effect in that they encourage clients to be active in the therapeutic process and to use their own language rather than just parroting the language of the therapist. It is especially important for the therapist to pay attention to the non-verbal aspects of the client's responses to such questions. When the client uses exactly the same language as the therapist the way in which the client responds can often serve as a guide to whether or not he or she has understood the therapist's communications. When the client uses the same words as the therapist in answer to such enquiries the therapist can usefully ask for example: 'What do you understand by the word awful. What other words in your mind are equivalent to this word?'. I have found asking for synonyms particularly revealing of clients' misunderstandings of the rational concepts I have been endeavouring to teach them. For example, a common 'synonym' that clients use for the term 'awful' is 'very bad'. The latter, of course, is not a synonym for the former in RET theory.

A helpful therapeutic strategy for making clear distinctions between constructive and destructive negative emotions while ensuring that client and therapist have a shared meaning framework while using the same verbal label is to define terms before implementing Disputing strategies. In particular, emotions should be linked with their evaluative Beliefs in any exposition of terms. For example, while trying to clarify whether a client is angry (damningly angry) or annoyed (non-damningly angry) I might say something like this, 'O.K. So you say that you are angry. Now, when you were experiencing that emotion, what was more likely to be going through your mind? Did you believe, for example, that that person who did that bad thing was no good and absolutely should not have acted that way, or did you believe that although their behaviour was bad, there was no reason why the person must not have acted that way. Also, did you regard <u>them</u> as bad or just <u>their behaviour</u> as bad?'. I have found that my clients can often more reliably distinguish between the two emotional states when I include their cognitive definitions than when such definitions are excluded. Clients rarely know spontaneously the RET theoretical distinction between these two emotional states. Thus, when discussing feeling terms with clients (particularly when one is distinguishing between constructive and destructive negative emotions) strive to include their cognitive counterparts.

RET therapists have much to learn from the work of George Kelly (1955) and his followers in personal construct therapy with respect to discovering the clients' idiosyncratic meaning systems. One such strategy derived from PCT concerns asking clients for polar opposites for their feelings. This is particularly useful while planning and carrying out Disputing strategies since it may help the therapist to discover why clients may not in reality wish to change an emotion that they claim they wish to change and which, according to RET theory, is a destructive negative emotion. Thus, for example, I once worked with a depressed client who claimed not to want to be depressed but was resisting my attempts to help her feel sad. I asked her what she associated in her mind as being the opposite of sad, to which she replied 'sensitive'. This highly idiosyncratic use of the word 'sad' as being in some way equivalent to being insensitive helped me to understand why my client resisted my attempts to encourage her to experience what RET theory states is a constructive negative emotion.

In conclusion I wish to emphasize that therapists should preferably be alert to the idiosyncratic ways in which clients use language and the equally idiosyncratic ways in which they may interpret and evaluate the rational concepts that RET therapists strive to teach them. It is important for RET therapists to internalise the language system of RET but in doing so they should not assume that their clients will magically share the meaning structure implicit in rational-emotive terminology.

Chapter Three

THE THERAPEUTIC ALLIANCE IN RATIONAL-EMOTIVE INDIVIDUAL THERAPY

WINDY DRYDEN

BORDIN'S (1979) CONCEPT OF THE THERAPEUTIC ALLIANCE

As a rational-emotive therapist I have found the work of Ed Bordin (1979) on the concept of the therapeutic alliance particularly helpful in developing a basic framework for the conduct of RET. Bordin argues that the therapeutic alliance refers to the complex of attachments and shared understandings formed and activities undertaken by therapists and clients as the former attempt to help the latter with their psychological problems.

Bordin has stressed that there are three major components of the therapeutic alliance: (a) *bonds* - which refer to the interpersonal connectedness between therapist and client; (b) *goals* - which refer to the aims of both therapist and client; and (c) *tasks* - which are activities carried out by both therapist and client in the service of the latter's goals.

I will consider each of these components separately and show that rational-emotive therapists have important clinical decisions to make in each of the three alliance domains so as to individualize therapy for each client and thus maximize therapeutic benefit.

At the outset it should be noted that Bordin (1979) has speculated that effective therapy occurs when therapist and client (a) have an appropriately bonded working relationship; (b) mutually agree on the goals of the therapeutic enterprise; and (c) both understand their own and the other person's therapeutic tasks and agree to carry out these to implement the client's goals.

Bonds

The major concern of rational-emotive therapists in the bond domain should be to establish and maintain an appropriately bonded relationship that will encourage _each_ individual client to implement his or her goal-directed therapeutic tasks. It should be underscored that there is no _single_ effective bond that can be formed with clients in RET; different clients require different bonds. This observation became clear to me when on a six months' sabbatical at the Center for Cognitive Therapy in Philadelphia in 1981. As reported elsewhere (Dryden, 1984a), I saw two clients on the same afternoon who benefited from a different bonded relationship with me. At 4 p.m. I saw Mrs. G., a fifty-year-old married business woman, who was impressed with my British professional qualifications and whose responses to initial questions indicated that she anticipated and preferred a very formal relationship with her therapist. I provided such a relationship by using formal language, citing the research literature whenever appropriate, wearing a suit, shirt and tie and by referring to myself as Dr. Dryden and to my client as Mrs. G. On one occasion I inadvertently used her first name and was put firmly in my place concerning the protocol of professional relationships. On another occasion I disclosed a piece of personal information in order to make a therapeutic point and was told in no uncertain terms: 'Young man, I am not paying you good money to hear about your problems'. Here, a therapist is faced with the choice of respecting and meeting a client's bond anticipations and preferences or examining the reasons why, for example, this client was so adamantly against her therapist's informality. In my experience the latter strategy is rarely productive and rational-emotive therapists are recommended to fulfil their clients' preferences for therapeutic style as long as doing so does not reinforce the client's psychological problems.

At 5 p.m. on the same afternoon I regularly saw Mr. B., a forty-two-year-old male nurse who indicated that he did not respond well to his previous therapist's neutrality and formality. Our therapy sessions were thus characterized by an informal bond. Before seeing him I would remove my jacket and tie that I wore for Mrs. G.; in sessions we would use our first names and would both have our feet up on my desk. We also developed the habit of taking turns to bring in cans of soda and my client referred to our meetings as 'rap sessions' while I conceptualized my work as therapy within an informal context.

I maintain that Mrs. G. would not have responded well to an informal therapeutic relationship nor would Mr. B. have done as well with a highly formal mode of therapy. Thus, I argue that it is important that rational-emotive therapists pay attention to the question: 'Which bond is likely to be most effective with a particular patient at a given time in the therapeutic process?'. Drawing upon social psychological principles, certain writers have argued that some clients show more progress when the therapeutic bond is based on liking and trustworthiness, while other flourish more when the bond emphasizes therapist credibility and expertness (Beutler, 1983; Dorn, 1984; Strong & Claiborn, 1982). Future research in RET, could fruitfully address the issue of which bond is effective with which clients. However, until we have such data, therapists could make decisions about what type of bond to foster on the basis of an early assessment of the client's anticipations and preferences in the bond domain and to try to meet such expectations, at least initially. This is one reason why I would caution novice therapists against emulating the therapeutic style of leading RET practitioners whose bond with clients may be based mainly on prestige and expertness. Rational-emotive therapists should thus be prepared to emphasize different aspects of themselves with different clients in the bond domain, without adopting an inauthentic facade, and to monitor transactions in this domain throughout therapy.

How can this best be done? One way would be to administer a portion of Lazarus's (1981) Life History Questionnaire which focuses on client's expectations regarding therapy. The items: 'How do you think a therapist should interact with his or her clients?' and 'What personal qualities do you think the ideal therapist should possess?' are particularly relevant and could usefully provide impetus for further exploration of this issue at the outset of therapy. If the client has had therapy previously, the current therapist could usefully explore what aspects of the previous therapist(s)' interactive style and behaviour were deemed by the client to be both helpful and unhelpful. Particular emphasis should be placed on the exploration of the instrumental nature of previous therapeutic bonds since statements such as: 'He was warm and caring' are of little use unless the client evaluated these qualities positively and attributed therapeutic progress to these factors.

Furthermore, and for similar reasons, I have found it helpful to explore clients' accounts of people in their lives who have had both positive and negative therapeutic influence on their personal development. Such exploration may provide the therapist with important clues concerning which types of therapeutic bonds to promote actively with certain clients and which bonds to avoid developing with others.

Therapeutic style is another aspect of the bond domain which requires attention. Interpersonally-orientated psychotherapists (e.g. Anchin & Kiesler, 1982) have argued that clinicians need to be aware that therapeutic styles have a 'for better or worse' impact on different clients. Rational-emotive therapists tend to be active and directive in their style of conducting therapy. This therapeutic style may not be entirely productive with both passive clients and, as Beutler (1983) has argued, clients who are highly reactive to interpersonal influence. Clients who tend to be passive in their interpersonal style of relating may 'pull' an increasingly active style from their therapists who may in turn reinforce these clients' passivity with their increased activity. Clients whose psychological problems are intrinsically bound up with a passive style of relating are particularly vulnerable in this regard. It is important that rational-emotive therapists be aware of the danger of becoming enmeshed in such unproductive vicious circles which have unfortunate self-fulfilling prophecy implications for their passive clients. These therapists need to engage their clients productively at a level which constructively encourages increased activity on their part but without threatening them through the use of an <u>overly</u> passive style of practising RET.

Beutler (1983) has argued that all approaches to psychotherapy can be viewed as a process of persuasion and this is particularly true of RET practitioners who aim to 'persuade' clients to re-evaluate and change their irrational Beliefs. As such, rational-emotive therapists need to be especially careful in working with clients for whom such persuasive attempts may be perceived as especially threatening (i.e. highly reactant clients). Here it is important that therapists execute their strategies with due regard to helping such clients to preserve their sense of autonomy, emphasizing throughout that these clients are in control of their own thought processes and decisions concerning whether or not to change them. At present, the above suggestions are speculative and await full empirical enquiry, but my clinical work has led me to question the desirability of establishing the same therapeutic bond with all clients and of practising rational-emotive therapy in an unchanging therapeutic style.

Goals

The major concern of rational-emotive therapists in the goal domain of the alliance is to ensure that there is agreement between therapist and client on the client's outcome goals for change. A prerequisite of such agreement concerns clients and therapists arriving at a shared understanding of the clients' most relevant problems as defined by the client (Meichenbaum & Gilmore, 1982). Difficulties may occur here when the therapist uncritically accepts the client's initial accounts of his or her problem since such accounts may well be biased by the client's internalized values, e.g. the views of significant others in the client's life. In addition, although most rational-emotive therapists consider that early goal-setting with the client is important, clients' initial statements about their goals for change may well be coloured by their psychological disturbance as well as by their internalized values concerning what these goals should be. Rational-emotive therapists need to walk a fine line between uncritically accepting clients' initial goals for change and disregarding them altogether. A helpful solution here involves establishment and maintenance of a channel of communication between client and therapist which deals with metatherapy issues (i.e. issues concerning matters relating to therapy itself). Dryden & Hunt (1985) have referred to the activities that occur within this channel as involving negotiations and renegotiations about therapeutic issues. Rational-emotive therapists need to take the main responsibility for keeping this communication channel open in order to monitor clients' goals over time and to determine the reasons for shifts in these goals.

Pinsof & Catherall (1986) have made the important point that clients' goals occur (implicitly or explicitly) in reference to their most important relationships and their therapists need to be mindful of the impact that these systems are likely to have on both the selection of such goals and the client's degree of progress towards goal attainment. Adopting this focus may well possibly mean involving parts of the client's interpersonal system in therapy itself. It also suggests that future theorizing in RET could profitably assign a more central role to interpersonal issues (cf. Kwee & Lazarus, 1986; Safran, 1984).

Tasks

As outlined in Chapter 1, rational-emotive practitioners tend to subscribe to the following therapeutic process. Initially, having agreed to offer help to the client, the therapist attempts to structure the therapeutic process for the client and begins both to assess his or her problems in rational-emotive terms and also to help the client to view his or her problems within this framework. Goals are elicited based on a rational-emotive assessment and therapeutic strategies and techniques are implemented to effect the desired changes. Finally, obstacles to client change are analyzed and, it is hoped, overcome, and therapeutic gains are stabilized and maintained.

Therapists have tasks to execute at each stage in the rational-emotive therapeutic process and these will now be outlined.

Structuring. Effective RET depends in part on each participant clearly understanding their respective responsibilities in the therapeutic endeavour and upon each agreeing to discharge these responsibilities in the form of carrying out therapeutic tasks. It is the therapist's major responsibility to help the client to make sense of this process by providing an overall structure of mutual responsibilities and tasks. It is important to stress that structuring occurs throughout therapy and not just at the outset of the process. Sensitive clinicians who pay attention to alliance issues will structure the process using language which the client can understand and analogies which make sense to each individual person. Thus, it is often helpful to discover clients' hobbies and interests so that apt and personally meaningful structuring statements can be made. Thus, if a client is interested in golf, ascertaining how that person learned the game may be valuable in drawing parallels between the processes of learning coping skills and learning golfing skills. Both involve practice and failures can be realistically anticipated in each activity.

Assessment and conceptualization of clients' problems. During the assessment process, rational-emotive therapists traditionally attempt to gain a full understanding of the cognitive and behavioural variables that are maintaining their clients' problems. During this stage two issues become salient from an alliance theory perspective. First, it is important for therapist and client to arrive at a shared definition of the client's problems (i.e. what these problems are). Second, as Meichenbaum & Gilmore (1982) have noted, it is important for them to negotiate a shared conceptualization of the client's problem (i.e. an explanation of what accounts for the existence of this problem) so that they can work productively together in the intervention stage of therapy.

When working towards shared problem conceptualization, I argue that it is important for RET therapists to use, wherever possible, the client's own language and concepts, particularly when providing alternative explanations of their problems. This helps therapists to work within the range of what clients will accept as plausible conceptualizations of their problems. If clients' own ideas about the origins of their problems and more particularly what maintain them are ignored, then they may well resist accepting their therapists' conceptualizations. As Golden (1985) has noted, sometimes therapists often have to accept initially, for pragmatic purposes, a client's different (i.e. to the therapist's) conceptualization of his or her problems in order to arrive later at a shared one. In addition, rational-emotive therapists may well privately (i.e. to themselves) conceptualize a client's problems in rational-emotive terms (irrational Beliefs) while publicly (to the client) using the client's conceptualization (e.g. negative self-hypnosis). To what extent the effectiveness of RET is based on negotiation or on the unilateral persuasion attempts of the therapist is a matter for future empirical enquiry

Change tactics. Once the therapist and client have come to a mutually agreed understanding of the client's problems, the therapist then discusses with the client a variety of techniques that the client can use to reach his or her goals. Here it is important to realize that both client and therapist have tasks to execute.

Effective RET in the task domain tends to occur when:

(a) Clients understand what their tasks are.
(b) Clients understand how executing their tasks will help them achieve their goals.
(c) Clients are, in fact, capable of executing

their tasks and believe that they have this capability.

(d) Clients understand that change comes about through repeated execution of their tasks.

(e) Clients understand the tasks of their therapists and can see the link between their therapists' tasks, their own tasks and their goals.

(f) Therapists adequately prepare their clients to understand and execute the latter's tasks.

(g) Therapists effectively execute their tasks (i.e. they are skilled in the techniques of RET) and use a wide range of techniques appropriately.

(h) Therapists employ techniques which are congruent with their clients' learning styles. Whilst some clients learn best through action, others learn best through reading bibliotherapy texts, etc.

(i) Therapists employ techniques that clients have selected (from a range of possible procedures) rather than unilaterally selecting techniques without client participation.

(j) Therapists pace their interventions appropriately.

(k) Therapists employ techniques which are potent enough to help clients achieve their goals. (e.g. using exposure methods with clients with agoraphobic problems - Emmelkamp, Kuipers & Eggeraat, 1978).

FAILURES IN RET

I have been practising RET now for over ten years in a variety of settings, I have worked in (a) a university counselling service; (b) a general practice; (c) a National Health Service psychiatric clinic; (d) a local marriage guidance council and (e) private practice. I have seen, in these settings, a wide range of moderately to severely disturbed individuals who were deemed to be able to benefit from weekly counselling or psychotherapy. While I do not have any hard data to substantiate the point, I have found rational-emotive therapy to be a highly effective method of individual psychotherapy with a wide range of client problems.

However, I have of course had my therapeutic failures, and I would like, in this final section, to outline some of the factors that in my opinion have accounted for these failures. I will again use Bordin's (1979) useful concept of the therapeutic working alliance as a framework in this respect.

Goals

I have generally been unsuccessful with clients who have devoutly clung to goals where changes in other people were desired. (In this regard, I have also failed to involve these others in therapy). I have not been able to show or to persuade these clients that they make themselves emotionally disturbed and that they ought to work to change themselves before attempting to negotiate changes in their relationships with others. It is the devoutness of their Beliefs which seems to me to be the problem here.

Bonds

Unlike the majority of therapists of my acquaintance, I do not regard the relationship between therapist and client to be the sine qua non of effective therapy. I strive to accept my clients as fallible human beings and am prepared to work concertedly to help them overcome their problems, but do not endeavour to form very close, warm relationships with them. In the main, my clients do not appear to want such a relationship with me (preferring to become close and intimate with their significant others). However, occasionally I get clients who do wish to become (non-sexually) intimate with me. Some of these clients (who devoutly believe they need my love) leave therapy disappointed after I have failed either to get them to give up their dire need for love or to give them what they think they need.

Tasks

In this analysis I will assume throughout that therapists are practising RET effectively and thus the emphasis will be on client variables.

My basic thesis here is that when therapist and client agree concerning: (a) the view of psychological disturbance as stated in rational-emotive theory, (b) the rational-emotive view on the acquisition and perpetuation of psychological disturbance, and (c) the rational-emotive view of therapeutic change, such agreements are likely to enhance good therapeutic outcome. Furthermore, the greater the disagreement between the two participants on such matters, the greater the threat that exists to the therapeutic alliance with all the negative implications that this has for good therapeutic outcome. I should say at the outset that this hypothesis has yet to be tested and should thus be viewed sceptically.

I will illustrate my points by using clinical examples from my experience as a therapist.

Conceptualization of psychological disturbance. Rational-emotive theory states that much psychological disturbance can be attributed to clients' devout, absolutistic evaluations (irrational Beliefs) about themselves, other people and life events. RET therapists assume that most clients do not enter therapy sharing this viewpoint and, thus, one of the therapist's major tasks is to persuade the client to adopt this viewpoint if effective RET is to ensue. Of course, not all clients will be so persuaded because they have their own (different) ideas about the nature of their psychological problems and what causes them and are not prepared to relinquish these. In my experience, the following clients are not good candidates for RET unless they change their ideas about the determinants of their problems; those who believe that their problems are caused by (a) external events (including events that happened in childhood), (b) physical, dietary or biochemical factors, (c) repressed basic human impulses, (d) fate or astrological factors and (e) blockages in the body.

I once had a referral from a social worker who confused RET with Reichian therapy. The client specifically wanted to work on his character armour, blockages in which he considered were at the source of his problems. I explained that an error had been made and that I was a rational-emotive therapist and gave him a brief outline of the rational-emotive view of his problems. He responded with incredulity, saying that he hadn't heard such intellectualised clap-trap in a long while and asked me whether I knew of anyone who could really help him. I referred him to a local bioenergetics therapist who, apparently, helped him considerably.

Acquisition and perpetuation of psychological disturbance. Rational-emotive theory de-emphasizes the value of understanding acquisition variables in helping clients change. Rather, it stresses the importance of understanding how people perpetuate their psychological problems. This is because the theory hypothesizes that while past events may well have contributed to clients' psychological disturbance, these did not make them disturbed, since people bring their tendency to make themselves disturbed to these events and experiences. Thus, clients who come to therapy in order to trace their psychological problems back to their roots tend not to benefit greatly from the present-centred and future-orientated focus of RET. Clients who are prepared to look for and challenge their currently held irrational Beliefs do much better in RET than clients who are preoccupied with discovering how they came to hold such Beliefs in the first place.

A 60-year old woman with agoraphobic problems was firmly convinced that the origins of her panic lay in buried childhood feelings towards her parents, who while kindly disposed to my client, had placed undue burdens on her as a child. Not only did we have different views concerning the 'causes' of her present problems, but we differed as to the most appropriate time focus for the therapy. I did discuss her childhood with her, but as a stimulus to help her re-focus on her present disturbance-perpetuating Beliefs, but to no avail. She quit therapy with me and started consulting a Jungian therapist who has seen her now for two years with little impact on her panic disorder.

Views on therapeutic change. RET can be viewed as a therapeutic system which has a 'Protestant Ethic' view of therapeutic change. Clients are urged to 'work and practise' their way to emotional health by using a variety of cognitive, emotive and behavioural methods designed to help them to change their irrational Beliefs. Clients who are not prepared to put in the necessary hard work usually have less successful therapeutic outcomes than clients who challenge repeatedly their irrational Beliefs in thought, feeling and deed.

It follows from the above that RET places most emphasis on the activities that clients initiate and sustain outside therapy as the major agent of change. Clients who consider that change will occur primarily from therapy sessions usually do not gain as much from RET as clients who are in accord with the rational-emotive viewpoint on this matter.

During my six months stay at the Center for Cognitive Therapy in Philadelphia, I saw briefly a client who had heard of cognitive therapy for depression and wished to try it. I was learning this approach at the time and was keen to do it 'by the book'. The client had recently moved to Philadelphia from Los Angeles where she had consulted an experiential therapist with whom she had had a very close relationship which, in my opinion, had encouraged her to be more dependent on love and approval than she was before she consulted him. The client had come to believe that therapeutic change depended on a very warm, close therapeutic relationship in which completing homework assignments and 'Daily Record of Dysfunctional Thoughts' sheets had no place. Despite my attempts to change her views on such matters, she left cognitive therapy to seek another experiential therapist.

Ellis's study on failures in RET. Ellis (1983e) has published some interesting data which tend to corroborate my own experiences of therapeutic failure in RET. He chose fifty of his clients who were seen in individual and/or group RET and were rated by him, and where appropriate by his associate group therapist, as 'failures'. In some ways, this group consisted of fairly ideal RET clients in that they were individuals (1) of above average or of superior intelligence (in Ellis's judgement and that of their other group therapist); (2) who seemed really to understand RET and who were often effective (especially in group therapy) in helping others to learn and use it; (3) who in some ways made therapeutic progress and felt that they benefited by having RET but who still retained one or more serious presenting symptoms, such as severe depression, acute anxiety, overwhelming hostility, or extreme lack of self-discipline; and (4) who had at least one year of individual and/or group RET sessions, and sometimes considerably more.

This group was compared to clients who were selected on the same four criteria but who seemed to benefit greatly from RET. While a complete account of this study - which, of course, has its methodological flaws - can be found in Ellis (1983e), the following results are most pertinent:

> 1. In its cognitive aspects, RET... emphasizes the persistent use of reason, logic, and the scientific method to uproot clients' irrational Beliefs. Consequently, it ideally requires intelligence, concentration, and high-level, consistent cognitive self-Disputation and self-persuasion. These therapeutic behaviours would tend to be disrupted or blocked by extreme disturbance, by lack of organization, by grandiosity, by organic disruption, and by refusal to do RET-type Disputing of irrational ideas. All these

characteristics proved to be present in significantly more failures than in those clients who responded favourably to RET.

(2) RET also, to be quite successful, involves clients' forcefully and emotively changing their Beliefs and actions, and their being stubbornly determined to accept responsibility for their own inappropriate feelings and to vigorously work at changing these feelings (Ellis & Abrahms, 1978; Ellis & Whiteley, 1979). But the failure clients in this study were significantly more angry than those who responded well to RET; more of them were severely depressed and inactive, they were more often grandiose, and they were more frequently stubbornly resistant and rebellious. All these characteristics would presumably tend to interfere with the kind of emotive processes and changes that RET espouses.

(3) RET strongly advocates that clients, in order to improve, do in vivo activity homework assignments, deliberately force themselves to engage in many painful activities until they become familiar and unpainful, and notably work and practise its multimodal techniques. But the group of clients who signally failed in this study showed abysmally low frustration tolerance, had serious behavioural addictions, led disorganized lives, refrained from doing their activity homework assignments, were more frequently psychotic and generally refused to work at therapy. All these characteristics, which were found significantly more frequently than were found in the clients who responded quite well to RET, would tend to interfere with the behavioural methods of RET,

Thus it appears from the above analysis that the old adage of psychotherapy applies to RET: namely that clients who could most use therapy are precisely those individuals whose disturbance interferes with their benefiting from it.

Chapter Four

COMPROMISES IN RATIONAL-EMOTIVE THERAPY

WINDY DRYDEN

INTRODUCTION

In this chapter I discuss the notion that while RET therapists prefer to encourage their clients to achieve a profound philosophic change by replacing their irrational Beliefs with rational Beliefs, this is not always possible. In such cases, RET therapists are advised to make various compromises in helping clients deal with their problems in ways which do not involve philosophic change. These alternative strategies are termed 'compromises' in that, while not ideal, they often bear more fruit than the preferred strategies of RET.

I should say at the outset that by RET in this chapter I mean those therapeutic activities which are designed to effect philosophic change - or what Ellis calls 'elegant', 'preferential' or 'specialized' RET. I personally consider that therapeutic activities which are designed to effect other kinds of change (e.g. inferentially-based change, behaviourally-based change or change in Activating events) are best referred to as derived from other approaches to cognitive-behaviour therapy, although Ellis considers such activities to be part of 'inelegant', 'non-preferential' or 'general' RET. Since terms like 'elegant' vs 'inelegant', 'preferential' vs 'non-preferential' etc. are value-laden and may offend other cognitively-orientated practitioners, I prefer to avoid their use and thus distinguish between rational-emotive therapy and other forms of cognitive-behaviour therapy. This distinction is more likely, in my opinion, to promote constructive dialogue among cognitively-orientated therapists than the one employed by Ellis (1980b).

Before discussing the various compromises that RET therapists sometimes are called upon to make, it is first important to distinguish between rational-emotive therapy and other approaches to cognitive-behaviour therapy.

DIFFERENCES BETWEEN RATIONAL-EMOTIVE THERAPY AND OTHER APPROACHES TO COGNITIVE-BEHAVIOUR THERAPY

As opposed to other approaches to cognitive-behaviour therapy, rational-emotive therapy:

(1) Has a distinct philosophic emphasis which is one of its central features and which other forms of cognitive-behaviour therapy appear to omit. Thus, it stresses that humans appraise themselves, others and the world in terms of (a) rational, preferential, flexible and tolerant philosophies and in terms of (b) irrational, musturbatory, rigid, intolerant and absolutistic philosophies.

(2) Has an existential-humanistic outlook which is intrinsic to it and which is omitted by most other approaches to cognitive behaviour therapy. Thus, it sees people 'as holistic, goal-directed individuals who have importance in the world just because they are human and alive; it unconditionally accepts them with their limitations, and it particularly focuses upon their experiences and values, including their self-actualizing potentialities' (Ellis, 1980b, p. 327). It also shares the views of ethical humanism by encouraging people to emphasize human interest (self and social) over the interests of deities, material objects and lower animals.

(3) Favours striving for pervasive and long-lasting (philosophically-based) rather than symptomatic change.

(4) Attempts to help humans eliminate all self-ratings and views self-esteem as a self-defeating concept which encourage them to make conditional evaluations of self. Instead, it teaches people <u>un</u>conditional self-acceptance (Ellis, 1972).

(5) Considers psychological disturbance to reflect an attitude to taking life 'too' seriously and thus advocates the appropriate use of various humorous therapeutic methods (Ellis, 1977b, 1977c, 1981c).

(6) Stresses the use of antimusturbatory rather than antiempirical Disputing methods. Since it considers that inferential distortions often stem from dogmatic musts, shoulds, etc., rational-emotive therapy favours going to the philosophic core of emotional disturbance and Disputing the irrational Beliefs at this core rather than merely Disputing antiempirical inferences which are more peripheral. Also rational-emotive therapy favours the use of forceful logicoempirical Disputing of irrational Beliefs whenever possible rather than the employment of rationally-orientated, coping self-statements. When feasible, rational-emotive therapy teaches clients how to become their own scientists instead of parroting therapist inculcated rational Beliefs.

(7) Gives a more central explanatory role to the concept of discomfort anxiety in psychological disturbance than do other cognitive-behavioural approaches to psychotherapy. Discomfort anxiety is defined as: 'emotional hypertension that arises when people feel (1) that their life or comfort is threatened, (2) that they _must_ not feel uncomfortable and _have to_ feel at ease and (3) that it is awful or terrible (rather than merely inconvenient or disadvantageous) when they don't get what they supposedly must' (Ellis, 1980b, p. 331). While other cognitive-behavioural approaches to psychotherapy recognise specific instances of discomfort anxieties (e.g. 'fear of fear' - Mackay, 1984), they tend not to regard discomfort disturbance to be as centrally implicated in psychological problems as does rational-emotive therapy.

(8) Emphasizes, more than other approaches to cognitive behaviour therapy, that humans frequently make themselves disturbed about their original disturbances. Thus, rational-emotive therapists actively look for secondary symptoms of disturbances and encourage clients to work on overcoming

these before addressing themselves to the primary disturbance.

(9) Has clearcut theories of disturbance and its treatment, but is eclectic or multimodal in its techniques. However, it favours some techniques (e.g. active Disputing) over others (e.g. cognitive distraction) and strives for profound philosophic change where feasible.

(10) Discriminates between 'rational' and 'irrational' negative emotions. Rational-emotive theory considers such negative emotions as sadness, annoyance, concern, regret, and disappointment as 'rational' affective responses to thwarted desires based on a non-devout philosophy of desire and it views them as healthy when they do not needlessly interfere with people's goals and purposes. However, it sees depression, anger, anxiety, guilt, shame/embarrassment, self-pity, and feelings of inadequacy usually as 'irrational' emotions based on absolutistic demands about thwarted desires. Rational-emotive therapy considers these latter feelings as symptoms of disturbance because they very frequently (but not always) sabotage people from pursuing constructively their goals and purposes. Other approaches to cognitive-behaviour therapy do not make such fine discriminations between 'rational' and 'irrational' negative emotions.

(11) Advocates therapists giving unconditional acceptance rather than giving warmth or approval to clients. Other cognitive-behaviour therapies tend not to make this distinction. Rational-emotive therapy holds that counsellor warmth and approval have their distinct dangers in that they may unwittingly encourage clients to strengthen their dire needs for love and approval. When RET therapists unconditionally accept their clients they also serve as good role models, in that they also help clients to unconditionally accept themselves.

(12) Stresses the importance of the use of vigour and force in counteracting irrational philosophies and behaviours (Dryden, 1984c, Ellis, 1979c). Rational-emotive therapy is alone among cognitive-behaviour-

al approaches to psychotherapy in stressing that humans are, for the most part, biologically predisposed to originate and perpetuate their disturbances and often thus experience great difficulty in changing the ideological roots of these problems. Since it holds this view it urges both therapists and clients to use considerable force and vigour in interrupting clients' irrationalities.

(13) Is more selective than most other cognitive-behaviour therapies in choosing behavioural change methods. Thus, it favours the use of penalization in encouraging resistant clients to change. Often these clients won't change to obtain positive reinforcements, but may be encouraged to change to avoid stiff penalties. Furthermore, rational-emotive practitioners have reservations concerning the use of social reinforcement in psychotherapy. They consider that humans are too reinforceable and that they often do the right thing for the wrong reason. Thus, they may change to please their socially reinforcing therapists, but in doing so they have not been encouraged to think and act for their own sake. RET therapists aim to help clients become maximally non-conformist, non-dependent and individualistic and would thus use social reinforcement techniques sparingly. Finally, rational-emotive therapy favours the use of in-vivo desensitization and flooding methods rather than the use of gradual desensitization techniques since it argues that the former procedures best help clients to raise their level of frustration tolerance (Ellis, 1983c).

Thus, as noted in Chapter 1, the major goal of rational-emotive therapy is an ambitious one: to encourage clients to make a profound philosophic change in the two main areas of ego disturbance and discomfort disturbance. This involves helping clients, as far as is humanly possible, to give up their irrational Beliefs and to replace these with rational Beliefs.

In summary, as was outlined in Chapter 1, in rational-emotive therapy, the major goals are (a) to help clients pursue their long-range basic goals and purposes and to help them do so as effectively as possible by fully accepting themselves and tolerating unchangeable uncomfortable life conditions. Rational-emotive practitioners further strive to help clients obtain the skills which they can use to prevent the development of future disturbance. In encouraging clients to achieve and maintain this profound philosophic change, rational-emotive therapists implement the following strategies. They help their clients see that:

(1) Emotional and behavioural disturbances have cognitive antecedents and that these cognitions normally take the form of absolutistic irrational Beliefs. RET therapists train their clients to observe their own psychological disturbances and to trace these back to their ideological roots.

(2) People have a distinct measure of self-determination and can thus decide to work at undisturbing themselves. Thus, clients are shown that they are not slaves to their biologically-based irrational thinking processes.

(3) People can implement their choices and maximize their freedom by actively working at changing their irrational Beliefs. This is best achieved by employing cognitive, emotive and behavioural methods - often in quite a forceful and vigorous manner (Ellis, 1979d).

With the majority of clients, from the first session onward, RET therapists are likely to use strategies designed to effect profound philosophic change. The therapist begins the process with the hypothesis that this particular client may be able to achieve such change and thus begins to implement rational-emotive methods which he or she will abandon after collecting sufficient data to reject this initial hypothesis. Rational-emotive practitioners regularly implement this viewpoint which is based on the notion that the client's response to therapy is the best indicator of his or her prognosis.

COMPROMISES

When it is clear that the client is not able to achieve philosophic change, whether on a particular issue or in general, the therapist often uses other cognitive-behavioural therapeutic methods to effect less 'profound' changes. Since, in such cases, these methods yield better results for the client than can be achieved by standard rational-emotive methods, they are regarded as compromises yielding an outcome between no change, on the one hand, and profound philosophical change, on the other.

Inferentially-Based Change

Inferentially-based change occurs when clients do not change irrational Beliefs but do succeed in correcting distorted inferences such as negative predictions, overly negative interpretation of events and the behaviour of others, etc.

A good example of such change was reported by a therapist of my acquaintance. He was working with a middle aged woman who reported feeling furious every time her ageing father would telephone her and enquire 'Noo, what's doing?'. She inferred that this was a gross invasion of her privacy and absolutistically insisted that he had no right to act in this way. The therapist initially intervened with the usual rational-emotive strategy by attempting to Dispute this client's dogmatic Belief and tried to help her see that there was no law in the universe which stated that he must not invade her privacy. Meeting initial resistance, the therapist persisted with different variations of this theme - all to no avail. Changing tack, he began to implement a different strategy designed to help the client question her inference that her father was actually invading her privacy. Given her father's age, the therapist inquired, was it not more likely that his question represented his usual manner of beginning telephone conversations rather than an intense desire to pry into her affairs? This inquiry proved successful in that the client's rage subsided because she began to re-interpret her father's motives.

Another example of inferentially-based change occurred with one of my clients, Robert, who was anxious lest people would stare at him for spilling his drink. His hands would shake whenever he attempted to drink in public. I first employed the customary philosophically-based RET strategy, encouraging him to assume the worst and imagine that people would actually stare at him when he spilled his drink. This yielded his irrational Belief: 'If they stare at me, it would prove that I would be a worthless freak'. However, I could not encourage him to Dispute this Belief successfully and he still adhered strongly to it after my varied Disputing efforts. Changing tack, I took him to several pubs and asked him to observe other people's reactions as I deliberately spilled drinks in public. From this, he came to realise that other people in general did not stare at me when I spilled my drinks and this helped him to change his own inference to: 'It is unlikely that most people will stare at me when I spill my drink'. This inferentially-based change enabled him to order and consume drink in public and reduce his social anxiety although he never did change his aforementioned irrational Belief.

Interestingly, in both examples, although my fellow therapist and I returned to Disputing our clients' irrational Beliefs _after_ helping them to modify their distorted inferences, we never succeeded in helping them to change these Beliefs. However, some clients are more willing to re-evaluate their irrational Beliefs after they have been helped to correct distorted inferences. Rational-emotive theory holds that irrational Beliefs are the breeding ground for the development of negative inferences and thus when clients succeed in changing their irrational Beliefs, spontaneous reduction in the negativity of inferences will follow. However, these two examples show that inferentially-based change can occur in the absence of philosophically-based change.

Behaviourally-Based Change

Behaviourally-based change occurs when clients do not change irrational Beliefs, but improve by effecting constructive changes in behaviour. Such behaviour change, in my experience occurs when clients (a) replace dysfunctional behaviour with constructive behaviour and (b) acquire constructive patterns of behaviour which previously have been absent from their skill repertoire. An example of each follows.

Replacing dysfunctional behaviour with constructive behaviour. Sylvia, a first year university student, sought therapy for extreme examination anxiety. She predicted that she would fail her first year exams, demanded that she must pass them and concluded that should she fail, this would be the 'end of the world'. No amount of Disputing her irrational Beliefs yielded any therapeutic gain, so I shifted attention to her test-taking behaviour. I discovered that Sylvia approached an examination in the following way. She would choose to answer the first question that she knew anything about; she would write everything she knew about that question without first making an answer plan and would often only answer two out of four questions in the entire examination. It thus transpired that her inferences concerning failure were accurate rather than negatively distorted. My subsequent therapeutic approach focused on teaching Sylvia the following examination techniques: allocating sufficient time to answer all questions; analyzing the wording of examination questions; making answer plans; answering all parts of a given question; and dealing with 'mind-blank' experiences through cognitive distraction. With the help of her department, I arranged for Sylvia to take several 'mock' examinations so that she could practise her newly acquired skills with the result that she performed very well in these examinations. These experiences helped Sylvia to predict success in her 'end-of-year' examinations rather than failure. This led to a significant decrease in her examination anxiety. However, although Sylvia did in fact do very well in her exams, she still held the same irrational Beliefs about failure as she did at the outset and did not want to focus on these later as she thought failure to be 'so unlikely that it's not worth considering'.

This example clearly shows that behaviour change often leads to inferentially-based change but not necessarily to philosophically-based change.

Acquiring new skills. Mrs. Anderson was referred to me with problems of anger and depression. Her husband and two teenage children expected her to go out to work, do all the housework without help and cater to their every whim. She had done this for several years, but had become increasingly angry and depressed. Her anger was based on the irrational Belief that they must not treat her this way and her depression stemmed from the Belief that she was no good for failing to please her family. Traditional rational-emotive Disputing methods failed to yield any therapeutic gains so I shifted the focus of therapy to a discussion of assertion and the value of politely declining to do the bidding of her family. Through role-play methods it transpired that Mrs. Anderson did not have assertive skills in her repertoire since she could only communicate in an aggressive and demanding manner. I thus trained her intensively in polite, negative assertive skills which she was able to put into practice with her family. Surprisingly her family responded quite well to her behaviour, began to share household tasks and made less demands upon her. The result was that Mrs. Anderson's depressed mood lifted appreciably and she became far less angry. As in the other examples in this chapter, I returned to Disputing her irrational Beliefs as outlined above but again without success.

This example shows that a client's behavioural changes can sometimes elicit constructive behaviour from others leading to healthy changes in the interpersonal system of which the client is a part.

Changing Activating Events

I concluded the above example with the observation that a client's change in behaviour can promote healthy system-based change. However, this does not always occur. In a similar case to that described above, I had to involve the client's husband and children in therapy and encourage them to change their behaviour towards the depressed client, Mrs. Curran, since her own assertive efforts did not on this occasion elicit constructive responses from her family members. Once they changed their behaviour towards Mrs. Curran for the better, her mood lifted accordingly. Again Disputing efforts aimed at helping Mrs. Curran to re-evaluate her irrational Beliefs, pre- and post-improvement, did not lead to philosophically-based change.

In another example of helping clients by promoting changes in Activating events, I helped Mr. Brown to overcome his depression by encouraging him to change his vocation from accountancy to law. He was depressed because he believed: 'I have to enjoy my job in order to be happy'. No amount of Disputing this Belief yielded any therapeutic gain so I switched the focus of the sessions to exploring his vocational interests and aptitudes. This led Mr. Brown to conclude that he would be happier working as a solicitor than as an accountant. Accordingly, he decided to go to law school. Years later, after he qualified as a solicitor, I met Mr. Brown who had effected a successful career change. He still believed that he had to be vocationally satisfied in order to be happy but since he was happy working in the law he considered that there was no need to re-evaluate this irrational Belief.

Challenging But Not Overwhelming: A Compromise in Negotiating Homework Assignments

Ellis (1983c) has recently criticized the use of

gradual approaches to helping clients overcome their emotional and behavioural problems. His argument is that the use of gradual methods in psychotherapy and behaviour therapy reinforces 'a philosophy that states or implies that (1) emotional change has to be brought about slowly and cannot possibly occur quickly or suddenly; (2) that it must be practically painless as it is occurring; and (3) that it cannot occur with the use of jarring, painful, flooding methods of therapy' (p.142). Thus, psychotherapeutic gradualism is seen by Ellis as counter-therapeutic in that it basically reinforces clients' discomfort anxiety or philosophy of Low Frustration Tolerance (LFT) which serve to perpetuate rather than ameliorate their problems. He thus prefers wherever possible the use of flooding or 'full-exposure' methods and homework assignments in RET, primarily because they help clients to overcome their discomfort anxiety and to raise their tolerance level for frustration.

However, 'wherever possible' is the important phrase to note here since not all clients will agree to execute flooding or 'full-exposure' homework assignments. That this should be rational-emotive therapists' initial approach to negotiating homework assignments is not questioned here. In taking this stance, therapists should explain the rationale for this type of homework assignment, emphasize the benefits of such an approach and encourage clients to implement these assignments after thoroughly Disputing clients' LFT ideas. What therapists are in fact saying is: 'Such methods are the most efficient means of helping you achieve your therapeutic goals'. It is not surprising that Ellis should recommend such assignments, given his belief in the value of efficiency in psychotherapy (Ellis, 1980c).

However, no matter how therapists try to encourage (or persuade) some clients to execute 'full-exposure' homework assignments, such clients steadfastly refuse to do so. In the face of such opposition, if therapists persist in their persuasive tactics, they will commit two therapeutic errors. First, they will threaten the therapeutic alliance between themselves and their 'resistant' clients. Bordin (1979) has noted that there are three major components of this alliance - goals, bonds and tasks. In such instances, the therapeutic alliance is likely to break down in the <u>task</u> domain. Although therapist and client may <u>have</u> a good collaborative relationship (effective bonds) and agree on the client's goals (shared goals), they disagree about the tasks that the client is prepared to do in order to achieve therapeutic goals. Second, such overly persistent therapists serve as poor role models since they tend to believe that clients must be 'efficient' in their approach to therapy and do 'full-exposure' assignments. Paradoxically, these therapists, by insisting that clients execute certain types of homework assignments are in fact being inefficient themselves. A breakdown in the therapeutic alliance often leads to therapeutic impasses which in turn often lead to clients dropping out of treatment.

In such cases, what should therapists preferably do? There is no need to return to therapeutic gradualism, for there is another alternative which allows therapists and clients to effect a working compromise. Whenever I encounter clients who steadfastly refuse to execute 'full-exposure' homework tasks and prefer gradual assignments, I explain this therapeutic compromise. I invite them to choose assignments which are sufficiently challenging to discourage reinforcement of their philosophy of Low Frustration Tolerance, but which are not overwhelming for them. I explain their choices thus:

> 'There are three ways that you can overcome your fears. The first is like jumping in at the deep end. You expose yourself straightaway to the situation you are most afraid of. The advantage here is that if you can learn that nothing terrible will happen then you will overcome your problems quite quickly. However, the disadvantage is that some people just can't bring themselves to do this and get quite discouraged as a result. The second way is to go very gradually. On the one hand, you only do something that you feel comfortable doing, while on the other, you don't really get an opportunity to face putting up with discomfort which in my opinion, is a major feature of your problem. Also treatment will take much longer this way. The third way is what I call 'challenging but not overwhelming'. Here you choose an assignment which is sufficiently challenging for you to make progress but not one which you feel would be overwhelming for you at any given stage. Here you are likely to make progress more quickly than with the gradual approach but more slowly than with the 'deep end' approach.'

I find that when clients are given an opportunity to choose their own rate of progress, the therapeutic alliance is strengthened. Most clients who refuse to execute 'full exposure' assignments choose the 'challenging but not overwhelming' approach and only very rarely do they opt for gradual desensitization therapy. When they do so I do try to dissuade them and frequently succeed. In the final analysis, however, I have not found it productive to insist that clients choose a particular way of tackling problems that is against their preferences.

Case example. Mary, a 23 year old, single woman came to therapy for help in overcoming her anxiety about eating in public. Typically she had both ego and discomfort anxiety-related Beliefs (Ellis, 1979b, 1980a), and in the early sessions I helped her to identify and Dispute such self-defeating attitudes as: 'I must not be anxious while eating'; 'If other people see me leave my food they will think I'm odd and I need their approval'; 'I am a shameful individual for having this problem'; 'There is something wrong with me because I have a small appetite' and 'I must not make a fuss and draw attention to myself'.

She claimed that her anxiety would be at its peak if she were faced with the prospect of not finishing her food in a crowded, fashionable restaurant. However, although she was successful at verbally Disputing both ego and discomfort-anxiety related Beliefs about this incident in therapy sessions, she could not initially conceive of putting this into practice in this particular setting even though I presented the rationale for 'full-exposure' homework assignments and emphasized the benefits that she would experience as a result. She literally could not imagine herself doing it (a good sign that such an experience would, in her terms, be too traumatic). She enquired whether there was not a painless method for overcoming her problems. I explained the dangers of such 'painless' methods and introduced her to the idea of 'challenging, but not overwhelming' tasks. She agreed, albeit with some reluctance, to select such an assignment. My hunch was that she would have terminated therapy if I had persisted in persuading her to expose herself fully to her anxieties. Over the following weeks she set herself and successfully executed the following 'challenging but not overwhelming' tasks while Disputing her salient irrational Beliefs. These tasks were in temporal order:

(1) Eating two squares of chocolate in a public place.
(2) Eating a meal of fish and chips on her own in a crowded restaurant, full of strangers.
(3) Eating out in a snack bar with her boy-friend.
(4) Eating out with her parents in a semi-fashionable restaurant.
(5) Eating out with her boy-friend in a fashionable restaurant.
(6) Deliberately asking for smaller portions in a fashionable restaurant.
(7) Eating out with a large group of friends in a very exclusive restaurant, sending back any portions that were too big.

As I have said, each task was seen by the client as 'sufficiently' challenging but not overwhelming and tasks 5, 6 and 7 were initiated by her in a planned break from therapy. This principle allows clients to take responsibility for their therapy quite early on, once they have fully understood it and experienced initial success. On follow-up, she was able to eat out in a variety of settings with a variety of people without anxiety.

Variations on a theme. While I have not used the 'challenging but not overwhelming' principle in planning a hierarchy of assignments before treatment commences, it can be used in this way. I have not found this necessary because what clients find 'challenging but not overwhelming' changes over time so that the initial hierarchy becomes redundant. Theoretically, therapists could also use SUDS ratings of hierarchy and/or non-hierarchy items, although, again I have not found this necessary.

While I have used this principle mainly in helping clients set appropriately challenging tasks to overcome their anxiety problems, I have also used it successfully in helping depressed clients set appropriately challenging behavioural tasks. In so doing I stress to clients the importance of defining what is challenging in personal terms in relation to their depressed state rather than in relation to their non-depressed state. The successful execution of small tasks deemed personally challenging by depressed clients when they are depressed, is highly encouraging for such clients and makes them more amenable to the subsequent use of more traditional cognitive change procedures (Beck et al., 1979).

In conclusion, the negotiation of 'challenging but not overwhelming' homework assignments is seen as a healthy compromise between therapists and clients when the latter are overly threatened by the prospect of fully exposing themselves to their anxieties. Such tasks enable clients to execute homework assignments without unduly reinforcing their low frustration tolerance ideas and help to preserve the therapeutic alliance between the protagonists. I maintain that in such circumstances it is a highly pragmatic and efficient approach to negotiating homework assignments in that it provides clients with the best available (acceptable) means to achieve therapeutic ends.

CONCLUSION

In this chapter I have considered the various compromises that RET therapists may be called upon to make when they cannot help their clients achieve philosophically-based change. Rather than persist with traditional rational-emotive methods that do not prove to be effective, RET therapists can still help their clients by encouraging them to change inferences, behaviour or Activating events.

There are, of course, problems associated with such compromises: (1) Clients who succeed in changing negative inferences may later encounter events that realise their inferences. As they have not changed their irrational Beliefs they may make themselves disturbed about such events. Thus the client of my colleague may later discover that her father in fact had been prying into her affairs and my own client with social anxiety (Robert) may later encounter a group of people who will notice his anxiety and stare at him. (2) Clients who do change their behaviour for the better may still encounter events which serve to activate their latent unchanged irrational Beliefs. Thus, Sylvia, my client with examination anxiety, may in the future fail an important examination and Mrs. Anderson's family may again make unreasonable demands upon her. (3) Clients who change or remove themselves from problematic Activating events may later re-encounter such situations which again may activate their latent unmodified irrational Beliefs. Thus, Mrs. Curran's family may later mistreat her and Mr. Brown's enthusiasm for the law may wane. Finally, (4) Clients who overcome their problems by using 'challenging but not overwhelming' methods are still vulnerable to 'overwhelming' situations.

While I have described cases where productive changes in inferences, behaviour and situations have not led to Belief change, other clients do later change their irrational Beliefs after effecting such changes. And yet although RET theory has emphasized the interdependence of ABC factors I have wanted to show here that change, particularly at the level of Beliefs ('B') does not necessarily follow changes achieved at 'A' or 'C'.

The implications of this chapter for empirical study is clear. It would be helpful to research questions such as: (1) 'With what clients, at which stages of the therapeutic process, are Belief change (inference change, behaviour change and situation change) methods appropriate?'; and (2) 'Under which conditions do changes in inferences, behaviour and situations lead to Belief change and when do they not promote such change?'.

Finally, given the way I have chosen to distinguish rational-emotive therapy from other approaches to cognitive-behaviour therapy and given my arguments about 'compromises' in RET, I conclude with the intriguing notion that RET therapists do not _only_ practise RET! Indeed it would be fascinating to research the question: 'When do RET therapists practise RET and when do they not do so?'.

Chapter Five

RET AS A THEORETICALLY CONSISTENT FORM OF ECLECTIC THERAPY

WINDY DRYDEN

INTRODUCTION

Theoretically consistent eclectics are therapists who have a particular theoretical perspective on human psychological disturbance but are prepared to use particular techniques developed by other therapeutic schools (Dryden, 1984b). In doing so they do not subscribe to the theoretical postulates of the other schools, but use their techniques for therapeutic purposes consistent with their own orientation. Although I consider myself a rational-emotive therapist in that I am in basic agreement with the theoretical tenets of RET, I also consider myself 'eclectic' in that, in the practice of psychotherapy, I select what appears to be best from diverse therapeutic sources, systems and styles to help my clients. The therapeutic practice of theoretically consistent eclectics is likely to be quite individualistic in that these therapists will draw from the aforementioned sources, systems and styles what *they*, individually, consider to be best. What guides them in their choices is as yet unknown and this area would be a fruitful one for research.

Before describing the case I have selected here to demonstrate my approach in action, I wish to outline the major elements that constitute my own brand of theoretically consistent eclecticism.

Rational-Emotive Therapy: My Theoretical Base

I am in basic agreement with the ideas of Albert Ellis (1984a) concerning the foundations of psychological disturbance. Rational-emotive theory posits that while emotions, cognitions and behaviours are interdependent processes, much human disturbance seems to stem from absolutistic, evaluative cognitions (irrational Beliefs) that profoundly affect how humans feel and act. These cognitions which are often couched in the form of 'musts', 'shoulds', 'oughts', 'have to's', etc. are termed 'irrational' by RET theory in that they very frequently impede people from reaching their basic goals and purposes. One of the major tasks of RET therapists is to help clients change their absolutistic evaluative cognitions to those which are non-absolutistic in nature. These latter cognitions are frequently couched in the form of 'wants', 'wishes', 'desires', 'preferences', etc. and basically help people achieve their goals and adapt constructively when their goals cannot be met.

While rational-emotive therapists have invented a whole range of cognitive, emotive and behavioural techniques which they routinely employ in therapy (see Chapter 1), RET-orientated eclectics, as mentioned above, go further and employ a number of techniques that are derived from other therapeutic schools to help clients effect a profound philosophic change, i.e. from devout absolute Beliefs to non-devout relative Beliefs. In my case, I often use methods and techniques derived from gestalt therapy, transactional analysis personal construct therapy, behaviour therapy and Adlerian therapy to name but a few. However, and this should be underscored, I use rational-emotive theory as a guiding framework for the selection of appropriate techniques. Equally important, rational-emotive theory helps me to decide which techniques _not_ to select (Dryden, 1984c). In the case that follows I will endeavour to show how I use rational-emotive theory as part of my therapeutic decision-making in this regard.

Therapeutic Alliance Theory

The second major element in my brand of theoretically consistent eclecticism concerns the application of what has come to be known as 'therapeutic alliance theory'. While the term 'therapeutic alliance' has been in use in the literature for over fifty years, the concept has recently been reformulated by Ed Bordin (1979) - see Chapter 3. Bordin has argued that there are three major components of the alliance between therapist and client.

Bonds, Goals and Tasks

First, the bonds between the protagonists must be considered. Alliance theory proposes that effective therapy occurs when the bonds between therapist and client are strong enough for the work of the enterprise to be executed. My over-riding concern here is to develop a type of bond with a particular client which will enable me to help that person without unwittingly perpetuating his or her problems. There are two important elements here. First, most clients (if not all) come into therapy with implicit (or explicit) preferences for a particular type of relationship with their therapist. Some, for example, seek a formal type of relationship while others prefer one which is more personal and intimate. I seek to meet clients' preferences to the extent that they do not perpetuate the client's problem. As will be shown in the case to be described, the client sought a formal type of relationship with me, which if offered, would have rendered me a less potent change agent. The second element, the relationship between the client's interpersonal style and his problems is to be found in the writings of interpersonal psychotherapists(e.g. Anchin & Kiesler, 1982). These theorists argue that clients bring a preferred interpersonal style to therapy and 'pull' a complementary response style from their (unsuspecting) therapists which reinforces both their own self-defeating style and their psychological problems. Thus, a client who presents herself as 'helpless' in therapy may well 'pull' an overly active-directive stance from the therapist which renders her more 'helpless'. Thus I ask myself: 'What interpersonal style will enable me to keep this client in therapy (clients' disconfirmed expectations here may lead to premature termination) while at the same time helping him (or her) to escape their self-imposed vicious cycles?'.

Second, the _goals_ of the enterprise must be considered. Effective therapy is deemed to occur when therapist and client agree on the latter's goals. Agreement on goals can occur at three levels. First, client and therapist can set _outcome_ goals which represent what the client wishes to achieve at the end of therapy. Second, _mediating_ goals can be set. These are the goals that the client needs to achieve before outcome goals can be reached. For example, a client may have to become proficient in a number of social skills before realistically being able to achieve the outcome goal of finding a partner. Finally, client and therapist can set goals for a particular session (i.e. _session_ goals). Alliance theory predicts that effective therapy is facilitated by the participants agreeing on each of these goals (where appropriate) and when they both can see the progressive link between the three levels (i.e. session goals ——> (leads to) mediating goals ——> (leads to) outcome goals).

Third, therapeutic tasks must be considered. Both therapist and client have tasks to carry out in therapy. Alliance theory predicts that effective therapy is facilitated when each person: (1) understands what tasks they have to execute; (2) can see the relevance of the other person's tasks; (3) is able to execute their respective tasks; and (4) acknowledges that the execution of these tasks will promote the attainment of the client's goals. In addition, the tasks must have sufficient therapeutic potency to facilitate goal achievement. Thus as a theoretically consistent eclectic, I need to know that the techniques I select from other therapeutic schools are sufficiently powerful to promote therapeutic change. For example, while exposure methods may well help clients overcome phobic reactions, Gendlin's (1978) focusing technique probably will not.

Finally, a channel of communication needs to be established between therapist and client so that alliance issues can be discussed and problems in the alliance resolved (Dryden & Hunt, 1985).

'Challenging But Not Overwhelming'

The third major feature of my eclectic approach involves a principle that I call 'challenging but not overwhelming'. I believe that people learn best in an atmosphere of 'creative challenge' and I endeavour to develop such an environment for my clients in therapy. Conversely, people will not learn as much in a situation which either challenges them insufficiently or overwhelms them. In this respect, Hoehn-Saric (1978) has shown that a productive level of emotional arousal facilitates therapeutic learning. For example, some clients are emotionally over-stimulated and here the therapeutic task is to create a learning environment which decreases the emotional tension to a level where they can adequately reflect on their experiences. With these clients I make use of a lot of cognitive techniques, and adopt an interpersonal style which aims to decrease affect. This style may either be formal or informal in character. These strategies are particularly appropriate with clients who have a 'hysterical' style of functioning. On the other hand, other clients require a more emotionally charged learning atmosphere. Such clients often use 'intellectualization' as a major defence and are used to denying feelings (see the case to be described). With such clients I endeavour to inject a productive level of affect into the therapeutic session and employ emotive techniques, self-disclosure and a good deal of humour. These 'challenging' strategies are best introduced gradually so as not to overwhelm clients with an environment which they are not accustomed to utilising. However, before deciding upon which interpersonal style to emphasize with clients, I routinely gain information from them concerning how they best learn. Some clients learn best through direct experience while for others more vicarious experiences seem to be more productive. I try to develop a learning profile for each of my clients, use this information to help me plan my therapeutic strategies and choose techniques to implement these strategies Care needs to be taken, however, that the therapist does not use a mode of learning that may perpetuate the client's problems.

The 'challenging but not overwhelming' principle is also appropriate to Ellis's (1979b, 1980a) concept of discomfort anxiety. Ellis has argued that many clients perpetuate their problems and deprive themselves of learning experiences because they believe that they _must_ be comfortable. Thus a major therapeutic task here is to help such clients to challenge this Belief and to carry out assignments while tolerating uncomfortable feelings. While this is a sound theoretical principle, I have found that it needs to be modified for pragmatic purposes. While it may be desirable for a client who is anxious about eating in public to go to an expensive restaurant and challenge their anxiety-creating cognitions in a situation where their worst fears may be realised, many clients will not do this. In such cases, I provide a rationale for a homework assignment which incorporates the 'challenging but not overwhelming' principle and contrasts it with gradual desensitization and implosion methods. This rationale is described more fully in Chapter 4.

Having outlined the major elements of my eclectic approach, I will now describe the case I have selected to demonstrate my approach in action.

THE CLIENT

The client whom I shall call Eric was a 31 year old,

white, unmarried man. He was born in the South of England, an only child of Peter and Margaret. His father was a ranking officer in the British Army and his mother did not work outside the home. At the time of treatment, Eric lived alone in a flat in Birmingham and worked as a computer programmer in a middle-sized business institution which manufactures electronic equipment. He was educated at a leading British university and has a Master's degree in computer studies.

Eric sought therapeutic help because he had increasingly come to feel that his life lacked direction and he had recently become concerned about his level of alcohol intake. This was the first time that he had sought help and there was no evidence of any psychiatric history. He enjoyed good physical health.

He initially reported his childhood to be uneventful; he saw his father infrequently due to the latter's army commitments and described his relationship with his mother as 'cordial but rather distant'. He was sent to boarding school at the age of ten where he remained until aged eighteen when he went to university. He said that he had many acquaintances at boarding school and university, but no real friends. He dated infrequently and reported no intimate relationships with women. He was sexually inexperienced and recently lost his virginity after having sex with a local prostitute. Describing this experience, he said: 'It was time, I thought, that I had sex with a woman; I felt a bit stupid being a 30 year-old virgin. I didn't enjoy it and wondered what all the fuss was about'. His main interest was in computers. He was fascinated by them and often worked late into the night trying to solve a problem thrown up by the latest programme he was working on. Of late, however, he said 'I can't seem to dredge up the enthusiasm any more'.

He was recommended to see me by his local G.P. who gave him the name of a number of therapists in the area. Explaining his choice of therapist, Eric said: 'I chose to come and see you because I was attracted by the name 'Rational-Emotive Therapy', I see myself as basically rational but there seems to be a breakdown in my logic at the moment. I'm hoping you can isolate the bugs in the system'. Perhaps unsurprisingly Eric's language reflected his interest in computers. My immediate impression of this tall well-groomed man was that he had almost become an extension of the computer he had recently lost interest in. His speech was very precise and his language lacked emotionally toned words. He was almost devoid of affect apart from allowing himself a little laugh when he drew attention to the fact that his surname was the same as a leading computer company.

His expectations for therapy were as follows. He anticipated that we would have an orderly discussion of his life's goals and why he had become 'stuck'. He further hoped we would find out why he started drinking more heavily than was his custom. He was pleased that I was not going to ask him to lie on the couch: 'I like to see who I am talking to'. I was left with the initial impression that here was a man who kept a very tight rein over his feelings from which he had become increasingly divorced. He seemed to employ intellectualization as a major defence in his life. Yet the cracks were beginning to appear. This marked the end of the initial interview at the end of which I offered to accept him for therapy. We would review progress after five sessions which would give him an opportunity to determine whether I was the kind of person who could help him. He accepted this contract.

THE THERAPY

What I shall do is to give an account of my work with Eric over the seventeen sessions I saw him. I will include at various points (a) my thoughts as a therapist which will help the reader understand my eclectic approach and (b) verbatim transcripts of our interchanges to illustrate (i) Eric's mode of functions (ii) 2 critical incidents and (iii) how I dealt with an incident concerning Eric's resistance to experiencing feelings.

Initial Phase (Sessions 1-4)

Initially I asked Eric to help me understand more deeply his predicament and what he would like to achieve from therapy. He reiterated the theme first raised in the intake session, namely that he wanted to regain his enthusiasm for his computer interest and was puzzled about why things had been going wrong.

Initially I wanted to test my hypothesis that his difficulties lay in the feeling domain so I decided to ask him to fill out a structural profile (Lazarus, 1981) to test this out and to demonstrate to Eric how he saw himself as a person.

Session 1 Transcript (Client Functioning)

Therapist: O.K. Eric, now throughout therapy I'll be sharing some hunches with you and it would be good if you could help us both by giving me honest reactions to these hunches. I see you and I as a team joining together to figure out what has gone wrong in your life and how you can find a more meaningful direction for you. How does that seem?

Client: Fine.

Therapist: Now, human beings have seven basic aspects. These aspects interact with one another to be sure but I want to understand how you see yourself on these aspects. I want to use a rating scale from 0-10, zero being an absence of this modality and ten being a high score on it. Now these modalities are behaviour, affect, sensation, imagery, cognition, interpersonal relationships and biological.[1] Now taking behaviour first ....

I then spent some time developing the structural profile with Eric (see Figure 3).

Therapist: O.K. What's your reaction to this profile?

Client: What do you mean?

Therapist: Well can you see anything that might be related to your current difficulties?

Client: Mmm. Well....I'm not sure.

Therapist: O.K. Let me share my reaction. I'm struck by the low scores on affect, sensation and interpersonal relationships. For example, I wonder if you would benefit from experiencing more feelings in your life. Let's start with that.

Client: Feelings? I'm not sure what you mean by that.

Therapist: Well emotions like joy, guilt, happiness, sadness, anxiety, depression, pleasure.

Client: Well, I used to get pleasure out of

Figure 3

Eric's structural profile (session 1)

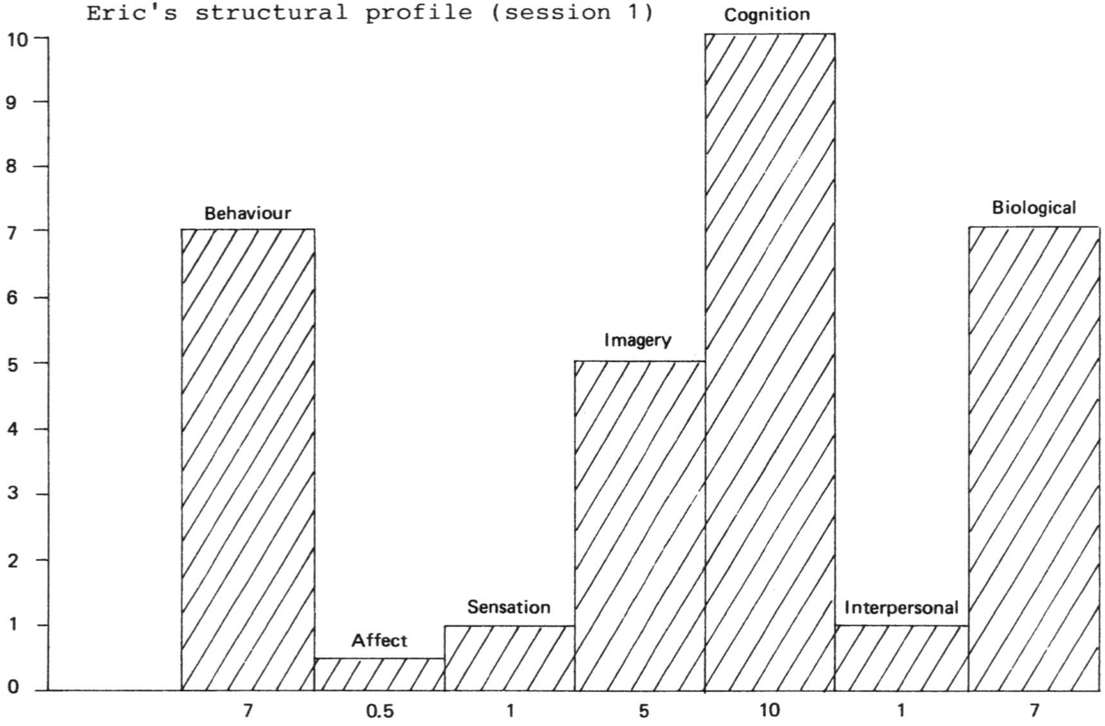

my computer but the others? I....Er. I'm not sure. I'm puzzled by that. Aren't feelings biological processes that originate in the hypothalamus or is it the thalamus?

Therapist: (ignoring the temptation to discuss the psychophysiology of emotion):
You seem to be finding it difficult to relate to these emotions.

Client: Yeah.

Therapist: Well is this an area we need to explore?

Client: (doubtfully): I suppose so.

A similar dialogue occurred on the topic of sensations with Eric speculating on their biological origins rather than on his experience. The following is the interchange concerning Eric's interpersonal relationships:

Therapist: Now how about your relationships with people?

Client: Well I've never sought people out.

Therapist: Have they sought you out?

Client: No.

Therapist: How do you feel about that?

Client: What do you mean?

Therapist: (noting the client's puzzled response to another feeling-orientated question): Well you describe your life as being empty of people. What do you think your life would be like if there were more people in it?

Client: It would distract me from my computer work.

Therapist: So you wouldn't like more people in your life?

Client: I wouldn't know what to *do* with them.

The above excerpt shows Eric's dilemma. Feelings are alien experiences and people are either an unwelcome distraction or a puzzle. He doesn't know what to *do* with them. I remember experiencing something of a dilemma myself at this point. How can I help this man entertain experiences that seem so alien to him.

I decided to share my dilemma in session 2

when we were talking about goals. This was an error since Eric could not relate to what I said to him. However, when I asked him: 'Could these areas be the bugs in your system?'. He reacted with visible (although transitory) alarm. I remember thinking that I was going to have to use his language to build the bridge between his affectless world and one which held most promise for him. An investigation into how Eric best learned revealed an over-reliance on books, radio and television. These would clearly be of little relevance in our therapeutic work since these media could well reinforce Eric's detachment and intellectualization. Other learning modes would have to be gradually introduced.

Although I like to set treatment goals early in therapy, I decided to postpone goal-setting for a while and work in a less structured way with Eric for two reasons. First, I did not consider that he would benefit from an early discussion about goals since he could not yet relate to issues about feelings, sensations and relationships. Second, I considered that he would initially benefit more from a more open-ended therapeutic contract. This would help him to widen his horizons and to loosen up a little.

In session 3 we talked about his thoughts concerning his structural profile and the 'bugs in his system'. He noticed that he tended to drink more at those times he found himself thinking about our sessions. I suggested that he refrain from drinking to experience whatever it was that he might be feeling at those times. I taught him Gendlin's (1978) focusing technique to help him in this regard. This technique is particularly helpful in that it directs clients' attention to their inner sensations and experiences and helps them to articulate what these experiences might be about. In session 4 I helped Eric to attach a feeling label to his experience. He was feeling sad. I helped him to realize that sadness can be a cue that there was something missing from his life, perhaps something else than computers. He nodded imperceptibly in agreement, but wondered what that was. I suggested it was our task to help him find out.

Up to now I would describe my approach to Eric as basically exploratory, I was beginning to 'challenge' him to look at his inner experience, but not in a way that would 'overwhelm' him and possibly scare him away. The two techniques I used in this initial phase were designed to help both of us move into what was for Eric the uncharted waters of his inner world. Neither of us could see at this stage that the next session would be so critical in the therapeutic endeavour.

Middle Phase (Sessions 5-14)

While reviewing my notes a few days prior to my fifth session with Eric, I noticed that Eric would have his 32nd birthday on the day of this session. I let my mind wonder and experienced a sense of sadness. I pictured Eric on his birthday alone in his flat and guessed that nobody would send him a birthday card. I decided I would buy him a card which I would give him at the beginning of the session. My decision was prompted by a sense of empathy but I also reflected on the therapeutic wisdom of doing so. Would he despise me for my open display of caring concern? Would he be affected? What might he experience? Empathy won the day, although I was somewhat apprehensive when I sat down at the beginning of the session. I want to stress that I did not see this purely as a technique. If I did not experience the concern I would not have given him the card. The following are excerpts from the session.

Session 5 Transcript (Critical Incident)

Therapist:	Eric, I noticed today was your birthday and I felt that I would like to give you this (handing over the card).
Client:	(puzzled): What is it?
Therapist:	Why don't you open it.
Client:	(opening the envelope): Oh! Er....Um.. I don't know.... what to say.
Therapist:	You seem agitated.
Client:	(clearly embarrassed): Yeah.... well.... That's....a....well...um (bursts into tears).

Eric wept silently for about five minutes and was clearly distressed. I felt both touched and concerned lest this was too overwhelming an experience for him at this point.

Therapist:	When was the last time you received a birthday card?

Client: (distracted): What?...Er...Well let me....see....Er. I can't remember.
Therapist: When I decided to buy you the card I felt kind of sad because I guessed that nobody would have sent you one.
Client: Pathetic isn't it.
Therapist: What is?
Client: Weeping like a baby over a silly card...Oh! I didn't mean...
Therapist: I know what you mean. How do you feel about weeping with sadness?
Client: I feel bloody stupid.

The rest of the session was spent helping Eric to see that he could accept himself for crying and that his sadness was perhaps an indication that some important desires were not being met. However, Eric remained somewhat distracted and I used these strategies to decrease the intensity of his experience (which I hypothesized would have otherwise been overwhelming for him) as well as a method of Disputing his irrational Belief: 'I am worthless if I cry'.

Towards the end of the session, I wondered aloud whether Eric would find it difficult to come back next session having expressed some strong feelings. He nodded and I said that I understood that feeling.

Indeed Eric did not show up for session 6. I was concerned about him particularly as he did not call to cancel his appointment. I decided to write the following letter:

Dear Eric,

I was sorry that you were not able to attend our session on Wednesday. My hunch is that you feel embarrassed about our last session. If I am right I can understand your feeling that way. If you recall, I mentioned at our second session that therapy may be difficult at times and there might be occasions when you might not want to come.[2] However, I feel it is important for us to talk about these experiences in person, so I look foward to seeing you for our next session at the same time next week. Please confirm that this arrangement is convenient.

Yours sincerely,
W. DRYDEN, Ph.D.

I received a reply from Eric, thanking me for my letter and confirming that he would attend our sixth session. The following is an excerpt from this session.

Session 6 Transcript (Critical Incident)

Client: You know when I got home, I found myself with a whisky bottle in my hand before I even knew what was happening. I remembered what you said about not drinking to see what feelings came up. I was overwhelmed with stomach cramps and I began to cry again. Somewhere at the back of my mind I remembered you asking me if I was worthless for crying. I was able to see that I wasn't and for the first time I let go. I cried and cried. I remembered my father saying things when I was a child like: 'Call yourself a boy, stop those tears'. I also remembered my mother getting agitated because I was crying and my father was due home soon.

Therapist: Sounds like a lot of hidden feelings came up for you.

Client: Yeah. When last Wednesday came I panicked. You were right I couldn't face you then. I went to my computer. I realised that I'd been using it as a friend, someone ... something rather that I could relate to... I also remembered what you said about your challenging but not overwhelming principle. I'd had enough challenge for a while and needed to have a rest. Sorry I didn't let you know.

And later in the session...

Client: I can see more clearly that I do need to get to know about some of those modalities that were low; you know affect and the others. That's what I'd like to focus on.

At the end of the sixth session I suggested that

Eric think about what kinds of experiences he would like to seek out. He came back with the following list at session 7:

- Learn to dance
- Find myself a girlfriend (about time)
- Go walking in the woods
- Join 18+ [3]

Eric devised his own programme and followed it through according to the 'challenging but not over-whelming' principle with good success. There were a number of occasions when he chose not to go to an event, using his computer as a kind of anxiety-reduction technique.

Mindful of the importance of using emotively-orientated techniques to help Eric I employed a number of these methods to help him focus on his avoidance behaviour.

For example in session 9, Eric reported that he couldn't be bothered to go to 18+ on club night and spent the evening working on his computer. I decided to use a gestalt empty chair technique to dramatize the situation to enable Eric to identify any possibly anxieties.

<u>Session 9 Transcript (Using a Dramatic Method to Uncover the Meaning of Eric's Avoidance Behaviour</u>)

Therapist: Let's see if we can understand if you were avoiding some important feeling. Now let me explain a drama technique to you. First can you imagine how you were feeling that night?

Client: Er...Yeah...Tired.

Therapist: O.K. So one of the players in this play is 'Tired Eric'. Now another one is your computer. Can you imagine 'Tired Eric' talking to his computer?

Client: (laughs): Just about.

Therapist: Good. Now see this empty chair. Imagine your computer on that chair. Got it?

Client: Yeah.

Therapist: Now strange as it might seem. I want you as 'Tired Eric' to talk to your computer. And, I'll play my-self in this. O.K.? Right. O.K. 'Tired Eric' it's time to go out

	to 18+.
Client:	(as 'Tired Eric'): I'm too tired.
Therapist:	(to computer): Is Eric too tired or might he be feeling something else? Eric change chairs and answer me as your computer
Client:	(as computer): Well, no he's scared.
Therapist:	(to computer): Scared of what?
Client:	(as computer): Well he's got his eye on a girl at the club but he's scared she might not want to know him.
Therapist:	(to computer): So why don't you tell him to go and face his fears.
Client:	(as computer): Er... because...
Client:	(as 'Tired Eric' and changing chairs after being prompted by the therapist): I know, because he doesn't think I'm strong enough to cope with rejection.
Therapist:	(to 'Tired Eric'): Is that true?
Client:	(as 'Tired Eric'): No, but why risk it if it's a possibility.

This dialogue helped Eric and me see that two important Beliefs were holding Eric back. One was: 'I'll only do things if its certain to work out' and the other was 'If I do things and they don't work out, I'm no good'. I then helped Eric to Dispute these Beliefs using traditional RET Disputing methods (see Chapter 1). He considered a more healthy alternative to both Beliefs to be: 'Things won't work out if I don't try. So I'd better increase the chances of getting what I want by going for them. If they don't work out tough. I'm no less a person'. Eric practised these new Beliefs by acting on them. He carried out a number of homework assignments between sessions 9 and 11 which were designed to help him accept himself in the face of failure and to help him work towards goals, the achievement of which could not be guaranteed.

In session 12 it emerged from reviewing these assignments that Eric feared losing control if he experienced strong arousal. His Belief here was: 'If I get excited I'll lose control and that would be awful'. In order to test out the prediction that he would lose control if he experienced a lot of arousal, Eric did several things between sessions 12 and 14. He did a number of shame attacking exercises (Dryden, 1984c). For example, he went into a large department store and shouted out the time. In addition in session 13, I got him to sprint up and down on the spot and then do a number of expressive meditation exercises designed to raise his arousal level. Finally, he went to a dance-therapy workshop and did a lot of vigorous dance exercises. All these experiences helped him to see that he could get highly aroused without losing control.

By session 14, Eric considered that he had made a lot of progress. He was feeling more in touch with his emotions the range of which had markedly increased. He gained pleasure from walking in the country and enjoyed experiencing a variety of country odours. He had taken up bird watching and had found a girl friend who also enjoyed these activities. He had made several friends at the 18+ club and was experimenting with a wide range of activities. His enthusiasm for his computer work had returned but he spent far less of his recreational time at his computer terminal.

End Phase (Sessions 15-17)

Eric suggested at the beginning of the 15th session that he would like to come less frequently and work towards termination. I outlined a number of ways we could terminate our work together. He chose to come twice more at monthly intervals. We spent these final sessions reviewing our work together and Eric reported that he had maintained the gains he had made in therapy. At the end of session 16, I suggested that Eric might bring to our last scheduled session a written account of what he had achieved in therapy. The following is a verbatim account of what he wrote under the heading: 'What I gained from therapy'.

What I Gained From Therapy

I have gained a great deal from seeing you, far more than I thought I would. You have opened my eyes to a whole new world of experience that I was only dimly aware of, if at all. I would say first and foremost I feel a more complete human being. Although I still respect my intellect - or the cognitive domain as the American man who invented those structural profile sheets calls it - I have learned to experience and gain respect for the other modalities. I have learned that it isn't unmanly to cry and feel sad. I've tried to discuss this with my father but perhaps predictably he doesn't understand what I'm talking about. I have learned that it's not so bad to try and achieve something and fail. Indeed, If a person doesn't try he certainly won't achieve. Obvious now but I didn't see that before.

I have also learned that control has little to do with feeling strongly aroused. To some degree looking back I was using my computer to shield me from life although of course I didn't realize that then. I guess I was using my computer as a substitute friend and yet it was a bit of a one-sided friendship. I now feel much more a part of the social world. 18+ has helped tremendously in that respect. Before, I wouldn't have thought I could have so much fun with others. I didn't even think of life as having fun. Strange isn't it! I still have to force myself to go out occasionally when I feel 'tired' but I can now distinguish between genuine tiredness and anxiety.

I've redone those modalities (see Figure 4) and have enclosed them within. I find the differences interesting. One last thought, I remembered being struck by the name of your therapy before I came to see you - Rational-Emotive Therapy. I was attracted to the word 'Rational'. I must confess that I'm now more attracted to the word 'Emotive'. I hope you find this instructive.

At the end of the seventeenth session, Eric and I agreed to have two follow-up sessions, the first one being 12 months after our last session. However, this has not yet taken place at the time of writing.

THERAPIST'S SUMMARY

From the point of view of rational-emotive theory, Eric had developed an unsatisfactory life style partly because he had little experience in the affect, sensation and interpersonal modalities but mainly because he held a number of irrational Beliefs which led him to avoid experiences in each of these areas. Namely he believed:

(a) 'Experiencing emotions and sensations are extremely dangerous and must be avoided at all costs'.

(b) 'I must be in control of myself. To lose control would be terrible'.

(c) 'I must be certain of achieving something before I try it'.

(d) 'I'm no good if I cry or if I fail to

Figure 4

Eric's structural profile (session 17)

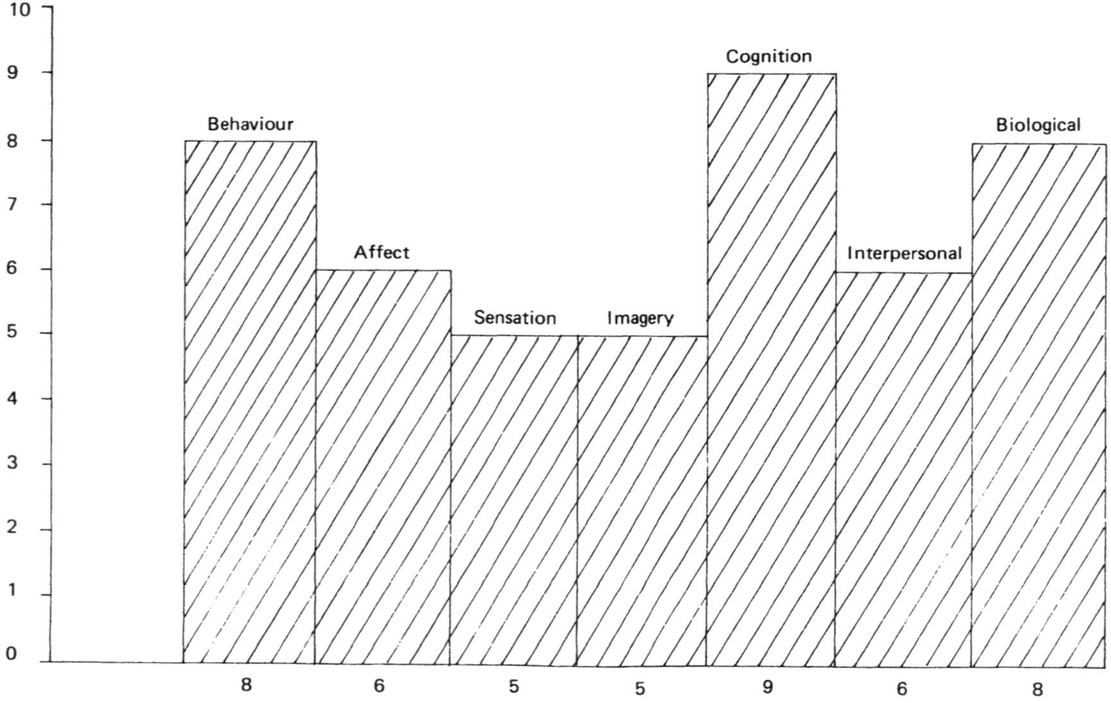

achieve important things'.

Adopting a theoretically consistent eclectic view based upon my rational-emotive conceptualizations, I decided to emphasize strategies and techniques that were dramatic, affective and expressive in nature. In doing so I was sensitive to avoid overwhelming the client, but to challenge him gradually at first and later increasingly so as therapy progressed and as he began to make significant gains. Thus I decided to use: 1) structural profiling as an assessment tool to help test my hunch about important deficits and to help Eric learn about these deficits; 2) such techniques as focusing - to help Eric to identify feelings and articulate what these feelings pointed to; 3) gestalt - two chair dialogue - to help identify the meaning behind his avoidance manoeuvres; 4) dramatic meditation and dance therapy - to help him learn that strong affective experiences were not dangerous and did not threaten his sense of control. All these methods were chosen in line with strategies consistent with my RET-inspired formulation and in keeping with my hunches about the importance for Eric to learn to become accustomed to the experiential-affective domain of human functioning.

From the point of view of alliance theory, I was able to develop a well-bonded relationship with Eric. Initially he viewed me as a rather distant 'expert' who would help him iron out the 'bugs' in his system. The 'birthday card' incident confronted him with the fact that I was also a human being who cared about his plight. This touched a deep chord in him and seemed to help him relate to me in a more affective manner. From session 6 our relationship was characterized by mutual respect and trust. I related to Eric in a moderately warm, informal manner without us both losing sight that we had various tasks to achieve.

With respect to the goal domain, I deliberately refrained from setting concrete goals at the outset of therapy. Initially, Eric worked to pursue goals which, in my opinion, would have not been constructive for him. He wished to strengthen his intellectualized defences and rid himself of the 'bugs' in his system which he hoped would help him shut out his increasing sense of isolation and dissatisfaction and hence to return to his computer. I did not attempt to deal explicitly with the self-defeating nature of these goals at the outset. I considered that to do this would have been unproductive and might have led to a futile 'intellectual' discussion which I wanted to avoid. There was also evidence at this initial stage of therapy that Eric would not have understood the importance of goals which emphasized becoming increasingly aware of his feelings and the healing aspects of interpersonal relationships. Indeed, I sidestepped the issue of goals by showing Eric the importance of looking at himself as a total individual (by using the structural profile) and how he was living his life against this backdrop. To some degree I think that Eric went along with me because he viewed me as an expert who knew what I was doing and because he was not too insistent about meeting his initial goals. Specific goal-setting followed Eric's increasing understanding of the importance that the affective, sensory and interpersonal modalities might play in his life.

As Eric gained this understanding, it was fairly easy to show him that the execution of various tasks could help him achieve his newly discovered goals. The more Eric derived benefit from being able to experience feelings, sensations and the pleasure of relating to other people, the more he was able to see the sense of the evocative techniques that I suggested to him and how they could help him achieve his goals. Interestingly enough, we rarely had to talk _about_ the relevance of therapeutic tasks. I believe he and I developed an implicit and shared understanding about these matters.

Following Bordin (1983), I believe that the repair of rifts in the therapeutic alliance can be most therapeutic. That Eric and I were able to sustain our relationship through the 'birthday card' and the 'missed session' incidents was, I believe, important for a number of reasons. I consider that Eric learned from these two incidents that the expression of strong feelings (i.e. his feelings) could be tolerated by another person and by himself and that no catastrophe would result. I also think that Eric learned that it was possible to talk about relationships with another person with whom he was involved and that rifts in these relationships can be repaired when both people show 'good faith'.

Applying the 'challenging but not overwhelming' principle to the case, I would like to make the following points. First, I attempted to provide a therapeutic environment which was increasingly charged with affect to encourage Eric to develop his potential to use the affective, sensory and interpersonal modalities. In this sense, I endeavoured to challenge Eric's use of intellectualization as a defence against such experiences without overwhelming him in this regard. The birthday card gift could have been an overwhelming experience for Eric and to some extent I underestimated the effect that it would have on him. However, it was not a damaging experience for him and indeed it contained important therapeutic ingredients for change (see section entitled 'Client Impressions'). Second, I explained the 'challenging but not overwhelming' principle outlined earlier, with respect to the execution of therapeutic tasks and Eric applied it to very good effect in his homework assignments. Indeed, as his own account in the next section shows, Eric has used this principle after therapy ended to maintain and extend his progress.

CLIENT IMPRESSIONS

Two months after formal therapy had finished, I wrote the following letter to Eric:

> Dear Eric,
>
> I hope this letter finds you well. I have been asked by Dr. J. Norcross of University of Rhode Island, U.S.A. to contribute a case study to a book he is editing entitled 'Casebook of Eclectic Psychotherapy'. With your permission I would like to write an account of our therapy and would like to request your permission for this. Your anonymity will of course be preserved.
>
> If you agree, Dr. Norcross also seeks to include the client's impressions of his/her therapy experiences. I would be grateful if you could write your impressions according to the following guidelines:
>
> (a) What were the most helpful and least helpful aspects of therapy?
>
> (b) What were your impressions of two critical incidents in therapy. Here I have selected (a) the session where I gave you a birthday card and (b) the session following the time you decided to miss our scheduled appointment (session 6).
>
> Please feel free to be as candid as you can in your account. I look forward to receiving your reply upon which I will send you a copy of my account.
>
> Yours sincerely, W. DRYDEN, Ph.D.

I received the following reply from Eric which I present as his verbatim account.

> Dear Dr. Dryden,
>
> Thank you for your letter. You have my permission to write about our therapy work. I am pleased to offer my perspective of my therapy experience. I hope that it may be helpful to your colleagues and their clients. I would be interested to see your own account when you have finished it.
>
> Most Helpful and Least Helpful Aspects of My Therapy
>
> As I look back over the period of my therapy I can think of many helpful aspects but only one or two experiences which perhaps weren't very helpful. So my account is somewhat skewed to the positive. The most positive aspect of the therapy was the fact that you helped me to discover the importance of feelings and personal relationships in my life. Up to seeing you, I had not considered that these had any place in my life. Indeed, I had not really given these matters much thought. Why this should be so is difficult to say, but I suppose it had something to do with my father's attitudes to feelings and the fact that my boarding school emphasized the value of hard work rather than the value of relationships between people.
>
> Your suggestion that I refrain from drinking to help me discover what feelings I was hiding from and that 'focusing' technique were particularly helpful in this respect. I also found some of the techniques you suggested that we try out together in our session helpful in aiding me to identify my feelings and some of the blocks I set up to stop me being uncomfortable. In particular those meditation exercises were good and I still do some of them from time to time.
>
> The other helpful aspects of my therapy were those exercises I did outside your office. I enjoyed immensely the dance workship you suggested I attend. In fact I have joined a regular dance therapy group which I find valuable in helping me to overcome my tendency to what you called 'intellectualization'. I didn't like that term when you first used it. I still don't like it but I know what you meant

by it. I call it 'cutting out'.

The therapy helped me to make much better use of outside resources than I would have done without therapy. Therapy helped me to form some important friendships; in particular my relationship with my girlfriend June, which is still flourishing. Therapy was like a release in this respect.

Looking back I think your patience and understanding was very important (I'll mention your concern for me as a person later). Your easygoing manner was good for me although at the beginning, I'm not sure, but I think I would have preferred seeing an older man, one who was more formal in style and dress. I realise now that these things are unimportant though. I also found some of your explanations helpful. The principle of 'challenging but not overwhelming' yourself was valuable and I still use it as a guideline in my life.

Now some not so helpful aspects, although these are minor. First at the beginning it might have been more helpful if you could have given me a clearer idea about what therapy was like. I was puzzled for about the first three sessions and was not sure what you expected me to do or say. Lastly, it might have been more valuable if we could have spent more time talking about my childhood and my experiences at boarding school. I don't know whether that would have been helpful but I think that it might.

Critical Incidents

I can understand why you selected these two incidents. They stood out for me too. I was shocked when you gave me the birthday card - shocked and very embarrassed that I reacted in the way that I did. Your concern for me hit me between the eyes. I wasn't prepared for it and just did not understand at the time why I reacted so strongly. That experience really made me stop and think about my life. It made the meaning of the first structural profile I did come alive and helped me to see what I had been missing in life. I was, as you suspected, too embarrassed and ashamed to face you the week after. Your letter helped me to come back. You understood what I was feeling and again your concern was an important fact in helping me to return the following week. To be honest, if you had not written I doubt whether I would have made the first move.

Coming back after the missed session was very important for me. You helped me feel that I wasn't a weak freak and also by not making too much of my missing the session you gave me important breathing space. Your matter of fact reaction gave me the impression that it was no big deal and also helped me think that you would not be shocked or startled by whatever I told you about myself. That attitude has remained with me and is also an attitude I can now apply to myself.

Well, I hope that you find these remarks of use. I'm very grateful to you for helping me in the way you did and am pleased to have had this opportunity to repay you in this small way.

Yours sincerely,
ERIC.

NOTES

1. See Lazarus (1981) for a full description of the structural profile and how to use it in therapy.

2. I frequently tell my clients that there may be times when they may wish to miss sessions. I do this partly so that I can remind them of the fact if and when the 'going gets rough' for them.

3. 18+ is a national social club for people between the ages of 18-30. A number of the members, however, are older than 30. It has branches throughout Britain.

Chapter Six

RATIONAL-EMOTIVE COUPLES THERAPY

WINDY DRYDEN

INTRODUCTION

Albert Ellis began his career in the helping professions as a sex, marital and family counsellor in the early 1940s. As a result of his experiences as a marital counsellor, he concluded that 'in most instances disturbed marriages (or pre-marital relationships) were a product of disturbed spouses; and that if people were truly to be helped to live happily with each other they would first have to be shown how they could live peacefully with themselves' (Ellis, 1962, p.3). This conclusion led Ellis to embark on intensive psychoanalytic training, believing then that psychoanalysis was the preferred mode of treatment for such disturbances. As has been already mentioned, in the early 1950s, Ellis became increasingly disillusioned with both the theoretical validity and clinical effectiveness of psychoanalytic treatment and began to see more clearly that human disturbance had profound ideological roots. Drawing upon the work of early Stoic philosophers (e.g. Marcus Aurelius and Epictetus) who stressed that people are disturbed not by events but by their views of these events, he began to develop a therapeutic approach based upon a perspective of human disturbance that stressed philosophic determinants and de-emphasized psychoanalytic psychodynamic ones and applied it to a number of therapeutic modalities including couples therapy.

Rational-emotive couples therapy (RECT) has not developed in a logical, stepwise direction since those early days. Up to the time of writing, there are no professional books or treatment manuals devoted to the application of RET to couple discord. However, a number of rational-emotive therapists have maintained an active interest in the field of RECT and there are a number of events that can be regarded as important in the history of its growth.

An early important development was the publication of Ellis's (1957) first book on RET: <u>How to live with a neurotic: at home and at work</u>. In this book he advances the thesis that partners could alleviate couple discord, first, by working to remain undisturbed about their partners' neurotic problems, and then, by experimenting with various solutions to help their partners get over their neurotic difficulties. In a later text written with Robert Harper, entitled: <u>A guide to successful marriage</u> (Ellis & Harper, 1961), Ellis developed this thesis and also made an important distinction between couple disturbance and couple dissatisfaction which has remained a cornerstone of RECT ever since. In the same book, Ellis & Harper also wrote on the important role that unrealistic expectations about intimate relationships play in the development and maintenance of both couple dissatisfaction and disturbance. While the term 'expectation' in psychotherapy is problematic in that it does not clearly differentiate between 'hopes', 'assumptions', 'predictions' of varying certitude, and 'absolutistic demands', they made the valid point that there is often a large discrepancy between what actually happens in intimate relationships and what one or both partners assume or predict will happen. Thus, unrealistic expectations are often the breeding ground for the later development of relationship problems.

In 1962, Ellis's seminal book: <u>Reason and emotion in psychotherapy</u> was published. This contained a chapter entitled 'A rational approach to marital problems' which was adapted and expanded from two earlier articles (Ellis, 1958, 1960). Here Ellis clearly outlined that one of the major tasks of the marriage counsellor was to 'tackle not the problem of the marriage, nor the neurotic interaction that exists between the marital partners, but the irrational ideas or beliefs that cause the neurosis à deux' (Ellis, 1962, p. 210).

As will be developed later in this chapter another cornerstone of RECT is its position on the role and treatment of angry and hostile reactions in intimate relationships. In 1976, Ellis published an important paper on this topic (Ellis, 1976c), in which he clearly outlined both the rational-emotive position on anger - namely that it is a dysfunctional emotion which severely interferes with relationship harmony - and its management in therapy.

Apart from Ellis a number of other rational-emotive therapists have made important contributions to the field of RECT. Amongst others, the writings of Church (1974) on the application of RET to divorce, McClellan & Stieper (1973) on a structured rational-emotive approach to group marital counselling, and Hauck on (a) the reciprocity theory of love and business theory of marriage (Hauck, 1981, 1983a) and (b) parenting styles (Hauck, 1977, 1983b) are particularly noteworthy. Special mention should be made of Walen, DiGiuseppe & Wessler's (1980) chapter entitled: _A practitioner's guide to rational-emotive therapy_. This chapter is unique in that it provides a clear set of procedural and technical guidelines for the practice of RECT. Also, recently, a special issue of the Journal of Rational-Emotive Therapy has been devoted to couples therapy (Grieger, 1986). Despite these developments there still appears to be an important place for a text which provides a comprehensive exposition of the theory and practice of RECT.

THEORY

The Nature of Disturbed Interpersonal Relationships

Rational-emotive therapists clearly distinguish between couple dissatisfaction and couple disturbance. Couple dissatisfaction occurs when one or both partners are not getting enough of what they _want_ from their partner and/or from being in an intimate relationship. Couple disturbance arises when one or both partners become emotionally disturbed _about_ these dissatisfactions. Thus, they may make themselves anxious, angry, hostile, hurt, depressed, ashamed, guilty and jealous - emotions that usually interfere with constructive communication, problem-solving and negotiation processes that aid the solution of couple dissatisfaction problems. In addition, when one or both partners are emotionally disturbed, they generally act in a self- and relationship-defeating manner, thus perpetuating couple disturbance. RECT theory states that, assuming they have the necessary constructive communication, problem-solving and negotiation skills, couples are likely to solve their dissatisfaction problems on their own. Where they are deficient in such skills, the focus of couples therapy is on training them to develop and use these skills. However, once couples are in the disturbance stage of a relationship, unless their emotional problems are dealt with, relationship problems usually remain, no matter how skilful one or both partners are in communicating, solving problems and negotiating workable compromises. Couples, interestingly enough, often misdiagnose their own problems. They often conclude that their problems are due to deficits in communication skills, while, in reality, they find it difficult to talk to one another when one or both are hurt, angry, depressed, anxious, etc.

Couple Disturbance

As has been shown in Chapter 1, emotional disturbance, 'C' according to RET's ABC theory, stems not from events at 'A', but mainly from a certain type of evaluative thinking or Belief at 'B'. This type of thinking which is absolutistic, devout and grossly exaggerated in nature, is called 'irrational' in RET theory, mainly to denote that it hinders people from actualizing their basic goals and purposes. Thus, irrational Beliefs that lead to such disturbed emotions as anxiety, anger/hostility, hurt, depression, shame and embarrassment, guilt and jealousy, stem, according to RET theory, from a thinking process known as MUSTURBATION. In the couple context, this processs is characterized by one partner making <u>absolute</u> demands and commands on self, the other partner and/or the relationship situation.

In the main, three further irrational (i.e. self-defeating) and grossly exaggerated thinking processes tend to stem from musturbation (Ellis, 1984a). Once humans absolutistically demand that something, for example 'MUST' not occur, they tend, if that event occurs, to conclude: that the event is 'awful', 'horrible', or 'terrible'; that they 'can't stand it' or 'can't bear it', and that the perpetrator of the event that must not have occurred is 'no good', 'worthless' (or 'less worthy'), or 'bad' - whether the perpetrator is self, another person or life conditions in general. Ellis (1983a) recently noted that these four thinking processes, known colloquially in RET literature as (1) MUSTURBATION; (2) AWFULIZING; (3) I-CAN'T-STAND-IT-ITIS; and (4) DAMNING, represent a philosophy of religiosity or devout Belief where the person adopts a God-like position and <u>insists</u> (not just desires or prefers) that the world (and the people in it) be as he or she wants it (or them) to be.

The rational (or self-enhancing) alternatives to these absolutistic Beliefs are framed within a non-demanding, non-absolute philosophy of desire. Here, in the relationship context, it is acknowledged that couples do have desires, are probably happier when these are met, and become dissatisfied when these remain unfulfilled. However, as has been stressed above, dissatisfaction is not synonymous with disturbance and the latter only develops if one or both partners escalate their non-absolute desires into absolute demands. Couple dissatisfaction occurs when one or both partners' important desires are not being fulfilled (and neither is insisting that they get what they want). Couple disturbance occurs when one or both partners demand that their desires must be met. Parenthetically, couples therapy is normally more difficult when both partners are emotionally disturbed about the relationship than when only one partner is thus disturbed.

The rational versions of the four irrational thinking processes are as follows:

(1) DESIRING (vs musturbation). Here the partner acknowledges his or her desires, does not insist that they be met, but is dissatisfied when they are not. Such dissatisfaction often serves to stimulate constructive attempts at problem solving which have a better chance of success with a spouse who is also not 'musturbating'. Rational thinking processes 2, 3, and 4 tend to be derived from non-demanding desiring just as irrational thinking processes 2, 3 and 4 are derived from musturbation.

(2) RATING AS BAD (vs awfulizing). RET theory holds that 'awful' really means more than 100 per cent bad since such a definition stems from the Belief: 'This _must_ not be as bad as it is.' Thus 'awful' is seen to be on a different continuum from 'bad'. If a partner is not getting what he or she really wants, but is not insisting upon it, this person will tend to define the deprivation as 'bad' but not 'awful'. The general principle is that the more important the unfulfilled desire, the more 'bad' the definition of the deprivation is likely to be. It is, thus, only under very unusual conditions that an event can be legitimately rated as 100 per cent bad. Non-absolutistically evaluating something as

'bad' but not 'awful' tends to lead the partner to try to ameliorate the 'bad' situation.

(3) TOLERATING (vs I-can't-stand-it-itis). 'I can't stand it' literally means disintegrating or dying on the spot. It more often seems to mean not being able to have any happiness whatsoever under any conditions, rather than actually dying. However, tolerating something means (a) acknowledging that some unwanted event has occurred and believing that there is no law that says it must not occur, (b) rating it as 'bad' but not 'awful', and (c) determining whether change is possible. If it is possible, constructive attempts are made to produce the desired change, while if change is not possible, the person accepts, but definitely dislikes this 'grim' reality. When partners are thinking rationally, they are likely to see that, while they can tolerate a bad relationship, there is no reason why they have to. Tolerating adverse conditions is an attitude conducive to constructive change attempts while I-can't-stand-it-itis leads to destructive manipulative strategies.

(4) ACCEPTING (vs damning). This attitude can be applied to self, others and the world. When a woman, for example, unconditionally accepts herself in this way, she recognises that she is a fallible human being who has an 'incurable error-making tendency' (Maultsby, 1984), meaning that she can and will make mistakes. If she is able to accept herself as such, she will more likely be able to acknowledge these errors, regard them as bad if they impede her goals, and take responsibility for committing them. Moreover, if she does not <u>demand</u> that her partner act well, she will more likely be able to accept him as fallible, dislike the fact that he is acting badly and initiate constructive negotiations for future improvement. Finally, if she does not dogmatically <u>insist</u> that her relationship be the way she wants it to be, she will tend to see it as a fallible institution with good and bad components which can only be improved but

not perfected.

As Young (1975) has shown, rational thinking can and does (especially in the arena of intimate relationships) lead to strong negative emotions, such as concern, annoyance, sadness, disappointment, regret and dislike. However, these emotions tend to motivate marital partners to take constructive steps to improve matters if their shared goal is to remain partnered.

Couple Dissatisfaction

RECT theory notes that there are two major contributing factors to couple dissatisfaction - relationship myths and important incompatibilities.

Couple dissatisfaction may occur if partners adhere to one or more myths (Ellis & Harper, 1961; Lazarus, 1985; Lederer & Jackson, 1968). Such myths tend to be unrealistic in that they idealize the state of the relationship and encourage partners to overestimate what they can realistically expect to derive from being partnered. Some examples of commonly held relationship myths[1] that are often implicated in marital dissatisfaction include the following: love equals good sex; romantic love will endure throughout partnership; my partner will be able to know what I want without me having to communicate my desires; good sex will always be spontaneous; I will not suffer any deprivations or penalties as a result of being partnered; my partner will help me get over my feelings of unworthiness; my partner will make up for my past frustrations; my mate will make allowances for my bad behaviour; my partner will always be on my side, always be loyal and always love me (no matter how badly I behave). If partners do not modify these myths in line with their experience, they will tend to become dissatisfied, as reality proves to be discrepant from their assumptions of what is 'expected' to happen in the relationship. Furthermore, it can be easily seen how such myths can further lead to couple disturbance when linked to a philosophy of musturbation.

Couple dissatisfaction may also occur when partners are revealed to be incompatible in one or more areas of the relationship. Generally, the more important the area, the greater the dissatisfaction, especially if negotiations for compromise fail to resolve the issues.

Couple incompatibility may stem from naive and superficial partner selection where partners do not really get to know one another, or may occur as a result of changes in outlook on the part of one or both of them. A commonly encountered example of emergent incompatibility occurs when a woman seeks to develop a more independent life-style. If this exceeds the role expectations of her partner, then neither are likely to get what they want in a significant area of their relationship. If she does not act on her newly discovered desire, she is likely to become dissatisfied and act less responsively toward him so that he becomes dissatisfied. However, if she spends less time in the house, he becomes dissatisfied, since his desires for a well-kept house are not being met and, if he begins to nag her, she becomes dissatisfied because her desires for support are not met. Dissatisfaction based on emergent incompatibility can often be a stimulus for constructive renegotiation of roles and responsibilities, but equally often, especially if the incompatibility occurs in a centrally important area for one or both partners, it may lead to relationship breakdown even if couple disturbance is not involved. In such a case, one or both partners conclude that the relationship no longer meets a very important desire and is not likely to in the future. If the incompatibility is in a less important area, it may lead to less intrusive dissatisfaction and may hardly affect the relationship, especially if the partners can find expression for the desire elsewhere and this is accepted by the other.

The Development And Perpetuation Of Couple Disturbance

RECT theory holds that couple disturbance can develop and be perpetuated in a number of different ways. Conflict may occur soon after the relationship has been established if one or both partners are quite disturbed as individuals. Similarly, conflict might develop at various stages of an on-going relationship when change occurs in the couple system. This change becomes a stimulus for one or both partners to bring their philosophy of musturbation to the new situation. Thus a dissatisfaction can quickly become a disturbance if, for example, a man demands that his mate _must_ not ask to see his pay packet or if the woman insists that her mate _must_ telephone to tell her that he will be staying late at the office. Here partners give themselves an emotional problem about the problem of dissatisfaction. In addition, partners may give themselves secondary emotional problems about their newly developed primary emotional problems (Ellis, 1984a). Thus, a man may get angry with his mate because he is demanding that she must not act in a certain manner; he may then notice his angry reaction and condemn himself for reacting in such a terrible manner. He thus becomes guilty for reacting angrily. It is unlikely that constructive communication or problem solving could ensue while he is experiencing anger alone, and doubly unlikely if he adds guilt to his emotional menu.

Irrational anger, stemming from the absolutistic demand that you, my partner, must not act this way either because it is 'wrong' or because it is a threat to my 'self-esteem', is probably the most prominent reason why couple disturbance is perpetuated (Ellis,1976c). Indeed, when both partners are damning each other, couple disturbance could be perpetuated indefinitely with little chance of a constructive solution being found. Another core reason why couple disturbance is perpetuated is anxiety over confronting basic issues. One or both partners may be scared that if they shared their feelings of dissatisfaction with one another that something 'awful' would ensue. They thus withdraw from one another and feel lonely, guilty and depressed about the growing distance between them.

Partners with emotional disturbances tend to act in dysfunctional ways (behavioural Cs). These then serve as the stimuli for the second partner's inference (INF). Vicious circles of disturbed couple interaction result when a dysfunctional behaviour (C) on the part of one partner serves as the trigger (INF2) for an irrational Belief (B2) of the other partner which in turn leads to disturbed feelings and behaviour (C2). This serves as a new trigger (INF3) for the first partner ... and so on. An example of such a vicious circle is shown in Figure 5. As this interaction pattern demonstrates, partners often make inferences of each other's behaviour (which have been included under INF). These inferences may be correct but, especially in the phase of couple disturbance, are likely to be faulty, coloured as they often are by irrational, evaluative thinking. Nevertheless, rational-emotive therapists do draw on Beck's (1976) work on 'cognitive distortions' and note that partners often make errors in processing interpersonal information and that these errors often serve to perpetuate couple disturbance (see Chapter 1). These also

Figure 5

The vicious circle of dysfunctional couple interaction

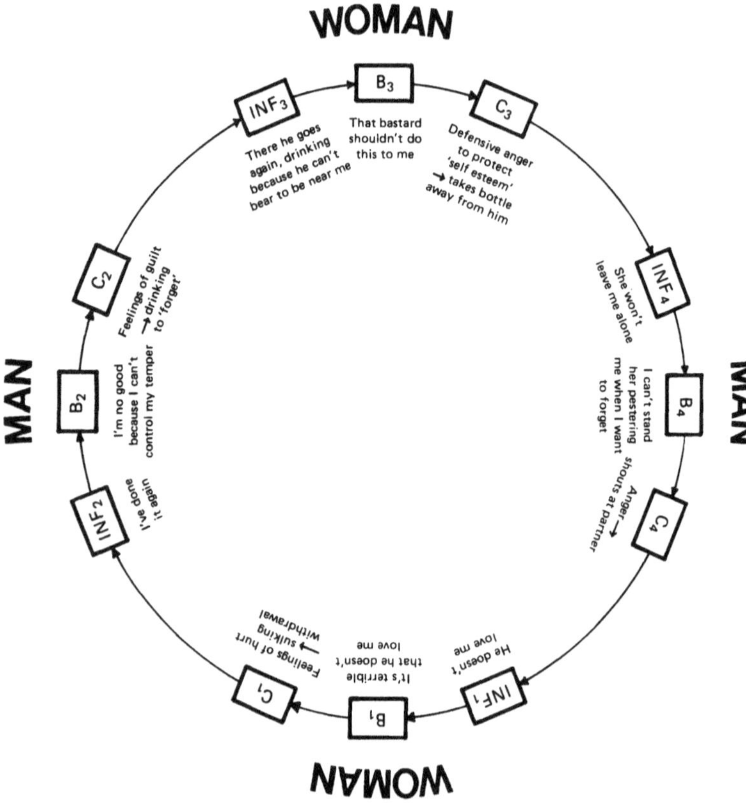

become the focus for therapeutic work, but normally after partners' musturbatory evaluative thinking has been tackled.

PRACTICE

Contextual Considerations

Rational-emotive therapists are guided by the principle of flexibility throughout the therapeutic process in working with couples. Thus, there are no absolute rules to guide RECT practitioners concerning whether to see partners conjointly, concurrently or consecutively in individual sessions. Therapeutic decisions concerning the working text are suggested by therapeutic exigencies. Ellis (in Dryden, 1984d) and Bard (1980), for example, consider that the decision whether to see both partners together or separately at the outset of therapy should preferably be made by clients themselves. However, individual sessions may be indicated for three main reasons:

(1) When the two partners persist in arguing non-productively in the context of conjoint sessions and thus negate the potential benefit of the therapists' interventions.

(2) When the joint presence of the partners in the therapy room unduly inhibits one or both of them. They may be so anxious about the possible negative effects of speaking their minds that they do not disclose significant material in therapy. In such cases, a period of concurrent individual sessions is often helpful.

(3) When the goals of the individual partners are sufficiently incongruent to preclude the establishment of a productive therapeutic alliance in conjoint therapy, e.g., when one person wishes to leave the relationship while the other wishes to preserve it.

When both partners wish to be seen together, share basically congruent goals, are not inhibited by their joint presence in therapy and can contain their strong angry feelings, then conjoint couples therapy is usually the most beneficial context for productive work.

Some RECT practitioners prefer to work concurrently with the partners in individual sessions in the 'overcoming couple disturbance' phase of treatment. They hypothesize that partners are more likely to disclose their genuinely held 'deep' feelings (e.g., of hurt, jealousy, anger and fear) if they see the therapist alone. Partners can thus give their full attention to the therapeutic process, while the therapist helps them to see the connections between their dysfunctional emotions/ behavioural patterns and their irrational Beliefs and helps them to Dispute and change these ideas. Since RECT is by nature an educational process, its practitioners are mindful of choosing environments that best facilitate learning. However, partners _can_ learn the ABCs of RECT in the context of conjoint therapy in the 'disturbance' phase. Here, while the therapist works with one partner, helping him or her to identify, challenge and change core irrational Beliefs, the 'listening' partner often learns the ABC framework of emotional/behavioural disturbance better than the 'working' partner.[2]

While RECT practitioners differ concerning their views about the supremacy of conjoint versus concurrent therapy in the 'overcoming couple disturbance' phase of treatment, they, generally, agree that the presence of both partners is highly desirable in the 'enhancing couple satisfaction' phase. In this phase, both partners have, ideally, made some progress overcoming their emotional disturbance about their differences and are ready to explore possible ways of improving their relationship, if they have decided to stay together. Rational-emotive therapists use a variety of methods to facilitate such exploration. Communication, problem solving and negotiation training are used in this phase, and the presence of both partners is highly desirable to enable the therapist to instruct them _both_ to communicate more effectively, solve problems and negotiate more constructively, so that they can improve the quality of their relationship.

Conjoint RECT is usually conducted with a single therapist, although there are occasions when a co-therapy arrangement would be desirable, particularly if, say, a woman feels unduly adversely affected by the presence of a male therapist. Here a female co-therapist would be helpful to strengthen the therapeutic alliance, and such a four-person arrangement might be particularly desirable in sex therapy.

In conclusion, the conduct of RECT is not bound by strict rules of procedure; flexibility is encouraged and changes in context may occur throughout the therapeutic process. Such changes are made according to therapeutic purposes which are generally made clear and agreed to by clients. It is in keeping with rational-emotive philosophy that RECT practitioners are against dogmatically insisting that therapy must be practised in any pre-determined context.

Developing And Maintaining A Therapeutic Alliance

It is important to note, at the outset, that RECT practitioners consider that their therapeutic contract is with the individuals in the relationship and not with the couple system (Harper, 1981; Walen, DiGiuseppe & Wessler, 1980). As Harper argues, the couple system is an abstraction, and, as such, RECT therapists have great difficulty seeing how a therapeutic alliance can be made with it. They prefer, whenever possible, to develop alliances with each of the involved partners. It is preferable if this is made clear to both partners at the outset of couples therapy so that they can see that the therapist is not interested in trying to preserve, or indeed destroy, their relationship. As has already been stressed, a primary objective of RECT therapists is to help both partners over their emotional disturbance about their situation and then help them work on forging a more mutually satisfying relationship, if this is their goal. However, partners often come into couples therapy with overt and hidden agenda, and it is often helpful to have separate interviews with each of the partners early in the process, to determine whether the goals of each partner are sufficiently concordant to make conjoint couples therapy - which is the best working forum for partners who have similar objectives - feasible. Since the therapeutic alliance is with the individuals and not with 'the relationship', the most appropriate therapeutic arena is sought to help the individuals actualize their goals.

Since therapeutic goals can be based on irrational as well as rational thinking, it is common RECT practice to explain to both partners that they are more likely to make productive decisions about whether to stay partnered (and, if so, what improvements are desired) or to separate, when they are not emotionally disturbed about what is presently happening in the relationship. Thus RECT practitioners prefer to set goals appropriate to particular phases of couples therapy. If the partners are disturbed, attempts are made to have them identify and set goals which involve minimizing such disturbance, and if they are dissatisfied, but not disturbed, attempts are made to work on relationship enhancement goals after a decision has been made by both that they wish to stay partnered. Too often non-RECT therapy founders because the therapist is working on couple enhancement goals when one or both partners are emotionally disturbed, with the result that goal sabotaging needlessly occurs.

Another common error made by non-RECT practitioners occurs when the therapist is only prepared to see the partners in conjoint therapy. Thus, if one partner wishes to preserve the relationship while the other has a hidden agendum to leave it, but will not declare this openly in the therapeutic triangle, such therapy is either terminated by the latter soon after its inception or is marked by little or no improvement, to the detriment of both partners. RECT therapists would be more likely to identify such a situation earlier in individual assessment interviews.

In the 'overcoming emotional disturbance' phase of RECT, it is important for the therapist to work with each partner individually either in conjoint therapy or in separate interviews. In conjoint therapy, the therapist gives each partner roughly equal amounts of time in order to maintain a productive alliance in the three-person situation - a social system which can easily be destabilized if the therapist, for example, excludes one partner for lengthy periods of time. The therapist explains at the outset of this phase that the goal is to help each of the partners overcome his or her own disturbance (intrapersonal focus) so that they can more productively work on their disagreements later (interpersonal focus). Productive RECT occurs when both partners clearly understand and agree to this modus operandi. Highly skilled RECT therapists who can present a convincing rationale concerning this important point are usually, but not always, successful at developing a good therapeutic alliance with both partners when such an alliance is based on this principle. Failure to form a productive alliance with both partners at the outset of therapy usually leads to problems later in the therapeutic process and does not bode well for successful outcome. Such failure is due to either (a) poor therapist skills, or (b) various partner factors which include: severe emotional disturbance; rigid adherence to the Belief that the other person is totally responsible for relationship problems; or various hidden agenda. In such instances, the therapist is advised to consider changing the therapeutic context or to consider various systems-inspired interventions which are designed to change 'A' factors in the ABC schema.

If the therapist can successfully manage the 'overcoming emotional disturbance' alliance, then the alliance necessary to effect productive change in the 'enhancing couple satisfaction' phase is much easier to manage, since both partners are in a position to make sound decisions about goals and are sufficiently free from emotional disturbance to work towards goal achievement.

Major Treatment Techniques

RECT is a multimodal form of therapy in that it employs a variety of cognitive (verbal and imagery), emotive and behavioural techniques to help partners overcome their emotional disturbances and couple dissatisfactions.

'Overcoming couple disturbance' phase. The goal of the RECT practitioner in this phase of couple therapy is to help each partner become relatively undisturbed about their problems so that they can constructively work, if they wish, to improve their level of relationship satisfaction. The therapist helps both partners to think rationally about themselves, their partner and their relationship, which means feeling appropriately frustrated, sorry, annoyed and sad about their predicament when their desires are not met - emotions which will motivate them to work to improve their relationship or separate without needless emotional pain.

In this phase, the RECT practitioner helps both partners to see how they are needlessly upsetting themselves about their problems and often adopts a 'let's assume' approach with both of them. Both partners are encouraged to assume that their inferences about, for example, their partner, are correct, for the time being, to offset unproductive arguments about what actually occurred at 'A' in the ABC framework. In this way, the therapist helps each partner to identify his or her underlying irrational Beliefs and replace them with their rational alternatives. The therapist would be wise to encourage persistently both partners to focus on their own upset if the goals of this phase of treatment are to be achieved. A variety of cognitive methods are used at this stage. Partners are shown how to use the logico-empirical methods of science to Dispute their irrational Beliefs. They are taught to ask themselves such questions as 'Where is the law of the universe that states that my partner _must_ do the housework perfectly well?'; 'How does it follow that she is _bad_ for acting badly?'; 'Is it true that I _cannot stand_ her behaviour?', etc. They are subsequently helped to see that there is no evidence for such absolute statements, only evidence for their 'preferential' form. A number of clients appear less able to perform this kind of Socratic questioning and here the therapist would help them to develop and employ rational coping statements such as: 'I don't like my partner's behaviour but there's no reason why she must not act badly'; 'She is a fallible human being who is doing the wrong thing'; 'I can stand her behaviour although I may never like it'. These statements can be further written down on index cards and rehearsed between sessions.

Some couples can be shown, similarly, how to Dispute each other's irrational Beliefs and thus serve as therapists for each other between formal therapy sessions. Other cognitive techniques employed in this phase of RECT include the use of: (a) general semantics methods (Korzybski, 1933); (b) rational self-help forms (see Chapter 1); (c) audiotape recordings (of the couple's therapy sessions or recorded lectures on rational themes); (d) bibliotherapy, especially the use of books which present the rational-emotive perspective on how to overcome emotional and behaviour disturbance and (e) a variety of imagery techniques (Lazarus, 1984).

Emotively, the therapist can employ several evocative and vivid methods of RET to help change the couple's irrational philosophies (Dryden, 1984c). Such methods include the use of: (a) rational-emotive imagery (Maultsby & Ellis, 1974) - where the partners deliberately imagine 'upsetting events' at 'A', and practise making themselves feel appropriately sad, annoyed, frustrated about these at 'C', which is achieved by spontaneously thinking more rationally at B; (b) vigorous and forceful repetition of rational statements (Ellis, 1979d); (c) role playing - to uncover hidden feelings which can then be traced back to the relevant irrational Beliefs and Disputed; (d) shame-attacking exercises - where couples deliberately seek our various 'shameful' experiences and practise accepting themselves for acting 'shamefully'; and (e) therapist self-disclosure and humour to help couples not take themselves and their partners <u>too</u> seriously.

Behaviourally, in this phase, partners are encouraged to face and not avoid potential problems so that they may have real-life opportunity to 'stay in' these situations until they have made themselves undisturbed about them (Grieger & Boyd, 1980).

<u>Enhancing couple satisfaction phase</u>. Once both partners have made some progress at helping themselves and their partner overcome their emotional disturbances about their dissatisfactory relationship, they are in a position to look constructively at ways of enhancing their degree of relationship satisfaction or to be helped to separate amicably. Assuming that they wish to stay partnered, there are a number of well-established methods that can be used to help them to live more happily together. These include communication training (Crawford, 1982; Guerney, 1977), negotiation training (Stuart, 1980) and a variety of behavioural techniques designed to help them to (1) develop appropriate relating and sexual skills and (2) get more of what they want from each other (Mackay, 1985). Bibliotherapy is often used in conjunction with these methods.

A hallmark of RECT is that homework assignments are negotiated to encourage couples to put into practice what they have learned in therapy. Assuming that such assignments are carefully designed by the therapist and agreed to by both partners, failure to execute them often reveals further emotional disturbance - particularly that which stems from a philosophy of low frustration tolerance (LFT). RECT practitioners are alert to such possibilities and strive to help both partners, if appropriate, overcome their LFT so that they can follow through on the difficult task of changing the nature of their relationship.

A final task for RECT practitioners in this stage is to address the topic of relationship myths (see the section 'Couple dissatisfaction' above) and help partners develop more realistic perspectives concerning what they can legitimately expect from intimate relationships.

<u>Problems Encountered In RECT And Their Solution</u>. The conduct of couples therapy is fraught with potential problems, no matter which approach the practitioner adopts. The more flexible the practitioner can be, the better, and in general it is highly desirable for RECT therapists to Dispute their own

irrational Beliefs concerning how therapy must proceed, how clients must behave and what harmonious relationships must be like. Practitioners would be wise not to be invested in either preserving or destroying relationships, if they are to truly help couples negotiate what is in their best interests. Apart from therapist-derived problems the following problems are often encountered in RECT.

Secrets. Because RECT therapists conceive their basic task to be one of helping individual partners, rather than the relationship, they will frequently see the partners alone in individual sessions particularly at the beginning of therapy. Consequently, they will sometimes be called upon to keep 'secrets'. They are prepared to do this and, in order to help both partners disclose what is really on their mind they will tell clients in individual sessions of their willingness to do so. This tactic also helps therapists to uncover 'hidden agenda' quickly. Consequently, they are advised to be mindful of what information is confidential to a particular partner and keep a mental note not to disclose this in front of the other. It should again be noted that this is done in order to develop productive contracts with both partners. Some RECT therapists stress to both partners that whatever is discussed in individual sessions is confidential to each partner concerned, so that if directly asked about what occurred in an individual session with the other partner, they can refer to this principle. Moreover, partners are advised to only talk about their individual sessions with each other in general terms rather than in detail.

Persistent other-blaming. It sometimes happens that one or both partners refuse to acknowledge that they make themselves disturbed about their mate's behaviour and cling rigidly to the assertion that their mate is the cause of their upset. In certain of these cases, it transpires that they are anxious that if they admit that they make themselves upset, their mate will not be motivated to change. In other cases, such 'defensiveness' is motivated by fear of self-criticism: 'If I admit that I make myself disturbed, as I must not do, then I will condemn myself'. In these two instances, effective RECT practitioners will test out such hypotheses rather than assume that their hunches are correct. Such 'defensiveness' can also be, in certain instances, a sign that the partner is profoundly disturbed. One technique that sometimes helps clients who persistently blame their partner, is to stress that if they want their partner to change, then one of the most effective ways of achieving this is to change their own behaviour first.

When Disputing fails. In certain cases, RECT therapists will fail to encourage one or both partners to identify, challenge and change their irrational Beliefs which mediate their disturbance. When this occurs, the practitioner can use some of the methods which are ideally intended for use in the 'enhancing couple satisfaction' phase. In the case where one partner is overcoming their emotional disturbance and the other is not, the therapist may focus his efforts on encouraging the former to be unusually nice to the disturbed partner to encourage that partner to change. Ellis (1957) originally advocated this tactic in his book, How to live with a neurotic, and it is one that sometimes proves successful. When both partners remain disturbed after Disputing fails, RECT practitioners may use a number of systems-theory-inspired interventions which are designed to change A. Thus, for example, reframing and various paradoxical procedures can be employed to help the couple extricate themselves from a vicious circle of negative interactions. If this is successful, it occasionally provides the stimulus for one or both partners to then focus on their disturbance-creating Beliefs. However, although such interventions may be successful in the short term, if both partners remain emotionally disturbed they might, as a result, experience more problems later, since unresolved emotional disturbance is the driving force behind the development and maintenance of disturbed interactions.

Extremely hostile interchanges. These are difficult to manage when they occur in couples therapy sessions, and when they become a regular occurrence it is advisable to see the partners individually. However, in dealing with such a situation at a given time, I have found it helpful to do something unusual to gain the couple's attention. Thus, I have, in the midst of a heated interchange, got up and commenced speaking to a picture on the wall, or tried to catch an imaginary mouse. These attention-getting techniques are, in my experience, generally more effective in defusing the situation than trying to shout the couple down which tends to increase the heat in an overly hot kitchen.

The Change Process

In the same way as a good navigator plots his favoured course but plans several different alternative routes, should they be needed, so do effective RECT therapists have their preferred and alternative game-plans. Since couples differ markedly, the RECT therapist who adheres rigidly to a single game-plan is likely to fail with a number of couple clients.

When therapy goes smoothly, RECT practitioners are able to keep to their preferred game-plan. In cases where this applies, they help both partners see that they have two different kinds of problems: those related to couple disturbance, and those related to couple dissatisfaction. They succeed at (1) showing the couple that it is better if they work on disturbance issues first; (2) explaining that their disturbance is due in the main to their irrational Beliefs about their unsatisfactory relationship; (3) inducing them to work at Disputing and changing these irrational Beliefs and replacing them with their rational alternatives; (4) inducing them to work at identifying whether their differences can be reconciled and, if so; (5) helping them to negotiate more satisfying relationship arrangements; and (6) encouraging them to work to actualize these desired alternatives. When both partners are only dissatisfied and not disturbed, only stages 4, 5 and 6 apply.

Problems still tend to occur even in this smooth change process, and can be generally attributed to one or both partners believing that change _must_ be easier than it is (LFT) or to one or both partners testing the solidity of change (Stuart, 1980). Here, the therapist (1) helps the couple to tolerate the discomfort that change almost inevitably brings and to see that change is rarely easily achieved, and (2) explains to the couple (preferably in advance) that 'testing' behaviour is a common occurrence in the change process, i.e. that one or both partners sometimes tests out the solidity of change by returning to dysfunctional patterns. When partners are prepared for this eventuality they are less likely to disturb themselves about it. The therapist also explains that change is rarely a linear process since humans easily return to well ingrained but dysfunctional patterns of behaviour, thought and emotion.

When both partners are disturbed at the inception of therapy and only one changes for the better in this respect, the therapist will often, as noted above, encourage that partner to make an extra effort for their own sake and for the sake of determining the future prospects of the relationship. This involves being unusually understanding and tolerant of the still disturbed partner, a tactic which often serves as the fulcrum and lever which encourages that partner to begin to change, for it sometimes happens that they need to see that their partner has shown an extra amount of 'good faith' before beginning to work on their own disturbance. If such a tactic fails to yield beneficial results for the disturbed partner, then the other partner has useful information when coming to determine the viability of the relationship.

As has also been noted above, when both partners remain disturbed even as a result of the therapist's interventions in the 'overcoming couple disturbance' phase of treatment, the therapist is prepared to use a variety of behavioural and systems-theory-inspired interventions to change 'A' in the ABC framework even though he or she acknowledges that is less desirable than producing philosophic change at B (Ellis, 1979c). If these interventions are successful, then the couple have been helped to see that they can extricate themselves from a negative pattern and thus may be encouraged to do so for themselves. There is always the danger, however, that if they re-encounter the original problem situation they will again become disturbed and thus may need further help to change 'A'.

It needs to be reiterated that RECT practitioners tend to be flexible in their use of different therapeutic contexts and thus may suggest changing the therapeutic modality at various points in the process of couples therapy (e.g. from conjoint couples therapy to concurrent individual sessions with each person). Such changes are usually instigated for positive therapeutic reasons, but can also be made if the therapy has become unproductively 'stuck' in a given modality.

The Personal Qualities Of Effective RECT Therapists

In the practice of couples therapy, effective RECT practitioners will be: (a) comfortable using the structure of RECT, but flexible enough to work in less structured ways when the occasions arise; (b) drawn to adopting an active-directive teaching style and credible enough to teach their client couples the principles of RET in ways appropriate to the learning abilities of the people involved; (c)'... authoritative without being authoritarian; ... bring up discussions of basic values without foisting their personal values on to clients; ... push, coach, persuade, and encourage clients to think and act against their own self-sabotaging tendencies' (Ellis, 1982b, p. 316); and (d) prepared to reveal their own feelings and Beliefs and show their clients that they are not scared to take risks in helping them over their marital difficulties. Moreover, they will tend to be philosophically inclined, scientific, empirical, multimodal and anti-absolutistic in their approach to the problems of their couples, and be drawn to RECT because it allows them to express these tendencies fully. They will be comfortable working with more than one person in therapy and raising difficult issues with both partners, particularly in the area of sexual relations.

While it is not essential for effective RECT therapists to have had first hand experience of cohabiting relationships, this is probably desirable for a number of reasons. First, they will be able to talk with clients about their difficulties from a more authoritative and credible position, particularly if they have been successful in dealing with some of their own. Second, they will tend to have a deeper understanding of the stresses of intimate relationships and see the potential for growth and for harm that such relationships hold. Finally, they will be able to share specific examples from their own experiences to help show their clients the advantages of a rational approach to coupled life. However, it is noted that some RECT practitioners are quite successful without such first hand experience.

A TYPICAL CASE EXAMPLE OF RECT

Mr. and Mrs. Rogers, married with no children, were seen when I worked as a part-time counselling psychologist for an East Birmingham (England) general practice. Mrs. Rogers, a 35 year old housewife, was initially referred to me for 'depression'. In an initial intake interview it transpired that she was depressed about what she described as her husband's cold attitude towards her. I decided, with her permission, to invite Mr. Rogers to come and see me to determine his opinions about his wife's depression and the marital situation. In cases where one partner is referred to me whose disturbance is rooted in an interpersonal context, I prefer to interview the significant other since this context facilitates their later involvement in therapy if this is indicated. Mr. Rogers, a 38 year old businessman, angrily complained about his wife's 'low mood'. He also expressed concern that he could not 'get through to her'. They both stated in these initial individual interviews that they would be interested to have counselling for their problems. They wanted to stay married, but both stated that they would like to be seen separately at first. I saw no reason to refuse their requests.

'<u>Overcoming Couple Disturbance</u>' <u>Phase</u>

I began by helping Mrs. Rogers to see that she was <u>insisting</u> in an absolutistic manner that she must have her husband's love and that she was unlovable since he did not seem to love her at present. I showed her that it was this attitude rather than the assumed lack of love on his part that determined her feelings of depression, and proceeded to help her to accept herself even if her husband did not love her. I helped her to <u>Dispute</u> her irrational <u>need</u> for love, but encouraged her to keep to her rational <u>desire</u> for his love, and showed her that she could be appropriately sad but did not have to be inappropriately depressed if her assumption proved to be correct now and/or in the future.

When working with Mr. Rogers I zeroed in on his demand that his wife <u>should</u> not be depressed and helped him to see that this was related to another demand that his wife <u>must</u> be supportive which in turn was related to his fear of failure at work. His wife used to help him by doing important typing and book-keeping and this helped him maintain a high standard of work performance. The fact that she was no longer assisting him in this way confronted him directly with his own anxiety, which, as often occurs, was masked by anger (Wessler, 1981). I encouraged Mr. Rogers to face this fear and helped him to Dispute his underlying irrational Beliefs, namely: 'I <u>must</u> do well and continue to do well at work or I'd be inadequate'; and 'I <u>must</u> keep getting promoted or I may not be able to improve our living standards which would be terrible'. For good measure, I showed him that, while he wanted his wife to support him, there was no law in the universe that decreed that she had to. Consequently, he became more tolerant and sympathetic towards his wife when she became depressed.

At this point it would have been tempting to bring Mr. and Mrs. Rogers together for conjoint sessions, since she was becoming less depressed and he was less anxious and angry. However, I decided to see them separately for two more individual sessions each to help them deal more thoroughly with the worst examples of 'A' in the ABC framework that they could imagine. This strategy, in fact, elicited Mrs. Rogers' acute fear of divorce. I helped her to identify and challenge her Belief that divorce would be 'awful' and helped her to see that she could lead an independent, happy life and therefore was not impelled to stay in the marriage.[3] I also helped Mr. Rogers deal with his morbid fear of unemployment and showed him (a) that his value as a human was not dependent on his work status and (b) that he could become vitally absorbed in other pursuits if he ever faced unemployment.

When I felt satisfied that they had made progress in dealing with their worst fears, I then arranged to see them in conjoint marital therapy, having seen them individually for six sessions each.

'Enhancing Couple Satisfaction' Phase

This phase of treatment began with a review of what Mr. and Mrs. Rogers had both learned in individual couples therapy. They reiterated their desire to stay together and work towards increased marital satisfaction. At the outset of this phase, Mrs. Rogers experienced a greater degree of dissatisfaction than her husband. Although she had made great strides in accepting herself, she stated that, in her opinion, he was still taking her for granted and expected that she would devote much of her life to helping him gain a managerial position to which he had always aspired. She said that she was no longer prepared to devote as much time to helping him in this respect and wanted more time to pursue her own emerging interests. Although Mr. Rogers initially appeared to understand her desire for self-actualization, his actual behaviour in subsequent weeks belied his words.

Despite the fact that I had helped them to negotiate a more equitable allocation of time to different tasks, Mr. Rogers failed to keep his part of the bargain. At this point, Mrs. Rogers decided to get tough with him. She was able to do this because she was less anxious about the prospect of being alone. When Mr. Rogers realized that his wife was really serious about pursuing her own goals he was jolted into realizing the implications of continuing to act in an unsupportive way towards her.[4] At this point, he was able to articulate his fears about what living with an independent woman might mean for him. He feared that she might find another man, whereas in reality Mrs. Rogers wanted not only to spend some time pursuing her own interests, but also to spend more time socially with him: 'I no longer want to be a doormat', she said.

At this point, I did some individual work with Mr. Rogers in the context of conjoint couples therapy. I helped him to see that he could still accept himself even if his wife did in fact leave him for somebody else, and that he could be relatively happy if this happened. Mrs. Rogers tried on several occasions to reassure him that she was not interested in other men, but I showed her and her husband that this was not the central issue and that the real point was that Mr. Rogers was anxious about the _prospect_ of this happening. As he successfully Disputed his irrational Beliefs about her leaving him, he calmed down and listened to his wife's desires with greater empathy. At this point, I taught them how to listen accurately and respond to each other's statements, and how to check out their hunches about the meaning of such statements rather than assume that their hunches were, indeed, facts (Guerney, 1977). I further helped them to consider the implicit contracts that they had made with each other at the time of their marriage about their roles as husband and wife, and showed them that these role expectations could be renegotiated (Sager, 1976). This led to a full discussion of their aspirations for themselves as individuals and as a couple, and they were able to determine for themselves how they could achieve 'I-goals' and 'We-goals'. At the end of ten conjoint sessions they decided that they had achieved enough to work on 'enhancing couple satisfaction' on their own.

Observations

This example clearly demonstrates the major features of RECT. Issues of couple disturbance were dealt with first, in this instance, in individual couples therapy sessions for both partners. Conjoint couples therapy sessions were employed to deal with issues of relationship dissatisfaction. Communication, problem-solving and negotiation training procedures were all employed in this second phase. The case also shows that RECT practitioners are often called upon to deal with further disturbance issues that emerge in the 'enhancing couple satisfaction' phase. As is commonly found, emotional disturbance is often uncovered as a result of the failure of one or both partners to execute carefully negotiated homework assignments. In this case Mr. Rogers's anxiety about his wife having 'affairs' was elicited as a consequence of his failure to follow through on an assignment that was negotiated on two separate occasions. He was helped to see that his 'excuses' were in fact defensive in nature and served to protect him from his own self-condemnation. Mr. Rogers confirmed my own hypothesis that it was my early focus on Disputing his irrational Beliefs in the first phase of treatment that encouraged him to disclose his core fear. In his words: 'I feel that I was helped to acquire the skills to actually deal with this particular fear. I doubt whether I would have revealed it if I felt unable to deal with it'.

Follow-Up

I conducted a follow-up session six months after treatment was terminated. Mr. and Mrs. Rogers maintained the gains which they had achieved in therapy, and, according to them, were experiencing the most productive period of their marriage. They reported that they were more able to express their desires to one another and be supportive of each other's goals as well as spend more time together. Mrs. Rogers had taken up voluntary work, pottery classes and yoga. She spent about an hour a day typing her husband's business correspondence as compared to the four hours daily work she used to do for him. She had not experienced any depressive episodes since treatment had ended. Mr. Rogers had still not acquired his coveted managerial position. He occasionally experienced bouts of panic about this fact, but said on these occasions he was able to identify and Dispute the underlying irrational Beliefs. He had come to realise that work was not the 'be-all and end-all' of his life and had started to manage a local junior soccer team. He seemed genuinely pleased with his wife's improvement, rarely got angry with her and she felt that he showed sincere interest in her activities. Together they had taken up ballroom dancing lessons and enjoyed regular Saturday evenings at the local dance hall. They reported that they were more able to challenge one another in a constructive way when problems began to emerge and that they were able to resolve matters without undue upset.

Interestingly enough, both Mr. and Mrs. Rogers pointed to the gains that they had made in the first phase of treatment as the most significant feature of their therapy experiences. Mrs. Rogers summed this up well when she said: 'Although it was painful, you helped me most by showing me that divorce wasn't the end of the world. I thought it was, you see. Yes, that really helped. Before, we stayed together more out of fear and obligation than anything else, but now we are together because we want to be together'. That statement beautifully encapsulates the goals and spirit of RECT!

NOTES

1. Partners often express such myths in idiosyncratic form.

2. A similar phenomenon often occurs in individual RET. When clients are given audiotape recordings of therapy sessions they often learn better the ABCs of RET after they have listened to these recordings than when they are in the therapy room. It may be that this is due to the fact that, later, they are less emotionally involved with the material and can thus listen more attentively to what the therapist is saying.

3. This procedure, known as 'de-awfulizing' divorce, is very helpful in reducing anxiety in partners who feel impelled to stay married out of obligation rather than out of desire.

4. I have often found that it is only when wives are prepared to take drastic action in pursuing their own goals that their husbands are 'shocked' into realizing the implications of not listening to them. This 'shock' is often the motivating factor for initiating constructive change.

Chapter Seven

RATIONAL-EMOTIVE CONCILIATION COUNSELLING

WINDY DRYDEN & DAVID McLOUGHLIN

INTRODUCTION

The past two decades have seen an international move away from 'fault-based' divorce legislation. This, in turn, has led to the adoption of a conciliatory approach to the resolution of disputes arising from separation and divorce, particularly those which centre on children. In Britain there are now around 22 voluntary and statutory agencies affiliated with the National Family Conciliation Council which offer a service to families. The conciliators staffing such agencies are drawn from a variety of disciplines including law, social work and psychology. Many have a background in areas such as marriage guidance or probation. Inevitably this has resulted in a somewhat eclectic approach to the practice of conciliation, theoretical concepts being drawn from a variety of sources. Parkinson (1985) lists six different perspectives which include psychoanalytic theory, family systems theory, crisis theory, communications theory, attachment theory, and conflict management theory. However, it seems that family systems theory is becoming the dominant perspective as it has been argued that, although conciliation is not therapy, the concepts and practices derived from it have much to offer the separating family (Horwill, 1983; Robinson & Parkinson, 1985). Nevertheless, there is a risk that such a perspective can in fact present disputes between separating spouses as being more complex than is necessary by focusing on the whole family system and there is room for alternative models. This chapter puts forward rational-emotive theory as a model from which conciliators can derive useful concepts and practices.

CONCILIATION

The National Family Conciliation Council (1984) describes the primary aim of conciliation as 'to help those couples involved in the process of separation and divorce to reach agreements, or reduce the area of intensity of conflict, on disputes concerning their children'. It is, however, necessarily vague on the question of how this aim should be achieved. Definitions of conciliation have been somewhat legalistic with Saunders (1977) describing it as 'a settling of disputes without litigation' (p. 71). Elsewhere Saunders (1969) has suggested that 'conciliation' has both a broad sense in which it covers the great variety of methods whereby a dispute is amicably settled, and a narrow sense in which it is a process of formulating proposals of settlement, where, after an investigation of the facts and an offer to reconcile opposing contentions, the parties are left free to accept or reject the proposals formulated. Such a definition allows conciliators broad scope in terms of the practices they can adopt under the heading of conciliation.

There have been attempts to provide clearer definitions of conciliation as it applies to the resolution of disputes arising from separation and divorce. In particular, distinctions have been made between 'mediation' and 'conciliation'. The former is seen as a simple level of affecting change in which the worker attempts to negotiate a limited practical solution to a presenting problem by acting as a go-between and does not deal with aspects of the parties' interaction; whereas conciliation is seen as a more complex process in which the worker acts as a barrier between the parties, preventing them from dealing with each other destructively on the problem (Preston et al., 1983). In attempting to describe the conciliation task Parkinson (1985) cites Madison's terminology thus:

> .... conciliation requires an assessment of the interaction between the couple, as a means of understanding the presenting problem. The counsellor works conjointly with the couple and facilitates their own efforts to reduce conflict, communicate and problem solve. The aim is to help the couple reach their own agreement with regard to the dispute and elements of their relationship that promote disputes between them. The method requires expertise in both the area of relationship

> skills and negotiation (Madison, 1983, p. 2).

As Madison was writing as a Director of Counselling within the Australian Family Court where conciliation counsellors are drawn from psychology and social work, and where 'mediation' by workers without expertise in relationship skills is being strongly resisted, such a definition with its focus on interaction and communication skills is understandable. However, his description of conciliation is as close as we have to a working definition, and does fit the present authors' understanding of it as practised in voluntary and statutory agencies in Britain. Further, it is a description of the conciliation task for which a number of psychotherapies, but particularly rational-emotive theory, can provide a model for conceptual analysis and practice.

BASIC PRINCIPLES OF RATIONAL-EMOTIVE THEORY

A major assumption of rational-emotive theory is that emotions are founded upon the evaluative Beliefs people hold towards themselves, other people and the world. An important distinction is made between irrational Beliefs and rational Beliefs.

Irrational Beliefs tend to sabotage the person's attempts to pursue constructively his or her basic goals and purposes and discourage the person from making a healthy adjustment if these cannot be achieved. They are absolutistic and devout in nature. Beliefs are often phrased as two parts of a syllogism - a <u>premise</u> and a set of <u>derivatives</u>. The premise form of irrational Beliefs is often couched in the form of 'musts', 'shoulds', and 'have-to's' (e.g. 'I must gain custody of my two children'). Typical derivatives that stem from such premises are couched in the form of 'awfulizing' (a magical rating that implies that something is more than 100% bad (e.g. 'It would be awful if I did not gain custody of my two children'); 'I-can't-stand-it' (another magical term that implies that I could never be happy again if I do not get what I must (e.g. 'I couldn't stand it if I did not gain custody of my two children'); and 'damning' of self, other(s) and/or the world (e.g. 'I - or my ex-partner - would be no good if I do not gain custody of my two children').

Rational Beliefs, on the other hand, tend to help the person to pursue constructively his or her basic goals and purposes and encourage the person to adjust if these cannot be achieved. They are relative and non-devout in nature. The premise form of rational Beliefs is often couched in the form of 'preferences', 'desires', and 'wants' (e.g. 'I really want to gain custody of my two children, but I do not absolutely have to'). Typical derivatives that stem from such premises are couched in the following forms: 'rating badness' (a realistic evaluation of 'badness' along a 0-100% continuum (e.g. 'It would be very bad if I did not gain custody of my two children, but it would not be awful if I didn't'); 'tolerating' (another realistic term that implies that even very bad situations are tolerable and do not preclude the experience of future happiness (e.g. 'I could tolerate it, but will never like it, if I did not gain custody of my two children'); 'accepting' self, other(s) and/or the world (e.g. 'If I do not gain control of my two children, I will still accept myself - or my ex-partner - as an unreliable, fallible human being').

Another important distinction made by rational-emotive theory concerns that between dysfunctional (or irrational) negative emotions (which tend to impede goal achievement and constructive adjustment) and functional (or rational) negative emotions (which tend to promote goal achievement and constructive adjustment). Furthermore, rational-emotive theory holds that irrational Beliefs underpin dysfunctional (or irrational) negative emotions and rational Beliefs underpin their functional (or rational) equivalents (see Table I).

A further basic principle of rational-emotive theory is that constructive communication, problem-solving, and negotiation - processes deemed central to successful conciliation - will tend to be impeded when one or both people concerned experience one or more of the dysfunctional (or irrational) negative emotions listed in Table I (which are underpinned by irrational Beliefs about self, ex-partner and/or the situation). For example, it is difficult for two ex-partners to engage in productive conciliation when one or both are angrily damning the other. Conversely, experiencing functional (or rational) negative emotions as listed in Table I (which are underpinned by rational Beliefs about self, ex-partner and/or the situation) will tend to motivate ex-partners to engage in constructive communication, problem-solving and negotiation, given that they both seek a conciliatory solution to their problems.

Finally, rational-emotive theory hypothesises that when a person holds an irrational Belief, he

TABLE I. Dysfunctional (irrational) and functional (rational) negative emotions and their cognitive correlates

Inference[1] Related To Personal Domain[2]	Type of Belief	Emotion	Type of Emotion	
Threat or danger	Irrational	Anxiety	Dysfunctional	(Irrational)
Threat or danger	Rational	Concern	Functional	(Rational)
Loss (with implications for future)	Irrational	Depression	Dysfunctional	(Irrational)
Loss (with implications for future)	Rational	Sadness	Functional	(Rational)
Breaking of personal rule (other or self); other threatens self	Irrational	Damning anger	Dysfunctional	(Irrational)
Breaking of personal rule (other or self); other threatens self	Rational	Non-damning anger (or annoyance)	Functional	(Rational)
Breaking of own moral code	Irrational	Guilt	Dysfunctional	(Irrational)
Breaking of own moral code	Rational	Remorse	Functional	(Rational)
Other betrays self (self non-deserving)	Irrational	Hurt	Dysfunctional	(Irrational)
Other betrays self (self non-deserving)	Rational	Disappointment	Functional	(Rational)
Threat to desired exclusive relationship	Irrational	Destructive jealousy	Dysfunctional	(Irrational)

..cont.

TABLE I (continued)

Inference[1] Related To Personal Domain[2]	Type of Belief	Emotion	Type of Emotion	
Threat to desired exclusive relationship	Rational	Constructive jealousy	Functional	(Rational)
Personal weakness revealed publicly	Irrational	Shame	Dysfunctional	(Irrational)
Personal weakness revealed publicly	Rational	Regret	Functional	(Rational)

1 Inference: an interpretation which goes beyond observable reality but which gives meaning to it; may be accurate or inaccurate.

2 The objects: tangible and intangible - in which a person has an involvement constitute a person's personal domain (Beck, 1976). Rational-emotive theory distinguishes between ego and comfort aspects of the personal domain although these aspects frequently interact.

or she is likely to make inferences (i.e. interpretations that go beyond the available data) about self and others that are more negatively distorted than if the person holds a rational Belief. Thus, if a woman believes: 'I must at all costs maintain control over access rights to my children', then she will tend to view her husband's attempts to gain access more negatively than she would if she held a rational equivalent of this Belief. It should be noted that this hypothesis awaits empirical enquiry.

BASIC GOALS OF RATIONAL-EMOTIVE CONCILIATION COUNSELLING

Once it has been established that both ex-partners understand the objectives of conciliation and the role of the conciliation counsellor and state that they wish to commit themselves to this process, then the counsellor has two basic goals. The first goal is called *overcoming couple disturbance*. This involves helping the clients to overcome their dysfunctional (or irrational) negative feelings by having them challenge their irrational Beliefs and replace these with their rational alternatives. Once the counsellor has helped both partners make significant progress in this area, they are then, normally, in a better frame of mind to work towards a conciliatory solution to their problems. The second goal is called *promoting constructive couple dialogue*. This involves the conciliation counsellor helping the clients to communicate clearly and constructively, identify possible solutions to their problems and to negotiate fairly with one another. During this process, the conciliation counsellor will also help the clients to correct any distorted inferences that interfere with the promotion of constructive couple dialogue.

It is important to reiterate, at this point, that attempting to promote constructive couple dialogue when one or both clients are experiencing dysfunctional (or irrational) negative emotions (based on irrational Beliefs) is usually unproductive *in the long term*. While it is possible to bypass such emotions in the short term during the conciliation process, and thereby to help the couple establish a given solution to their problems, later sabotage of any such agreements is likely to occur in this circumstance. This tends to happen when one or both ex-partners re-experience dysfunctional (or irrational) negative emotions. Because these have not been dealt with during the conciliation process, the clients do not have the skills of getting over such feelings, i.e. by identifying, challenging and changing the irrational Beliefs which underpin them. These dysfunctional negative emotions then tend to foster old destructive communication patterns which, when brought into play, in turn tend to destroy the good faith that may have been developed between them during the conciliation sessions.

THE PROCESS OF RATIONAL-EMOTIVE CONCILIATION COUNSELLING

Eliciting Commitment To The Process

When a couple seeks conciliation, the rational-emotive conciliation counsellor's initial tasks are to explain the objectives of the process, to correct any misconceptions the couple may have about the enterprise (e.g. it does not seek to effect reconciliation), to outline the likely course the process will take, and to explain the role of the conciliation counsellor. This is done to enable the couple to make an informed decision whether or not to commit themselves to the process.

Case illustration. Mr. & Mrs. Smith had been separated for 9 months and until recently Mr. Smith had wanted little contact with Clare, their 5-year old daughter. He then requested weekend-long access, this being strongly resisted by Mrs. Smith. They were referred for conciliation counselling by their respective solicitors.

The conciliation counsellor outlined that his role was to help them to overcome the obstacles that were preventing them from effecting a mutually agreed solution to this current impasse, assured both clients that he would not take sides, and explained that the process normally involves helping both people to get into the right frame of mind to make sound decisions. As with most couples seeking conciliation, Mr. & Mrs. Smith were somewhat ambivalent about the process. They both wanted a solution to their dispute but did not want to 'lose'. They committed themselves to the process after being assured that this was a common sentiment among couples seeking a conciliatory solution to their disputes.

Overcoming Couple Disturbance

At this stage, given that such commitment has been elicited, the counsellor helps the clients to: (a) identify any dysfunctional (or irrational) negative emotions that they may be experiencing, (b) see how such emotions will probably sabotage the process of conciliation as well as being self-defeating, and (c) commit themselves to work on overcoming their disturbed feelings before working towards an agreed solution to their problems. It is important for the counsellor to stress that the goal of this stage is to help the clients experience functional (or rational) negative emotions which serve as healthy responses to negative events as well as serving as motivating forces to stimulate a conciliatory solution to their problems, rather than to eliminate all feelings about their situation.

The counsellor's next task is to help the clients see the link between their dysfunctional (or irrational) negative emotions and the irrational Beliefs that underpin them. Once this has been understood, the counsellor is in a position to help the clients to Dispute these Beliefs using the methods of Socratic dialogue (Dryden, 1984c). In conciliation counselling, the focus is not only on philosophic Disputing (helping the clients learn that there is evidence in support of their rational Beliefs, but none in support of their irrational Beliefs), but also on pragmatic Disputing (helping clients see that continued adherence to their irrational Beliefs will sabotage their own interests as well as the interests of their children).

During this stage, the conciliation counsellor can choose to work conjointly with the couple or see each person individually. This decision is, in part, influenced by the wishes of the couple and the degree to which they can work productively at this stage in conjoint sessions. Thus, if their anger is such that very hostile interchanges ensue or if one or both clients are very withdrawn and refuse to communicate, then it would be wise for the conciliation counsellor to see them separately, at least initially. Otherwise, conjoint sessions are probably indicated.

Case illustration. Mr. & Mrs. Smith both wanted to be seen separately at the beginning of conciliation counselling and the conciliation counsellor had two individual sessions with each of them.

Mr. Smith's 'sudden' desire to have weekend-long access was prompted by his parents' urgings. He felt very guilty about 'neglecting' his daughter and was desperate to 'make up for lost time'. He was helped to see that his feelings of guilt would interfere with his negotiating constructively with his wife, and these were targeted for change. The conciliation counsellor helped him to Dispute the irrational Belief underlying his guilt: 'I'm bad for neglecting my daughter' and encouraged him to accept himself as a fallible human being who did the wrong thing. He was then able to understand that his 'neglect' was linked to his past anxiety about being a good father. At the end of the two individual sessions, he was feeling much less guilty and less desperate to make up for lost time with Clare. He still wanted access but was prepared to accept less time than he originally requested.

Mrs. Smith was angry about her husband's sudden change of heart towards access to his daughter, but, as often occurs, her anger was underpinned by feelings of anxiety that her daughter might eventually want to live with her father and his parents. Mrs. Smith was first asked to assume that her daughter did express such a desire. She was then helped to identify her underlying irrational Belief: 'My daughter must not want to live with her father. If she did this would prove that I'm a poor mother and worthless'. She was then helped to Dispute this Belief and showed that she could accept herself as a fallible human being even if she was deficient as a mother. Once she accepted this she calmed down appreciably, became more open to consider some kind of access arrangement but expressed concern about her husband's competence in looking after Clare.

<u>Promoting Constructive Couple Dialogue</u>

Once both clients have made sufficient progress at replacing their irrational Beliefs with their rational alternatives and are experiencing functional (or rational) negative emotions much of the time, the process then shifts to promoting constructive dialogue between ex-partners. The focus here is on the skills of effective communication (empathic listening, 'owning' feelings, 'I' statements, etc.), problem-solving (brain-storming, evaluating possible solutions, etc.), and negotiation (developing compromises, considering the interests of children against self-interest, etc.). The counsellor may have to teach one or both clients these skills if these are not in their repertoire. Because this stage of conciliation has a decided interpersonal focus it is very important that clients are seen in conjoint sessions. Another task of the conciliation counsellor at this stage is to help one or both clients to correct any distorted inferences they may have about themselves, the other person and other involved parties.

It is important to note that the counsellor may have to return occasionally to the tasks of the overcoming disturbance phase during this stage since one or both clients may disturb themselves about what their ex-partner says as they strive to reconcile their differences.

Case illustration. At the beginning of the first conjoint session, the conciliation counsellor summarised what had occurred in the individual sessions. This was done with each client's permission. Both Mr. & Mrs. Smith were interested to learn that they were, in fact, grappling with a similar issue - self-condemnation for perceived deficits - and could see how this influenced their inferences about each other's motives. Mr. Smith had inferred that his wife's refusal to agree to any access arrangements was due to her desire for revenge for him leaving her. Mrs. Smith had inferred that her husband wanted to turn Clare against her. Mrs. Smith also voiced concern that her 'in-laws' were against her but was assured by Mr. Smith that in fact the opposite was the case. This lessened her concern that they were allies in her husband's plot against her.

During the second conjoint session, the conciliation counsellor occasionally had to intervene to aid both clients to negotiate without anger by helping them to see that there was no evidence that the other person must not hold 'wrong' opinions. They were helped to 'own' their opinions (e.g. 'From my perspective, I disagree that your suggestion would be good for Clare') rather than make negative attributions about the other's character (e.g. 'You're callous for suggesting that'). This helped to refocus the couple on the task of problem-solving.

With respect to Mr. Smith's care-taking ability, Mrs. Smith (a) conceded (albeit grudgingly) that his mother was 'good with Clare' and could help him to look after their daughter and (b) agreed to educate her husband concerning Clare's likes and dislikes.

Formulating Agreed Solutions and Trouble-Shooting

The next stage of the conciliation process concerns the formulation of agreed solutions to the couple's problems. Ideally, these need to be as detailed as possible and phrased using language and in a form that is acceptable to both partners. The relationship between both sets of solicitors often becomes a focus for discussion at this point.

One additional task, at this stage, concerns the counsellor helping both partners to identify possible future obstacles to maintaining productive communication. These are dealt with by reminding both clients that they can use the cognitive and interpersonal skills that they have developed during conciliation and by asking them to imagine using these skills to overcome the obstacle. Here, the couple are reminded to use the cognitive skills of Disputing irrational Beliefs before the interpersonal skills when they experience dysfunctional (or irrational) negative emotions. The more the couple can involve themselves in this trouble-shooting task the more it is likely that they will be able to deal productively with such obstacles if and when they occur in reality.

Case illustration. In the third conjoint session, the couple agreed on the following access arrangements: 'Mr. Smith will collect Clare at 10.00 a.m. every other Saturday morning and return her by 6.00 p.m. that day. For the first 3 months Mr. Smith's mother will be available to help Mr.Smith with looking after Clare'.

The conciliation counsellor helped both clients to identify possible future obstacles that were related to anger and anxiety and reminded them first to Dispute their underlying irrational Beliefs and then to share their concerns with the other by 'owning' their feelings and opinions.

Reviewing The Process

The final stage of conciliation involves the counsellor undertaking with the couple a review of what they have learned from the process. A particular focus here is on underscoring the fact that the couple have not only made agreements on specific issues but have also learned how to restore and maintain channels of constructive communication with one another. This latter point is important, since although they may have divorced, they will continue to have a relationship with one another as parents to their children.

Case illustration. In the final session, the conciliation counsellor helped Mr. & Mrs. Smith to see that they had acquired skills which they could use to: (a) Dispute irrational Beliefs underlying dysfunctional (or irrational) negative emotions; (b) communicate opinions rather than attributing negative traits to the other person and (c) formulate a mutually agreeable arrangement. They were urged to use these skills to solve future problems that might arise between them and in their own separate lives.

REGARDING THE INVOLVEMENT OF CHILDREN

As issues concerning children are those most frequently dealt with in conciliation their direct involvement in some way is often a necessary prerequisite to dispute resolution. Involving children can be helpful in a number of ways including providing them with an opportunity to put forward their own perceptions and opinions providing opportunities for the observation of relationships, and facilitating communication between parents and children.

In rational-emotive conciliation counselling the direct involvement of children can contribute to the process of identifying dysfunctional (or irrational) negative emotions, irrational Beliefs and distorted inferences. By involving children directly through separate interviews, or having them participate in sessions with their parents the irrationality of one or other partner's Beliefs and the distorted nature of their inferences can be demonstrated to them. A simple example where inferences can be tested would be a situation in which a mother is denying a father access to his children because she has come to infer that they are afraid of him, and has become anxious about their welfare as a result. Providing such a mother with the opportunity to observe the positive interaction between the children and their father in a 'safe' environment can enable her to question her inference that the children are afraid of their father.

The direct involvement of children does need to be handled carefully, however, as it can place them in a very vulnerable position. They may, for example, wish to say things which will upset one or other parent and have to deal with the threat, real or perceived, of retribution. Even separate interviews with a counsellor do not guarantee children protection as under present British law confidentiality cannot be promised because conciliators can be called to give evidence in Court.

CONCLUSION

We have proposed here that rational-emotive conciliation counselling can effectively deal with disputes arising out of separation and divorce. The illustrative case example shows that both the immediate problem and the underlying Beliefs and emotions can be dealt with despite a relatively short intervention and, as most client contact with conciliation agencies is short-term, this has much to recommend it. Further, the nature of rational-emotive conciliation counselling is such that, whilst dealing with immediate problems, couples are taught skills which will prevent them from becoming entrenched should other disputes arise in the future.

Chapter Eight

PROBLEMS IN LIVING: THE FRIDAY NIGHT WORKSHOP

WINDY DRYDEN & WOUTER BACKX

INTRODUCTION

The role of the counselling psychologist as remedial counsellor/psychotherapist is well defined in the literature, even in Britain where the debate concerning the professional status of counselling psychology continues to rage. But, the role of the counselling psychologist as psychological educator is less well defined. As Nelson-Jones (1982) has argued, psychological education is not a unitary phenomenon and he lists six activities that fall under this general heading. One of these activities concerns educating the public in psychological matters.

In this chapter, we will describe an event pioneered by Albert Ellis that has run continuously for the last twenty years or so. It combines both remedial counselling and that aspect of psychological education which endeavours to educate the public in the rational-emotive view of the nature of psychological disturbance, how people perpetuate their emotional and behavioural problems and how they can overcome them. This event has come to be known as 'The Friday night workshop'.

THE FRIDAY NIGHT WORKSHOP

Every Friday night (except when he is 'out of town'), Albert Ellis demonstrates the rational-emotive approach to counselling and psychotherapy by interviewing separately two volunteers from an audience of up to a hundred people at the Institute for Rational-Emotive Therapy in New York. Each volunteer is interviewed for about 30 minutes on a specific psychological problem (or problems), after which the members of the audience who wish to do so are actively encouraged to speak to the volunteer and to the therapist concerning aspects of the volunteer's problem(s) and the interview that they have witnessed. The workshop lasts for about 1½ hours and is followed by a coffee hour. Ellis conducts therapy in this format in a very similar manner to how he would conduct therapy in his private office, with the possible exception that he uses more humour in these public demonstrations.

RATIONAL-EMOTIVE THERAPY (RET)

RET is well suited to this form of public workshop. It is a non-mystical type of therapy where the therapist is very open about his or her interventions. It is also an educational form of therapy which strives to teach both the volunteer and the members of the audience the ABCs of RET - i.e. it is not 'A' (the event, or the person's inferences about the event) that determines the client's psychological problems (emotional and/or behavioural) at 'C' but rather it is 'B' (the client's irrational Beliefs about the event) that seems to more adequately account for the presence of these problems. In the course of the public demonstration, the volunteers are helped to identify, challenge and change their irrational Beliefs which take the form of dogmatic musts (shoulds, oughts or have to's) and one of three irrational derivatives. These derivatives take the form of (a) _awfulizing_ (rating an event as more than 100% bad - an evaluation which stems from the Belief: 'This bad event _must_ not be as bad as it is '; (b) _I-can't stand-it-itis_ (believing that one cannot tolerate an event and/or that one cannot be happy again as long as the event exists); and (c) _damnation_ (giving oneself, other people or the world in general a negative, global damning rating - (Dryden, 1984c, 1987; Ellis, 1985a; Ellis & Dryden, 1987). It is a feature of the Friday night workshop that while Ellis is working intensively with a particular volunteer, the audience is simultaneously being educated concerning the cognitive underpinnings of their emotional and behavioural problems, and how these underpinnings can be identified, challenged and changed.

THE PROCESS OF A PUBLIC DEMONSTRATION WITH A VOLUNTEER

We have both witnessed dozens of Ellis's interviews conducted in the Friday night workshop and have identified a discernible process to such interviews. First, Ellis elicits the client's major emotional and/or behavioural problem at 'C'. He then links this to a relevant activating event at 'A'. From there he proceeds to identify the client's major irrational Beliefs and starts to Dispute these in a strong, evocative and often humorous manner (here it is the client's Beliefs that are ridiculed, not the client). During this process, Ellis often uses self-disclosure to illustrate a number of points (as is shown in the transcript to be presented later in this chapter). Then, Ellis instructs the client how to use rational-emotive imagery (REI) - a technique whereby the client vividly imagines the troublesome event at 'A', is instructed to make him or herself disturbed at 'C' and then is asked to change this inappropriate (or irrational) emotion (e.g. depression, anxiety, guilt or anger) to an appropriate (or rational) negative emotion (e.g. sadness, concern, regret or annoyance). When the client is successful in using this technique he or she is practising spontaneously changing irrational Beliefs to rational Beliefs (which are expressed in the form of non-dogmatic desires and preferences). The client is then asked to practise REI for 10 minutes a day for 30 days and is given what Ellis calls 'operant conditioning' to motivate him or her to carry out this task. In 'operant conditioning',the client forgoes an enjoyable activity until he or she has practised REI and penalizes himself or herself if he or she forgoes such practice (e.g. carries out an unpleasant task like cleaning the toilet). At the end of the counselling session the audience is invited to ask questions and the client is given a tape of the session for later review. Listening to the tapes of their sessions has two major benefits for clients. First, they often gain increased understanding of issues that were discussed in the public session. This is valuable since talking about one's problems in a public setting can be distracting for some clients. Second, clients often learn how to challenge their irrational Beliefs more effectively after listening to Ellis's Disputing interventions on tape.

We next present a verbatim transcript of an interview conducted by Ellis with one of us (WB) in the setting of the Friday night workshop to show this approach in action.

A PUBLIC THERAPY SESSION CONDUCTED BY ALBERT ELLIS

(Friday Night Workshop 19th of July 1985 in front

of an audience of 100 people).

Th: (to the audience): Please be as compulsively quiet as you can be right now. Later you will get into the act and be able to say anything, but not right now. So shut your big mouths right now or else you'll have to listen in the John, which is a nice place to listen but not as good as in the auditorium. So quiet now and then later you'll be able to talk up and to say practically anything you want.
(to client): O.K. Do you want to give them your first name?

Cl: Wouter.

Th: Woulter, Wouter?

Cl: Yes say Walter.

Th: Yeah, we would say Walter in English, but W-O-U-T-E-R in your language, right? O.K. Walter or Wouter, what problem would you like to start with?

Th: Well, I have a problem about doing things on time, especially when I have to take an examination or something like that, and eh...

Cl: So in plain English you procrastinate, is that right? We call it procrastination; I don't know what you call it in Holland or Germany but we call it procrastination. Right?

Cl: That is possible.

Th: Give us an example recently when you sat on your ass and procrastinated...

Cl: Oh well when I came to the United States I had to finish an essay about the philosophy of science; and eh... well, I had to finish it and I did not make it, I did not get it ready.

Audience: (murmurs to client)

Cl: Sorry?

Audience: (says something about the microphone that the client is using not being turned correctly).

Cl: Like this?

Th: No, no. When you turn to me, it does not turn with you. If you turn around that way, then you face me. But it does not turn your turn. We haven't trained it properly yet. We are training it to turn properly, we are giving it therapy every week on how to turn. But so far we are failing and we may have to give up and kill ourselves. Unless we become rational and stop depressing ourselves about the goddamned mike! Anyway, so this time you could have done the paper...

Cl: Yes that is right.

Th: ... and you delayed, you procrastinated. Because when you were about to do it and you didn't, what did you say to yourself? What negative self-statement?

Cl: Oh, 'I have a lot of time. I'll do that easily'.

Th: That's what we call a rationalization, which means horseshit in English. That is horseshit, because you did not have that much time. You lied to yourself.

Cl: That's right.

Th: But what was the <u>reason</u> underneath the <u>rationalization</u>? You said something about the <u>hardship</u> of doing it. What do you think that was?

Cl: Well, it could be that I had delayed so much that I did not have sufficient time to do it. So I was afraid to find out. Or realized that it was very difficult, instead of what I originally thought, that it was easy.

Th: Yeah ...

Cl: I was a little bit afraid of not having enough time left in which to do it after I first delayed.

Th: Alright, but let us try the issue of difficultness first. Because your not having time enough was <u>after</u> you had already delayed. When you started delaying instead of doing it, you were saying, 'It may be difficult to do'. But if you didn't do it, that would be difficult too. Right?

Cl: That seems to be - yeah, that is right.

Th: Yeah. So therefore you would probably do it. But what were you saying in addition to 'It may be or will be difficult'? You were saying something in addition to that. And what is that?

Cl: 'If I fail I'll feel worse, I'll feel bad. I'll feel like a bad person.'

Th: So you were putting yourself down in case you failed.

Cl: That's right.

Th: Alright, we'll start with your fear of failing first. I'll then get back to the difficulty of the task because that is usually important with procrastination - the difficulty of doing it and your reluctance to deal with that. But let us say, let us suppose you do the task quickly and immediately and it is not so hot and you fail. Why would *that* be terrible? Why would you be a bad person, a Failure with a capital F for failing?

Cl: Well, eh...

Th: Yes?

Cl: ... that's difficult. Well, I should, must be able to do that!

Th: Oh you *should*! That is right: you *should* do it. But why *should* or *must* you?

Cl: And it was my fault not to arrange it in a way that I could do it.

Th: That is correct, it was your fault. Let us assume that. Nobody made you, put a gun to your head and made you procrastinate. But since it was your fault, your failure, how does it make *you* a failure, a shit, a no goodnick for having that failing?

Cl: Now I cannot find a good reason, but ...

Th: You believe it. You still believe you *must* not fail and are no good if you do.

Cl: Yes I do believe it, really. That is ...

Th: And as long as you *believe* it you are going to procrastinate.

Cl: That is right.

Th: You see. Now how can you give up that bloody idea? Not the idea that 'It is my fault if I fail', but the idea that 'I am then a total failure'. How can you give up that horseshit?

Cl: By telling myself something different.

Th: Exactly! What? 'I am a real failure'?

Cl: No, 'I am not a real failure, but I am just failing at this moment'. Or 'I am about to fail this time'.

Th: 'If I do it badly', - which you may not, you may do well - 'and I fail, I'll be failing at this moment with this essay. But I am never a failing person. I am never a rotten individual'. Right. Now you said the right thing, but do you really believe it? That you could fail at this essay but are not a real failure?

Cl: Well, the problem is when I try to tell myself this it is very difficult. I don't make it. I am thinking, 'Well it is not that bad to put it off at this moment'.

Th: Yeah.

Cl: So I go on delaying it ....

Th: Yeah, but that is for the other reason; we'll get to that in a minute, the hardness of it. But could you really believe that if you did it steadily and you kept failing, didn't do as well as you could do, do you really believe you would not be a failure, you would not be a worm? Do you really believe that?

Cl: I think so, to some extent.

Th: Yeah to some extent! But how could you believe it stronger? Like all these people in the audience believe it about you, but not about themselves. How could you believe it stronger? 'I am never a failure, a louse, a worm, even when I try my best and still fail'. How can you believe that?

Cl: Well, I can stop making global evaluations about myself. That's right.

Th: Well, eh ...

Cl: Because after I fail I can still do very many good things. So it is impossible to say what will be any final or global evaluation or rating of me by the time I die.

Th: Once you fail, you have the possibility to do many successful things in the future.

Cl: That is right.

Th: That is correct. So you are never a Failure. If you were a Failure, that would mean that you always deserve to fail and will fail because you failed this time. Is that correct?

Cl: That's right, yeah. That's right, I would deserve punishment or whatever.

Th: But why do you deserve punishment if you fail? If you try your best and you fail this time?

Cl: But I did not try my best.

Th: But suppose you did do your best. Why would you deserve punishment for failing? Why would you?

Cl: No, I don't deserve it. That is right.

Th: Even if you did not try, you don't. Suppose you tried very little and you fell on your face. Why would you still not deserve punishment for failing?

Cl: Well, I have freedom of choice. I can choose.

Th: You could choose not to rate yourself and not to consider yourself undeserving. Right. And the universe does not give a shit if you fail. It really does not care.

Cl: Really?

Th: Yeah really. Don't be surprised that the powers up there and the powers down there really don't give a fuck whether you succeed or not. They have their own quaint ideas. They are only interested in their own navels, not in your bellybutton. So if you really thought about it you could convince yourself that 'It is bad to fail, it is unfortunate, it is poor behaviour. But I am not a Failure and I don't deserve punishment or anything like that. I just deserve whatever I can get: such as good things in life. And when I get bad things I can live with them'. But now let us go down back to the hardness of doing the essay. You said rightly before that it is easy to put it off till later and to pretend: 'I'll do it later, I'll do it soon. I'll do it when it is easier'. Because it is *hard* to do it right now, right? But it is hard if you *don't* do it right now. In fact it is harder. Is it not?

Cl: Well, sometimes it comes out that it is easier to do it later.

Th: Yeah, *how many* times?

Cl: Yes, well ...

Th: Well, what percentage of times is it *easier* if you put it off?

Cl: Well, I don't ... Ja ...

Th: Yeah, yeah! Out of a hundred times you put it off, how many times does it *really* become easier and a rare delight?

Cl: Ja, that's right. But on the short term it is. That is the problem.

Th: Aah, yeah. That *is* the point. That is what we want you to see. It is easier *in the short run*.

Cl: That's right.

Th: If you would really believe that, and would remind yourself how hard it is in the long run. If you write down on a piece of paper or a card the disadvantages of putting it off instead of the advantages of putting it off, which you have solidly instilled in your head, then you would tend not to put essays and things like that off. Now could you do that? Really write down on a piece of paper the disadvantages of putting it off, of doing it later and the advantages of doing it right now?

Cl: I can do that.

Th: And would not that help you?

Cl: I think so, ja.

Th: Is there any other reason which we may have omitted for your not doing the essay? Can you think of any other reason why you don't do it quickly, get it over with and that is that, which is what sensible people like me do?

Cl: Well, sometimes I think something like, 'Why do they bother me with this kind of stuff?'.

Th: 'Oooooh, oooooh! Those lousy bastards! How could they give a nice guy like me that crummy paper to do?'. Right?

Cl: That is right!

Th: And what is the answer to that question? How _can_ they give a nice guy like you that crummy paper to do? How can they?

Cl: They are a little bit stupid. They don't know better.

Th: They can _easily_ do what they do! They have _no trouble_ giving you those stupid papers! Do they?

Cl: No they don't.

Th: And they are surviving very well!

Cl: That is right.

Th: So you are rebelling and saying to yourself, 'Because it is such a pain in the ass and such a stupid assignment, such a stupid paper to write, therefore they _should_ not give it to me!'. But they _should_ give it to you! Do you know why they _should_ give it to you, that stupid paper?

Cl: Because they choose to give it.

Th: Yes. Because _that is their nature_, to give out stupid papers! Do you expect them to give out intelligent papers to do or give you sensible things to do? How ridiculous!
So you see you have got three major musts to produce your procrastination: One, 'I _must_ do it very well and if I don't that would be terrible! I would be no good'. Two, 'They must not give me that goddamned stupid paper! So I'll fix their wagon by not doing it or by doing it later, when I feel like doing it'. And three, 'It is too goddamned hard to do! It _should not_ be so hard! Therefore I'll put it off and I hope and pray to God

almighty that it becomes easier some day'.

Cl: That's right. I do say these things.

Th: But that is not working. And you see that your irrational Beliefs are all musts. 'I must do well! They must treat me well! And conditions, the work itself must be easy!'. You are demanding and commanding that things must be your way. Now that is very unlikely!

Let me say how I did the opposite, when I was in college. I realised that they gave us term papers, especially in English which was really my major because I took more courses in English than in anything else. So the first day of the term they gave us a list of topics to write a term paper on and everybody else would fart around like you did, till the last day of the term or the day after the last day. But I did my paper immediately. I went to the library to work on it right away. First of all, nobody else was in the library and all the books were there, so that was good. Secondly, I could take any length of time I wanted to do the paper and finish it at my leisure. Thirdly, my professor almost dropped dead when he got the paper the second week of the term, was very grateful to get it so soon and thought I was a very noble person and a scholar. It was the first time in his or her history that that had ever happened and I could coast for the rest of term, having nothing hanging over my head. No worry, no problems. So I figured out that it was much more advantageous for me to do my term papers that way. So I did them immediately. But you are not figuring what I figured out. You are deluding yourself that it is advantageous to delay your essays. And it very very rarely, practically never is.

Let us try you with rational-emotive imagery. We have up to now been doing Disputing and asking 'Why <u>must</u> it be easy and where is it written that you <u>have to</u> do a perfect paper?' And 'Who says that those bastards <u>must</u> not give you stupid papers?' So we have been questioning and challenging your irrational Beliefs and you had better keep doing that. But let us also give you rational-emotive imagery. Close your eyes and imagine that the bastards give you another lousy, crummy paper to do which they probably will; and imagine that this paper is really a pain in the ass, it is very stupid that they give it to you, and it is hanging over your head to do. Can you vividly imagine that happening?

Cl: Yes.

Th: How do you feel in your gut as you imagine that paper hanging over your head, the days passing, and you keep telling yourself 'Tomorrow, tomorrow, manana, manana'. How do you feel?

Cl: I feel anger at those people who gave it to me.

Th: Now get in touch with your anger and really make yourself feel very angry at those idiots for giving you this stupid paper. Make yourself feel very angry. Are you now feeling very angry with them?

Cl: Right.

Th: All right. Now they are still making you do it, your image is still the same. But make yourself feel only sorry, only disappointed at what they are doing to you. Not angry at them. Tell me when you only feel sorry and disappointed, not angry.

Cl: I do.

Th: Open your eyes. That was quick, really quick. Tell us how you changed your feeling. How did you change?

Cl: I eh... first of all turned away from those stupid people and secondly by telling myself, 'Well it is not nice to have to do that paper, but O.K. I'll do it and I will certainly not die whatever bad things may happen in the world, I can stand it. And when

I pass it is O.K.'

Th: Alright. Now that was really good. Now all you have to do if you follow this, is every day for the next 30 days you imagine the worst you can think of, make yourself very angry or depressed or anything like that - anger is one of the things that shows how you feel, so that is O.K. - change it into being sorry and being disappointed the way you did and other ways that may occur to you. Now will you do that for the next 30 days at least once a day? You may do it 10 times a day but do it at least once. Would you really want to do that?

Cl: Let us say before I go to bed?

Th: Well any time in 24 hours once a day, do you want to do it?

Cl: Oh, whether I _want_ to do it, I thought you asked when.

Th: Yeah. No, no, I am not telling you that, you can do it any time once a day. Now in case you don't we are going to give you reinforcement - operant conditioning. What do you like to do that you do almost every day in the week? What do you really enjoy doing? You enjoy something you do almost every day. What is it?

Cl: Well, reading a book.

Th: Alright. No reading for the next 30 days until after you do that one or two minutes rational-emotive imagery because that is all it takes you. What do you hate to do that normally you avoid doing because you hate it?

Cl: Doing the laundry and things like that.

Th: Alright. For the next thirty days if bedtime arrives and you have not yet done your rational-emotive imagery you are to stay up another hour to do the laundry. But if you do the rational-emotive imagery you don't have to do the laundry. And if your laundry gets too clean, you can then do your neighbour's laundry!

Cl: I am working at a youth camp, so that won't be difficult to arrange.

Th: That is right! At a youth camp there

is plenty of laundry to do! Now, is there anything else about this problem that we may have omitted?

Cl: Well, sometimes I do just the reverse of what you now tell me. When I feel depressed, I do things I like instead of trying to do things ...

Th: ... that you don't like?

Cl: Yeah. I do the things that I have to do or that I want to do.

Th: Yeah, that would be all right temporarily, just temporarily for a while. But you could make sure that you later do the things that you don't like to do, in case you avoid performing the rational-emotive imagery. But it would even be better when you are depressed, to do the goddamned things you don't like. They would preoccupy you, help you get distracted from your depression. Also you can then do work at eliminating the depression. Now another thing when you don't do the work, don't write your essays, how do you feel about yourself for procrastinating, for not doing it?

Cl: Well very bad. Shit, shit.

Th: Alright. So some of your depression stems from your self-downing. And you could ask yourself not 'Why am I not doing the work?', but 'Why am I a shit for not doing this work?'. And your answer would be what?

Cl: There is no reason.

Th: Yes, there is no reason. 'I am a fallible fucked up human being who is not doing the work right now. So I'd better move my ass and do it!'

Let us now get the audience's comments and discussion about this problem.

AUDIENCE PARTICIPATION

We have noticed that the types of issues/questions raised by the audience can be placed into a number of categories.

Practical Advice

A number of participants offer practical suggestions

or advice concerning what the volunteer can do about his or her problem. Thus, good suggestions concerning how to overcome procrastination and how to approach members of the opposite sex, for example, are often put forward. Ellis endorses those practical suggestions that he considers of merit and points out problems in other pieces of advice. However, he generally urges the volunteers (and thus indirectly teaches the audience) to change irrational Beliefs before attempting to solve the practical aspects of their problems. In doing so, Ellis highlights an important point in rational-emotive theory that when people are disturbed by holding irrational Beliefs about an event, this impedes them from thinking clearly and thus from implementing effective solutions to change the event or to adjust to it.

Challenging Inferences

One feature of RET that distinguishes it from other forms of cognitive-behaviour therapy is that RET therapists in general first encourage their clients to assume that their inferences about a situation are true (in order to identify latent irrational Beliefs) before challenging these inferences at a later stage. Members of the audience often ask volunteers questions which are directed to the truth or falsity of the latter's negative inferences. Ellis generally endorses such interventions but stresses why it is important to first challenge irrational beliefs before challenging negative inferences.

Assessing The Impact Of Self On Others

A number of questions and points are addressed to volunteers concerning the possible impact that their behaviour has on others. These often prove to be valuable interventions since Ellis does not frequently address himself to such material in the course of the 30 minute public demonstration interviews. Thus, volunteers who present with problems of maintaining or developing inter-personal relationships are asked to reflect on the possibility that some aspects of their behaviour impedes the quality of their relationships. Some members of the audience are quite astute at picking up cues from the demeanour of volunteers that are worthy of consideration.

Anti-RET Viewpoints

Some members of the audience ask questions which are

based on therapeutic philosophies that are antithetical to RET. Here Ellis is quick to show the questioner, the volunteer and the rest of the audience the problems which are inherent in such viewpoints. In doing so, Ellis is quite vigorous in his criticisms of opposing viewpoints, for example, labelling them as 'psychoanalytic horseshit', etc. He does this to stress to the audience the dangers he sees in such positions. While some claim that Ellis is dogmatic in his expressed views on these subjects, Ellis defends himself by distinguishing between dogma (which he denies) and strongly held viewpoints (which are non-dogmatically expressed in a powerful manner). After voicing his criticisms, Ellis proceeds to offer the RET position on these issues.

Catching Ellis Out

A few members of the audience are extremely knowledgeable in RET theory and practice and delight in pointing out to Ellis that he has omitted some aspect of RET theory and practice in his presentation. Ellis takes these points in very good spirit and uses them to teach the audience the neglected aspect of the rational-emotive approach.

While no systematic research has been done on the effect of the Friday night workshops on audience learning, Ellis claims that members of the audience are often helped by observing such interviews to solve their own problems by using the same methods that they have watched Ellis employ. This would certainly be a fruitful area for future research.

FURTHER ISSUES

It can be seen from the presented interview that Ellis's approach reflects his New York origins. Several writers have made the point that one does not have to sound like Albert Ellis in order to practise RET effectively (e.g. Meichenbaum, 1977). Indeed, one reason we believe that RET has not attracted a large following among British counsellors and psychotherapists is that these practitioners equate the practice of RET with Ellis's forthright and earthy style. So if a British version of the Friday night workshop were ever to be held, a less forthright and earthy approach may have to be adopted to obviate such negative effects. On the other hand, it may be that the British public are less sensitive about such matters than British counsellors and psychotherapists!

Such workshops obviously raise issues concerning confidentiality. Our preference would be to announce at the beginning of such workshops that client material should be respected as confidential and should not be discussed with other people outside the workshop other than in general terms. Certainly no names should be linked to discussions of client material. That Ellis does not make such an announcement is something we would criticize.

It is interesting to observe that disclosing their problems before an audience of strangers does not seem to inhibit the volunteers who choose to discuss their problems in New York. Obviously some material might not be disclosed and it is important to stress at this point that such demonstrations are not designed to replace individual therapy. Indeed, a number of volunteers at Ellis's Friday night workshops later seek help from Ellis himself or from one of the other therapists at the Institute. Whether British people would feel as free to volunteer to discuss their problems in public in such interviews, and whether they will show the same lack of inhibition in their disclosures remains to be seen.

Chapter Nine

USING RET IN THE SUPERVISION OF COUNSELLORS

WINDY DRYDEN

INTRODUCTION

Dryden (1981) discussed some of the advantages of employing audio-tape procedures in counselling and supervision. It was pointed out in that article that listening to trainee counsellors' accounts of their counselling sessions and hearing audio-tapes of these sessions often reveals important discrepancies. For example, in a group supervision session, one trainee told the group about the interventions she employed with a client experiencing extreme examination anxiety. She stated that she covered a number of important concepts with the client. She discussed with him: a) the important healing qualities of unconditional self-acceptance; b) the mediating effects that cognitions have on emotional experience; c) the value of focusing on task - relevant cognitions and editing out task - irrelevant thoughts in evaluative situations; d) the benefit of concentrating on one piece of revision at a time rather than on the entire revision schedule; and e) the importance of taking regular short breaks from study. She indicated that the client understood these concepts and received great benefit from the discussion. However, while listening to the tape of the session, it emerged that the trainee covered all of these points in one long ninety-second statement. While the client claimed to understand these concepts, it was obvious to all that he was confused. The value of recording counselling sessions is therefore apparent.

However, trainees often experience anxiety about using cassette recorders in counselling and supervision and this theme will be developed in the present chapter.

MANIFESTATIONS OF TRAINEE RECORDING AND SUPERVISION ANXIETY

Supervision of trainees' audio-taped counselling sessions was a central component of the one-year postgraduate diploma in counselling in educational settings' course offered at Aston University (1970-1984). Prospective trainees were informed of this and they knew that places on the course were contingent upon their agreement to make tapes of actual counselling sessions. In the first term of the course trainees taped their peer-counselling sessions and thus became quite familiar with being recorded while counselling. They should have thus achieved a fair measure of habituation to making audio-tapes of counselling sessions before seeing clients on placement. However, a significant number of trainees initially experienced debilitating anxiety which interfered both with their counselling work and with their ability to learn from supervision. This anxiety generally took several different forms.

Showing Overconcern For Clients

A number of trainees expressed exaggerated concern for the impact that recording counselling sessions had on clients. They feared that clients would be psychologically damaged if they even raised the topic of tape-recording. In my many years experience of asking clients for permission to record sessions, the vast majority readily agree and, as far as I am aware, none were damaged by my request. My practice is to be thoroughly honest in my request. I point out that it is helpful for me to listen back to sessions and to receive supervision on them. I guarantee that only my supervisor and supervision group will listen to them and that the tapes will be wiped clean afterwards. I tell clients that while taping sessions is helpful to me, my primary concern is for their well-being. If they prefer not to have sessions recorded, their wish will be respected and I emphasize the primacy of their decision. When I discussed this with trainees, they were often then able to express their own anxiety underlying their stated concern for clients - anxiety concerning the impact that recording counselling sessions would have on *them*.

'I Don't Have A Tape This Week'

In my experience of supervising tapes, I have been impressed with the range of 'reasons' which trainees give either for not making tapes or for not having audible tapes of counselling sessions for supervision. This occurs despite the fact that they receive clear instructions concerning the attainment of clearly audible tape-recordings. The 'reasons' I have received can be grouped as follows:

(a) Plug faults:- the plug did not contain a fuse;
- the plug contained a defective or incorrect fuse;
- the plug wires were not properly attached.

(b) Mains faults:- the mains lead was not attached to the recorder;
- the mains lead was not inserted into the wall socket;
- the socket switch was not turned on.

(c) Microphone faults:- the external microphone was not attached (or not properly attached) to the recorder;
- batteries were not inserted into the battery-operated microphone;
- the microphone was placed incorrectly so that clear recording could not be obtained;
- the external microphone was not powerful enough to clearly register voices.

(d) Battery faults:- batteries were not inserted into the battery-operated recorder;
- 'dead' or fading batteries were used (batteries not regularly checked);
- batteries were incorrectly inserted into the recorder;
- too few batteries were inserted into the recorder;
- batteries were left in the recorder causing corrosion;
- the battery pack had not been recharged;
- the battery pack had been incorrectly inserted into the recorder.

(e) Recording faults:- incorrect controls were depressed while 'recording';
- no controls were depressed while 'recording';
- a radio programme was recorded instead of the counselling session (when a radio-cassette recorder was used);
- an indistinct recording was made (either because an internal microphone was

employed which was not sensitive enough to record clearly or because recording and erasing heads were not regularly cleaned).

(f) Recorder faults:- the recorder was faulty in 'recording' mode;
- interference was present on the recording;
- the recorder picked up local police or taxi broadcasts in 'recording' mode which masked the recording of the counselling session.

(g) Tape faults:- no tape was inserted into the recorder;
- the tape was incorrectly inserted into the recorder;
- the tape was inappropriate for recording purposes.

Trainees who were not particularly anxious about recording counselling sessions generally made clearly audible cassette recordings which they regularly brought to supervision. Thus, it is probable that anxious trainees tacitly (i.e. outside their awareness) developed self-defeating ways of defending against their own anxiety. Helping these trainees to acknowledge their anxiety proved difficult but was best done by encouraging them to explore how they would feel if they had made audible tapes which they would then present for supervision.

Trainee Behaviour In Counselling Sessions

The behaviour that anxious trainees manifested in counselling sessions often provided clues to their recording and supervision anxiety. Such trainees were often 'forgetful'; they 'forgot' to take their recorder (microphone, cassettes or mains lead) to the sessions or they 'forgot' to introduce the topic of recording at the beginning of counselling interviews. When they did remember, they claimed that their clients were 'far too upset' to make clear decisions concerning recording. When they did introduce the topic to clients, they did so hesitantly or ineptly so that their clients refused.

When they did record their sessions they tended to: a) play safe, by being extremely passive in interviews or by parroting client statements verbatim; b) talk too much and ask irrelevant questions when silences occurred; c) display many paraverbal clues to anxiety and d) often misunderstand what their clients were trying to express.

Trainee Behaviour In Supervision

Trainees who were particularly anxious about recording their counselling sessions often displayed typical behaviour patterns in supervison. They often: (a) 'forgot' to bring in tapes for supervision; (b) brought in the 'wrong' tape; (c) tried to engage the supervisor and/or the supervision group in theoretical discussions about the counselling process; (d) opted to present their tapes last hoping for a truncated period of supervision; (e) spent considerable periods of supervision time trying to find the precise segment of tape which they wished to play; (f) tended to deny or distort positive feedback; (g) played segments of counselling sessions which contained plenty of client talk but little counsellor intervention and (h) played numerous 'games' that have been admirably documented by Kadushin (1968) which were designed to distract supervisors' attention from their actual counselling work.

UNDERSTANDING TRAINEE RECORDING AND SUPERVISION ANXIETY

It was important in attempting to understand trainees' anxiety about recording counselling sessions to focus on the inferences that they made and the Beliefs they held about the recording and supervision process.

Inferential Distortions

Inferences are cognitive processes that are either interpretative and/or evaluative in nature, but do not themselves account for people's emotional experiences. They indicate how people interpret the data that is available to them in their perceptual field. Inferences can of course be accurate or distorted. They are best regarded as hypotheses about the nature of reality and can thus be subjected to empirical enquiry. Unfortunately, anxious trainees often regarded their inferences as facts and thus not amenable to such enquiry. Since anxiety is an emotion which generally involves anticipations of future threat, it is not surprising to find that anxious trainees frequently made a number of distorted inferences concerning the future implications of their present behaviour. Identifying such inferential distortions was done by either examining trainees' in-vivo automatic thoughts (Beck et al., 1979) or by helping them to articulate the private meanings that the recording and supervision process held for them. Burns (1980) has developed the pioneering work of Aaron Beck (c.f. Beck et al., 1979) on the common forms of inferential distortions that depressed and anxious clients typically make. Burns's 'ten forms of twisted thinking' will be used as a framework for presenting the most common inferential errors that anxious trainees made concerning the personal implications of the recording and supervison process.

(a) All-or-nothing thinking. Here trainees typically employed black-or-white categories to process information. All-or-nothing thinking commonly leads to perfectionism and feelings of failure. Thus, one trainee reported observing herself making an inaccurate summary of her client's concerns and concluded: "I've ruined this interview completely".

(b) Overgeneralization. Anxious trainees often saw a single event as a perpetual pattern of defeat. Words like 'always' and 'never' are clues that overgeneralizations were being made. Such trainees often become easily discouraged and hopeless about their ability to learn and internalize constructive counselling skills. One trainee reported thinking that if he did not master the technique of systematic desensitization quickly, then he would never learn it.

(c) Mental filter. Commonly, anxious trainees focused on a single negative detail and dwelt on it obsessively so that their ability to make objective perceptions of reality became impaired. One trainee became so anxious about gaining her clients' approval that she habitually gave them extra time instead of terminating sessions punctually. She reported having the thought that if one of her clients showed disapproval then she would continually focus on this, thus editing out the total picture which indicated that many of her clients were benefiting quite well from their counselling sessions with her.

(d) Disqualifying the positive. Anxious trainees tended to reject positive experiences when they occurred by saying that they didn't count. Such processes frequently occurred in supervision groups. For example, one trainee consistently denied that he was doing well with a socially anxious client (he was in fact helping her quite considerably), insisting that it was such an easy case (which it wasn't) that anybody would have been successful.

(e) Jumping to conclusions. Anxious trainees often acted as if they had extra-sensory perception. They consistently interpreted events in a negative manner in the absence of corroborating evidence. There are two major types of 'conclusion-jumping': (i) Mind-reading. Here anxious trainees predicted that their clients would have negative thoughts about them, the counselling process and the issue of tape-recording. They regarded such inferences as 'facts' as opposed to 'hypotheses' and thus rarely attempted to test their validity. For example, one trainee came to supervision in a distressed state because she was certain that one of her clients had not kept an appointment because he regarded her as a 'useless novice'. It transpired that the client had been involved in a minor traffic accident, had tried to contact the counselling service by telephone to cancel his appointment but could not get through. In counselling, practitioners are not commonly in a position to ascertain reasons for client non-attendance and drop-out. Consequently such ambiguity contributes to the perpetuation of self-defeating mind-reading. (ii) Negative prediction. Anxious trainees often anticipated that counselling sessions would turn out badly and thus they frequently predicted disasters. One trainee predicted that he would fail to understand his new overseas client, got into an anxious state which severely interfered with his ability to listen and empathize with the client. As can be seen, negative predictions often become self-fulfilling prophecies.

(f) Magnification and/or minimization. In magnification, anxious trainees exaggerated the importance of their difficulties in learning and internalizing counselling skills. They 'forgot' that most people would be uncomfortable learning new techniques and methods and regarded their discomfort in a very negative light. In minimization, trainees undervalued their own skills and talents while praising their fellow trainees for these very same skills and talents.

(g) Emotional reasoning occurs when people assume that their feelings constitute evidence as to the nature of reality. Thus, anxious trainees concluded that their anxiety was valid proof for their inadequacy as counsellors. One trainee argued that taping counselling sessions was dangerous because he felt anxious about it.

(h) Labelling is an extreme form of overgeneralization. Instead of acknowledging that they merely made errors or poorly executed counselling interventions, anxious trainees were much more likely to conclude that they were 'inadequate counsellors' than did less anxious trainees. The latter were more likely to acknowledge their errors in skill and technique without placing a perjorative label on their ability as counsellors.

(i) Personalization. Here anxious trainees were prone to assume almost total responsibility for the counselling process when it was going badly and virtually no responsibility when it was going well. They tended to be constantly looking for evidence that their clients were dissatisfied with their services. This vigilance perpetuated their anxiety which consequently impeded their learning. Trainees who were to be seen frequently checking for the arrival of unpunctual clients often made such personalizing inferences.

Personal Worth And Fate Control

The analysis presented above provides a helpful way of classifying the inferential distortions made by trainees anxious about recording and presenting their counselling interviews for supervision. Most frequently, trainees' inferential distortions reflect concerns about either personal worth or fate control. It is important to note that the same inferential distortions may therefore reflect these very different underlying concerns. For example, consider Jack and Sylvia, two counselling trainees who were both anxious in case what they considered to be poor examples of counselling technique would incur the disapproval of their respective supervisors. Both prdicted that such disapproval was virtually certain to occur. However, while Jack was anxious because he was basing his personal worth on his supervisor's anticipated response, Sylvia was anxious that her supervisor's disapproval would influence him to give her poor job references which would, in her mind, ruin her career in counselling before it had commenced. Sylvia thus viewed her supervisor as having enormous control over her fate, while Jack viewed his supervisor as having enormous control over his personal worth.

Trainees who experienced 'personal worth' anxiety tended to predict that their errors (which they inevitably made in learning how to counsel) would lead their supervisors and fellow trainees to make negative judgments of not only their counselling ability but also of their personal worth. They thus implicitly construed other people as harsh critics, intolerant of human fallibility. This (as will be shown later) was really a projection of their own intolerant attitude towards themselves. They were really harsh critics of themselves. On the other hand, trainees with 'fate control' anxiety predicted that their supervisors would note their errors and use this information against them in ways which would adversely affect their future aspirations (e.g. by giving them failing grades or writing them poor references etc.). They did not consider that their supervisors viewed such errors as an inevitable part of learning new skills. They thus construed their supervisors as malevolent individuals who would not make allowances for the fundamental processes of human learning. Again, as will be shown later, this view was generally a projection of their own attitude towards themselves and the world. They believed that they must not make errors and when they did, they would consequently be punished. They sometimes did fail to gain their counselling qualification, but this was to a large extent a self-fulfilling prophecy since their 'fate control' anxiety seriously impaired their ability to learn from the feedback that they were given.

Irrational Beliefs

It is a fundamental assumption of RET that inferential distortions stem from people's irrational Beliefs (Ellis, personal communication). Irrational Beliefs are evaluations of personal significance couched in devout, dogmatic and absolute terms. They reflect a philosophy of demandingness and are stated as 'musts', 'shoulds', 'oughts' and 'have-to's' and generally account for people's emotional experiences.

Dryden (1984a) has argued that there are two fundamental human disturbances - EGO DISTURBANCE and DISCOMFORT DISTURBANCE - which of course take a myriad of different forms. Trainees who experienced 'personal worth' anxiety, were clearly exemplifying ego disturbance. They profoundly believed the idea: 'that you can give yourself a global rating as a human and that your general worth and self-acceptance depends on the goodness of your performances and the degree that people approve of you' (Ellis, 1977f). They tended to make global ratings of their 'selves' which were conditional on (a) their counselling abilities, (b) the extent to which their clients improved and (c) the feedback they got from their supervisors and, to a lesser extent, their fellow trainees. overgeneralized from rating their present performance as trainee counsellors to rating their full potential ability as counsellors and thence made global ratings of their 'selves'. If they could articulate their underlying philosophy it would be thus: 'Because I am not doing very well at the moment in my counselling, I will never do well and therefore will always be an ineffective counsellor which will prove that I am worthless'. The statement: 'I am worthless' is derived from the premise: 'I must do well and be approved'. Believing this, they remained anxious even when they performed well since they further believed that they **must** maintain that good performance in the future. These irrational Beliefs underpin the inferential distortions that this group of anxious trainees made concerning the reactions of their clients, supervisors and fellow trainees. Since they were harsh critics of themselves, they once again predicted that others would make similarly harsh judgments of them.

Trainees who had discomfort disturbance wanted to enter the counselling profession, but escalated their desires into absolute demands. Their underlying philosophy was 'I must get what I want at all costs'. If they did not get what they believe they must, they concluded that **it was awful** and that they **could not stand** being deprived. Since they regarded getting what they wanted as absolutely necessary, they tended to be extremely sensitive to perceived threats to goal attainment. This underlying Belief then accounted for their inferential distortions, since even constructive negative feedback constituted a severe threat to what they believed they must have. Other people, and as has been noted particularly their supervisors, were thus seen as malevolent individuals who would deprive them of their sacred goals and consequently were viewed as having enormous control over their fate. These trainees did not necessarily attach their personal worth to the attainment of their goals although some may have also done this. Trainees with 'pure' discomfort disturbance believed that they must get what they wanted merely because they desired it, while other trainees with ego disturbance believed that they must get what they wanted in order to prove to themselves that they were worthwhile individuals.

As Dryden, Trower & Casey (1983) have shown, ego disturbance and discomfort disturbance are often interacting processes. Thus, one trainee who believed that she must do well in counselling interviews (ego disturbance) became anxious. This anxiety activated her Belief that she couldn't stand feeling anxious (discomfort disturbance), which in turn triggered her further Belief that such heightened anxiety proved her worthlessness (ego disturbance). Indeed many trainees trapped themselves in the interlocking web of their ego and discomfort-related Beliefs

In the previous section, trainee anxiety about the recording and supervision process was considered. The manifestations of this anxiety were detailed and a framework for understanding its determinants was outlined. The emphasis of this section will be on how supervisors can help trainees overcome the debilitating effects of recording and supervision anxiety so that they can maximize their learnings.

OVERCOMING OBSTACLES TO TRAINEE LEARNING: FOSTERING A HELPFUL CLIMATE IN SUPERVISION

It is important to realize that while not all trainees will be anxious about presenting audiotapes of their counselling sessions for supervision, virtually all will be apprehensive. As a supervisor I have found that applying the following principles is most beneficial in fostering a helpful climate in both individual and group supervision sessions. The promotion of a helpful climate is highly desirable if anxious trainees are to be encouraged to acknowledge and deal with their anxieties.

Unconditional Acceptance

It is beneficial if supervisors show that they can unconditionally accept their trainees as fallible human beings. This means that while supervisors may rate certain aspects, behaviours or skills that their trainees may display, they endeavour not to rate the 'personhood' of trainees (Ellis, 1984a). For example, I once had occasion to reproach one of my trainees thus for consistent unpunctuality at counselling sessions.

> Look, frankly I consider your behaviour in this regard to be pretty bad. We've discovered some of the reasons for it and though you claim to understand why you do it, you keep doing it. However, I want you to know that while I dislike your behaviour, I really don't feel badly at all about you as a total complex ever-changing person. While I think your behaviour stinks, you're not a stinker. And of course we've discovered that you have a lot of assets in your counselling. Now the reality is that counsellors who aren't punctual...

The trainee, in question, appreciated the honest expression of my annoyance concerning her behaviour and realised that I was not either in tone or words damning her as a person.

Supervisors would be wise to Dispute their own internal intolerant demands about the behaviour of their trainees and replace these with their honest undevout preferences. In this way they will be able to effectively communicate unconditional acceptance of trainees, while honestly expressing their positive and negative reactions to trainee behaviour, when appropriate.

Supervisor Self-Disclosure

Anxious trainees often view their supervisors as infallible and fantasize that such superhuman beings learned how to counsel effortlessly and without error. It is important for supervisors to refuse to be seduced into this fantasy and openly acknowledge their past and present counselling errors. This serves to help trainees learn that: (a) errors are an inevitable part of becoming skilled counsellors; (b) counsellors do not suddenly stop making errors after completion of training; (c) it is possible to acknowledge errors openly without defensiveness and self-blame and (d) supervisors who are tolerant of their own errors are likely to be tolerant of trainees' errors.

Explaining The Nature Of Human Learning

It is often helpful if supervisors discuss the nature of human learning with trainees at an early stage in the supervision process. It is important to stress that making errors is a natural and inevitable stage of learning any new set of complex skills - including counselling. In fact, I have found it useful to introduce a note of levity into this discussion. I usually add that any trainee who does not make errors will be ceremoniously thrown out of the supervision group. I also challenge and overthrow the myth that trainee counsellors will seriously damage clients by their errors - adding of course that this group will be the exception and I shall thus order several ambulances to stand by to ferry quivering clients to the nearest sanctuary called 'The Dryden Home for Clients Damaged by Trainees'. I, of course, stress that there is usually a long waiting list!

Employing The Judicious Use of Humour

As can be seen from the above, I sometimes judiciously use humour in running supervision groups in a similar manner as I do in counselling. I do so because I basically agree with Ellis (1977b) who argues that one way of viewing emotional disturbance is that it stems from people taking themselves, others and the world <u>too</u> seriously. Anxious trainees definitely take themselves, the counselling role and the counselling process <u>too</u> seriously. I have found it highly therapeutic to challenge this viewpoint directly and indirectly with humour. I am often the butt of my own jokes (it is helpful to introduce humour into supervision in this way) and show in this manner that I do not take myself <u>too</u> seriously both in and out of counselling sessions. I show that I can laugh at some of the stupid things I have done while taking a compassionate and accepting attitude towards myself. The therapeutic use of humour with trainees had better be done within a spirit of unconditional acceptance. My intention is to direct my humour comments to what trainees <u>do</u> and never at who they <u>are</u>. It is important for supervisors to elicit feedback from trainees concerning the impact of humorous interventions. Not all trainees appreciate it and find it helpful!

Giving Balanced Feedback

I have found that trainees benefit most from receiving <u>both</u> positive <u>and</u> constructive negative feedback from their supervisors concerning their counselling work. Supervisors who consistently focus on trainees' errors unwittingly reinforce the self-defeating attitudes of trainees with 'personal worth' and 'fate control' anxieties. Receiving consistent negative feedback encourages trainees with 'personal worth' anxiety to blame themselves for their errors and those with 'fate control' anxiety to think that their future aspirations are being seriously threatened, since the supervisor concerned will surely give them failing grades. On the other hand, receiving consistent positive feedback does not encourage either group of trainees to believe that they are learning very much about counselling. While such feedback may not directly evoke their respective anxieties, it does lead to a different kind of anxiety. Such trainees are reasonably sure that they are making counselling errors but are never told what they are. They either become anxious about this uncertainty or anxious about their own inability to determine their errors for themselves.

I thus strive to provide a balance between positive and constructive negative feedback given in a spirit of unconditional acceptance of trainees as persons. I even reinforce this with humour by saying to trainees with 'personal worth' anxiety: (a) 'that was a good response, but it doesn't make you a great person' and (b) 'that wasn't a very good response, but it doesn't make you a rotten person'. To trainees with 'fate control' anxiety I may say: (a) 'that wasn't a particularly good response, but we won't throw you out just yet', and (b) 'that was a good response, we'll definitely throw you out if you keep that standard up'.

Parenthetically, when giving trainees either positive or constructive negative feedback, it is best to make such feedback as <u>concrete</u> as possible. Vague feedback does not encourage trainees to identify what they are doing right or wrong and in the latter case they are not helped to consider specific alternatives.

Explaining 'Personal Worth' and 'Fate Control' Anxieties

It is beneficial to explain to trainees at an early stage the nature of 'personal worth' and 'fate control' anxieties and to point out that these are both common, albeit dysfunctional experiences. Providing such explanations makes it easier for trainees to honestly admit to these fears and thus undercuts trainee defensiveness. This is particularly so when trainees can see that others in the group share similar anxieties. It is this factor of 'universality' that helps the supervision group become a therapeutic milieu for its members (Yalom, 1975). When trainees see that they are not alone in experiencing anxiety about the recording and supervision process, they tend to feel less shameful of these fears and thus become less defensive about their experiences.

OVERCOMING OBSTACLES TO TRAINEE LEARNING: DEALING WITH TRAINEE ANXIETY IN SUPERVISION

While it is important to delineate boundaries between supervision and personal therapy, I find that the two processes sometimes necessarily overlap. When the factors described in the previous section do not help to allay fully trainees' fears, it is beneficial if supervisors help trainees to identify and deal with their anxieties if the latter are to maximize their learning from the supervisory experience. However, these therapeutic encounters are generally restricted to an exploration of trainees' anxieties about recording and supervision, and supervisors had better not deal with trainees' other personal problems in the supervision group since this tends to lead to difficult role-conflict problems. When I attempt to deal with trainees' recording- and supervision-related anxieties in supervision groups, I find it best to first seek permission to do this. I explain to the trainee in question that we could deal with the issue here in the group setting or if the trainee prefers, the issue could be dealt with outside in personal therapy with someone else. If permission is not sought and granted, trainees may become understandably defensive during the ensuing discussion. Once permission is granted, my role is then to help trainees identify, challenge and change the inferential distortions and the irrational Beliefs that underline their anxieties and negative inferences.

The following segments, then, represent two examples of how to deal with trainees' anxieties about recording and supervision in the context of supervision groups.

Dealing with 'Personal Worth' Anxiety

Stephanie, the trainee in question, had on several occasions failed to bring audio-tapes of her counselling sessions to the group for supervision.

Supervisor: O.K. Stephanie I would like to say something here. My guess is that you may have some anxiety about making tapes or presenting them for supervision here and this issue needs addressing in some context. What do you think?

Trainee: Well.... I guess you are right... I know I don't like making tapes. It does seem to be valuable ... for other people. I guess I'm anxious about it. It certainly is on my mind a lot.

Supervisor: O.K., look. We can either discuss it here and now or if you wish you can discuss it with someone else... I mean ... with someone else not concerned with your evaluation. (The supervisor gives the trainee a <u>choice</u> to deal with the issue in the group or elsewhere. He seeks <u>permission</u> to discuss it further).

Trainee: Well... since we're here, why don't we do it now.

Supervisor: All right. Now would you agree with my hunch that you're anxious?

Trainee: Yes, that's right.

Supervisor: What are you anxious about specifically?

Trainee: Well ... if I knew, no-one would listen to my tapes, I wouldn't mind recording my interviews. It's just ... the thought of ... well ... you all hearing my counselling.

Supervisor: So you're anxious about the group listening to you on tape. What's scary about that?

Trainee: Oh God! ... well ... it's the ... thought I guess about what you all ... no perhaps more about what you specifically are going to think of me.

Supervisor: Right. You're scared that I'm going to think you're a great girl and a scholar. Is that correct? (General laughter. The supervisor uses humour to loosen the trainee up a little).

Trainee: (laughs) Well hardly. I guess I'm scared ... that ... you would think badly of me if I presented a lousy tape.

Supervisor: But let's assume that. Let's suppose you played a lousy tape, what sort of things do you think I would think of you? (The supervisor checks out the nature of the trainee's inferences).

Trainee: Well ... (pause) ... the thing that comes to mind is that ... well the word idiot comes to mind.

Supervisor: So you're scared that you'd present a tape and I'd think what an idiot you were for doing a lousy job? Is that it?

Trainee: Yes.

Supervisor: Now let's assume that I actually do think you're an idiot. Do you also get the sense that I would act on that thought in some way? (The supervisor seeks to go deeper into the trainee's inference structure. He wishes to assess what type of anxiety - 'personal worth' or 'fate control' - he is dealing with).

Trainee: I'm not sure ... what do you mean?

Supervisor: Well, for example, do you think that I might shout at you and say something like: 'Stephanie you're an idiot', or do you think I'd fail you, or ...?

Trainee: Oh, I see ... No, I don't think you would shout at me. I don't think you'd fail me either. It's just ... I guess that your opinion is pretty important to me. (The trainee provides clues that it is 'personal worth' rather than 'fate control' anxiety that she is experiencing).

Supervisor: Pretty important in what sense?

Trainee: Mmm... That I need you to think well of me.

Supervisor: And if I don't?

Trainee: Then I'd feel pretty lousy.

Supervisor: Could you zero in on that feeling a little more and let me know what kind of lousy feeling it would be?

Trainee: I'd feel depressed.

Supervisor: What would you dwell on in that depressed lousy feeling?

Trainee: On ... what a failure I am.

Supervisor: So if I understand you. You would play a lousy tape. I would think you were an idiot, you would define yourself as a failure and feel lousy. Is that how it would go?

Trainee: Yes, that's it.

Supervisor: O.K. Now as I see it, whether I think you are an idiot is important but not the real issue. You probably need to check it out, however, at some point. Can you see though the link between that definition 'I am a failure' and that lousy depressed feeling? (The supervisor focuses the trainee on her irrational Belief, while indicating also the importance of testing inferences).

Trainee: Yes I see it. It's what you said in your lecture on RET, isn't it?

Supervisor: Right. Now what I also said in that lecture is the importance of checking out whether that Belief holds water. As Ellis might say, we want evidence that you would be a failure if you fail to impress me or fail to give a good performance.

Trainee: Well there isn't any. I guess I'd be what you called a fallible human being who is failing to do well at the moment.

Supervisor: That's correct, but look at how hesitantly you said that. You acknowledge it but don't really believe it.

Trainee: Exactly.

Supervisor: How do you think you could really work on believing it?

Trainee: By going over it as you said in the lecture.

Supervisor: Right. Really show yourself that (a) you don't need my approval and (b) if you were a failure you would do what?

Trainee: Fail continually.

Supervisor: At everything? Now if you really worked on that, would you feel anxious about my defining you in my own head as an idiot?

Trainee: No, but I still wouldn't like it.

Supervisor: Quite.

Trainee: But I wouldn't be anxious.

Supervisor: O.K. Now if you really believed that, would you then be so sure of what I would be thinking of you?

Trainee: Let me see ... No ... I would still have doubts though.

Supervisor: Right. How could you check out your hunch about what I was thinking?

Trainee: By asking you?

Supervisor: No, by consulting the tea leaves. (General laughter).

Trainee: (laughs) O.K.! O.K.! I get your point.

Supervisor: Why don't you do that work and let us know how you get on next week. O.K.?

Trainee: O.K.

Stephanie really worked on her 'personal worth' anxiety, started to accept herself unconditionally and began to bring in tapes regularly for supervision and did very well in her final assessment.

Dealing With 'Fate Control' Anxiety

Ralph, another trainee, did bring in his audio-tapes for supervision, but wasted an inordinate amount of time by discussing theoretical points, by trying to find the exact segment of tape he wished the group to hear and by extending other trainees' supervision time, so that his counselling work wasn't heard.

Supervisor: Well, Ralph. You seem to be doing it again. We're interested in hearing your counselling, not your excellent grasp of theory. Listen. Let me honestly ask you. Why are you so reluctant to play your tapes in here? You say you're not, but your behaviour belies your words.

Trainee: I'm not reluctant.

Supervisor: Let me put it another way. Close your eyes a moment. Really picture this scene. We are going to devote the whole three-hour session to listening to your tapes and we won't allow you to interrupt or anything ... Now really picture that scene. How do you honestly feel? (The supervisor uses the imagery modality to bypass the trainee's tendency to deny feelings (Lazarus, 1984)).

Trainee: Quite uncomfortable.

Supervisor: O.K, Now I'd like to explore that feeling more so that I can help you participate more in the group and play your tapes, but I don't want to force you. Would you like to explore this discomfort here and now? (The supervisor asks for permission to explore the issue further).

Trainee: O.K. (The trainee is hesitant, but the supervisor decides to go along with his stated agreement).

Supervisor: Now what would you be uncomfortable about?

Trainee: About you lot listening to my tapes.

Supervisor: If you really focus on that discomfort, what kind of feeling would it be?
Trainee: ... A mixture of anger and anxiety.
Supervisor: Anxiety about what?
Trainee: Being evaluated.
Supervisor: By whom?
Trainee: Mmmh... mainly you. Yes by you.
Supervisor: And the anger?
Trainee: Towards you for making me do it.
Supervisor: O.K. Let's go back to your anxiety. What kind of evaluation would you be afraid of getting?
Trainee: A bad one.
Supervisor: O.K. Now let's assume, and I want to stress that we're assuming now, let's assume that I do listen to your tapes and give you a bad evaluation. What would be scary about that?
Trainee: I'd be scared that I wouldn't get my counselling diploma.
Supervisor: Let's assume that for the moment. If you don't get your diploma what would that mean? (The supervisor is aiming to 'chain' the trainee's inferences to get at his core irrational Belief).
Trainee: That would be awful.
Supervisor: Why is that?
Trainee: Counselling is really what I want to do. I've set my heart on it.
Supervisor: But let's say you were barred forever from your first choice, what then?
Trainee: ... well ... I don't know ... I'd hate it. It's a feeling that ... I just have to get ... my first choice. (The trainee reveals in halting fashion his discomfort disturbance).
Supervisor: O.K. So you start by saying that counselling is really important to you and then you jump, if I understand you correctly, to you <u>have to</u> do it. Am I hearing you accurately?
Trainee: Yes.
Supervisor: So your Belief is: 'Because it's important to me, I have to get it' or to put it another way, 'I have to get what I want'.
Trainee: That's right.
Supervisor: And then I guess, in your mind, I'm the obstacle.
Trainee: Right. It's funny, that's why I get angry with you. I often see you as

	kind of in control of ... my future almost. (The trainee clearly reveals his 'fate control' anxiety).
Supervisor:	Is there any feeling at all, that if you don't get to be a counsellor that you'd be less worthy or anything like that. (The supervisor is testing to see whether 'personal worth' anxiety is involved in the trainee's concerns).
Trainee:	No. It's much more the feeling of being deprived of what I want. I'd really hate that.

The supervisor then helped Ralph over subsequent weeks to acknowledge his desire to enter the counselling profession, but to Dispute the Belief that he <u>had to</u> get what he wanted. Ralph was further helped to imagine his future without counselling and eventually began to see that he could be happy in his second or third career choice although not as happy as he would be working as a counsellor. This helped him to view his supervisor as less of a threat, although some direct interventions were still necessary to help him correct some of his inferential 'fate control' distortions. He passed the course with average grades.

While I have chosen to present examples where trainees revealed 'personal worth' and 'fate control' anxieties in their pure form, in reality much trainee anxiety is a subtle blend of the two. Furthermore, while I have detailed two interviews where the entire dialogue occurred between the trainee in question and myself as supervisor, commonly other group members participate in this process as well. In conclusion, the overall aim of supervisors, on their own or with other group members is to help anxious trainees: (a) acknowledge their anxiety; (b) identify and challenge the inferential distortions and irrational Beliefs which underlie their anxiety and (c) replace these with more accurate inferences and rational Beliefs. When this is done successfully, trainees normally become less anxious, regularly present their audiotapes for supervision in a non-defensive manner and generally benefit greatly from supervisory feedback.

Chapter Ten

WHERE IS THE EVIDENCE? PROMOTING QUALITY RET RESEARCH

WINDY DRYDEN

INTRODUCTION

Since its inception, RET has become an influential force as a therapeutic system. It is practised throughout the world and its founder, Albert Ellis is recognized as one of the world's leading contributors to the field of psychotherapy. There is no doubt that much has been achieved since RET was first developed in 1955. However, has RET been adequately investigated? I will argue that it has not and will offer some reflections on the need for better research on RET.

THE HERITAGE OF RET'S DEVELOPMENT

As I have pointed out elsewhere (Dryden, 1984c), the development of RET has been marked by its application to a wide variety of clinical syndromes and problems of living. While RET *has* attracted research attention (DiGiuseppe, Miller & Trexler 1979; McGovern & Silverman, 1984) this research literature has not kept pace with the breadth of RET's practical applications. In my opinion this is due in large part to Ellis's decision to pursue a career as a full-time practitioner, part-time lecturer and trainer and prolific writer. He has neither carried out much research on RET himself, nor has he directed any significant research programmes on RET. He has sought to show how RET can be widely applied and in particular to demonstrate how it can serve as a system of self-help therapy. He has thus written many books and articles for the general public as well as for professionals.

Perhaps taking their lead from Ellis, leading RET theorists and therapists have largely contributed to the psychotherapeutic literature by writing papers, chapters and texts which have a 'discussion' as opposed to an 'evaluation' focus (Kendall, 1984a, 1984b). Thus, it seems that the heritage of the way RET has developed is one which, in part, emphasizes descriptive, practical developments and de-emphasizes well-designed empirical research. It is not that RET has not received research attention, but most of this research has not been of a particularly high quality (DiGiuseppe, Miller & Trexler, 1979; Hollon & Beck, 1986; McGovern & Silverman, 1984; Smith & Allred, 1986; Zettle & Hayes, 1980).

This position contrasts sharply with the development of Beck's Cognitive Therapy, for example, which is marked by careful well designed studies both on the psychological processes within clinical syndromes (e.g. depression and anxiety) and on the effectiveness of therapeutic procedures applied to these syndromes. It is perhaps no surprise that Beck has been at the fore of these developments. In comparison, informed observers of developments in the cognitive therapies have all commented on the dearth of sound research on the theoretical postulates of RET and its effectiveness as a therapeutic system (Hollon & Beck, 1986; Kendall, 1982, 1984a, 1984b; Smith, 1982; Smith & Allred, 1986; Zettle & Hayes, 1980).

In my opiniion, if this situation continues, RET will lose credibility as a therapeutic system which purports to hold dear the logico-empirical methods of science. While RET therapists routinely ask their clients: 'Where is the evidence...?', it is apparent that either they have not asked themselves such questions concerning rational-emotive inspired hypotheses or they have not sought to investigate them. As Kendall (1984b) has suggested, it may be that RET practitioners evaluate less but debate more.

DEVELOPING A RESEARCH COMMUNITY

It is apparent that, at present, there exist few centres of excellence which regularly produce well designed research on the theoretical basis of RET and its effectiveness with clinical populations (an exception here is the work carried out by Howie Kassinove at Hofstra University). This again is in marked contrast to Beck's Cognitive Therapy which has been investigated at a number of centres of excellence (including the Universities of Edinburgh, Oxford, Pennsylvania, etc.). It is my opinion that the development of an international RET research community is of the utmost importance if RET is to be seriously considered as an empirically-minded therapeutic system in the future.

There are three ways in which this can be done: (a) attracting quality researchers to the parent Institute for RET in New York; (b) encouraging more research submissions to the Journal of Rational-Emotive Therapy; and (c) holding national and international conferences.

Research At The Institute for RET (New York)

The Institute for RET has for many years offered one- and two- year clinically-orientated post-doctoral fellowships. While there is a research component to such fellowships, little research of note has emerged from the 'Fellows' over the years. It may be that the Institute might be wise to offer research fellowships as well as clinically-orientated fellowships which would hopefully stimulate more research at the parent Institute.

Another development here could be the appointment of a full-time Director of Research at the Institute whose sole job would be to direct research programmes on RET. The Institute has never had a full-time Director of Research. The present incumbent, Raymond DiGiuseppe, holds this position in a part-time capacity but also serves as part-time Director of Training as well as maintaining a large private practice. It is unreasonable to expect DiGiuseppe to direct major research programmes given his other duties. However, it is interesting to note that he has recently pioneered a large outcome study which is at present being carried out at the Institute, the first that has been organized there. I await with interest the results of this study. If it is carried through to fruition it may stimulate further studies at the Institute, which hopefully will attract research funding.

The 'Journal of Rational-Emotive Therapy'

Since 1966, RET has had its own journal. From 1966 until 1983 it was called 'Rational Living', changing its name to the 'Journal of Rational-Emotive Therapy' in 1983. From 1966 to 1984 the journal was published by the Institute for RET in New York; in 1985 it was taken over by Human Sciences Press but remains sponsored by the Institute. Table 2 shows a breakdown of the total number of articles published by the journal and the number of research articles that have appeared. It can be seen that 15.47% of the total number of articles that were published in

TABLE 2: Total Number of Articles Published by 'Rational Living' and the 'Journal of Rational-Emotive Therapy' and the Number of Research Articles that have Appeared.

RATIONAL LIVING

Year	Volume Number (2 issues per year)	Total Number of Articles Published	Research Articles
1966	1	15	0
1967	2	20	0
1968	3	15	3
1969/1970	4	14	1
1970/1971	5	9	1
1971	6	12	2
1972	7	17	2
1973	8	17	2
1974	9	17	6
1975	10	20	2
1976	11	21	6
1977	12	15	4
1978	13	14	2
1979	14	13	1
1980	15	15	2
1981	16	13	4
1982	17	12	1
1983	18 (only one issue published)	6	2
		265	41 (15.47%)

JOURNAL OF RATIONAL-EMOTIVE THERAPY

Year	Volume Number	Total Number of Articles Published	Research Articles
1983	1 (only one issue published	6	
1984	2	12	3
1985	3	11	3
1986	4	14	3
		43	10 (23.26%)

'Rational Living' were research articles; this percentage increasing to 23.26% in the new 'Journal of Rational-Emotive Therapy'.

Given the importance that I am giving in this chapter to promoting more RET research of higher quality, I would like to see the 'Journal of Rational-Emotive Therapy' aim to attract more of such articles.[1] I consider 50% to be a reasonable percentage to aim for in this respect, given the additional need for also publishing in the journal articles that document new theoretical and practical developments in RET.

RET Conferences

An additional method of promoting higher quality RET research is to hold more national and international conferences on RET. In 1975 the first national RET conference was held followed by a second conference in 1977 and a third in 1980. These conferences attracted large numbers of RET theoreticians, practitioners and, to a lesser extent, researchers and were an excellent forum for bringing together people who might otherwise not have the opportunity to dialogue on theoretical, practical and research matters. However, no further RET conferences have been held since 1980 and none are planned in the future as far as I am aware.

I have on several occasions suggested to key personnel at the Institute for RET in New York that further conferences are needed but my suggestions have attracted little active interest. Common reasons given for not organizing such events have centred on the 'hassle' involved. I consider such 'reasons' to be shortsighted, given the potential benefit that may accrue from such events. Ironically, key RET personnel who, in other arenas, regale against the irrationality of the philosophy of low frustration tolerance seem to display such an attitude when it comes to organizing national/international conferences.

I would like to see biennial national or international conferences held which would have, as a major goal, the provision of a forum for the planning of key RET research programmes. Given the fact that the vast majority of RET practitioners are American, it would make sense for such conferences to be held in the U.S.A. at least initially. Furthermore, given that the Institute for RET in New York is at present at the centre of RET operations worldwide, it would make sense for that organization to be involved in the planning of such biennial events at least until the principle for organizing regularly-held conferences has been established.

While it is true that two international conferences on cognitive psychotherapy have recently been held which followers of RET could attend, in practice this has not been the case. For example, at the 2nd International Conference on Cognitive Psychotherapy held in Umea, Sweden, in 1986, I was the only RET advocate present!

WHAT KIND OF RET RESEARCH IS NEEDED?

Given that a number of commentators have bemoaned the dearth of quality RET research (e.g. Kendall, 1982, 1984a, 1984b) what kinds of studies are needed? I will focus here on two areas: (a) developing better measures of irrationality/rationality and (b) improving the quality of RET outcome research.

Towards The Development of Better Measures of Irrationality/Rationality

Timothy Smith (e.g. Smith, 1982; Smith & Allred, 1986) has observed that existing measures of irrationality have their problems. First, both the 'Rational Belief Inventory' (Shorkey & Whiteman, 1977) and the 'Irrational Beliefs Test' (Jones, 1968) - the most frequently used measures of irrational Beliefs seem to lack discriminant validity. For a measure of irrational Beliefs to have discriminant validity it 'should correlate, as predicted by the theory, with measures of distress, but not as highly as it correlates with a second measure of irrational beliefs' (Smith & Allred, 1986, p. 66). Thus the development of measures of irrationality that demonstrate discriminant validity seems to be a priority if valid conclusions are to be drawn for example, on the relationship between irrational Beliefs and emotional disturbance.

Second, existing measures of irrationality (in particular the 'Irrational Beliefs Test' which is the most frequently used measure of irrationality used in RET research) contain items which pull for affective judgments. In other words, their items do not just reflect Belief statements but are also worded in terms of behaviour and affective responses. Thus, in my opinion, they do not demonstrate acceptable face validity. Kassinove (1986) has recently developed a new measure of core irrational Beliefs, the 'Personal Beliefs Test' which aims to correct this deficiency.

Finally, no existing measures of irrationality adequately discriminate between irrational Beliefs and rational Beliefs. This is a major deficiency which, to my mind, calls into question much of the research that has been carried out which has employed measures of irrationality/rationality. In my opinion, an irrational Belief item should contain both an irrational premise and an irrational derivative from that premise (e.g. 'I must be approved by my best friend and it would be terrible if he/she disapproves of me'). In addition, a rational Belief item should be keenly differentiated from an irrational Belief item in both its premise and derivative form (e.g. ('I would like very much to be approved by my best friend but he/she does not have to approve of me. It would be bad if he/she disapproves of me, but not terrible').

To reiterate, the development of a better measure of rationality/irrationality is a matter of priority. Such a measure should (a) contain items which are worded to reflect cognitive content rather than affective and/or behavioural content; (b) contain items which are clearly statements of irrationality and rationality in both premise and derivative form, and (c) demonstrate acceptable discriminant validity.

Towards The Design Of Better Outcome Studies With Clinical Populations

Kendall & Bemis (1983) in reviewing the outcome literature on RET made the following statement:

> 'The few controlled trials that have been carried out have often included analogue subject population treated by inexperienced therapists using poorly specified and unmeasured intervention techniques with outcome judged on the basis of inadequate dependent variables and no provision for follow-up assessment' (p. 570).

Hollon & Beck (1986) in the 3rd edition of the 'Handbook of Psychotherapy and Behavior Change' reviewed the outcome literature on different variants of cognitive-behaviour therapy and made the following comment: 'RET appears to have the least clear empirical support of any of the major variants, although that state of affairs may derive as much from the fact that the bulk of the trials involving that approach were earlier, less rigorously conducted efforts' (p. 476).

The most recent comprehensive review of RET outcome study was conducted by McGovern & Silverman (1984) who reviewed 47 such studies carried out between 1977 and 1982. Their conclusion concerning the effectiveness of RET was more optimistic than those made by Hollon & Beck (1986) and Kendall & Bemis (1983). However in their article, they included 33 out of 47 studies which were Ph.D. theses summarized in 'Dissertation Abstracts International'. Until those studies are published in prestigious peer review journals it is difficult to ascertain their quality. Of the remaining 14 studies in McGovern & Silverman's review, nine were published in prestigious journals.[2] Of these studies only four found significant differences in favour of the RET treatment.

In one study, Jenni & Wollersheim (1979) found that the group RET treatment was more effective than a group stress management treatment for subjects who had the highest degree of Type A characteristics on self-report measures. Neither treatment reduced subjects' cholesterol level or blood pressure. Unfortunately, behavioural dependent measures were not employed in this study which was a significant weakness in the design since: 'Type A persons are reported to cling tenaciously to their behaviour pattern ....' (Jenni & Wollersheim, 1979, p. 71). Given this weakness, the effects achieved by the short-term RET intervention (six 90-minute group sessions) must be viewed with caution. In addition, no longer term follow-up assessment was undertaken so it is not possible to determine whether or not the RET subjects maintained their gains. Subjects in this study were either referred by their physician or recruited through advertisement and thus it is arguable whether they constituted a clinical population.

In the second study, Carmody (1978) compared rational-emotive assertion training, self-instructional assertion training and behavioural assertion training. The first two treatments also included behavioural rehearsal. All treatments took place in a group format comprising four 90-minute sessions. All treatment groups showed improvement but 'only the RET group proved significantly better on the self-report measure of unproductive cognitions and only the RET group demonstrated significant generalization of treatment gains in an in vivo test-of-transfer during a post-test follow-up' (McGovern & Silverman, 1984, p. 14). Carmody did conduct a three month follow-up and found that all groups maintained their treatment gains. However, since all subjects were recruited via an advertisement this group cannot be considered representative of a clinical sample. This may explain why Carmody's subjects achieved more gains than subjects in Wolfe & Fodor's (1977) study where an RET-based approach to assertion training did not prove to be more effective than a behavioural treatment in facilitating generalization of treatment gains. Wolfe & Fodor's subjects were more representative of a clinical sample.

In the third study, Kassinove, Miller & Kalin (1980) found that prospective psychotherapy clients receiving rational-emotive bibliotherapy showed significant reductions on measures of neuroticism and trait anxiety, while those assigned to a rational-emotive audiotherapy group did not. Both groups, however, made significant gains on a measure of acceptance of irrational ideas. Only self-report measures were employed in this study and no follow-up assessment was employed. This study however, did not focus on RET as a treatment approach but rather as a preparation for later therapy.

Finally, Lipsky, Kassinove & Miller (1980) did employ a clinical population in researching the effectiveness of RET (RET; RET plus rational-emotive imagery and RET plus rational role reversal[3]) compared with relaxation training. Results showed that RET alone or in conjunction with rational-emotive imagery or rational role reversal was superior to relaxation training and to a no-contact condition on a variety of self-report measures. However, no extended follow-up assessment was conducted and only self-report dependent variables were employed which both constitute weaknesses in the design of the study.

Given the problems associated with these four studies and given that they were selected to represent research published in respected journals which demonstrate some measure of effectiveness for RET, it is appropriate to adopt a sceptical attitude concerning the efficacy of RET. This is particularly so since the remaining studies reported by McGovern & Silverman (1984) were either not published in respected journals or did not show significant results in favour of RET over other treatments and/or other groups.

Recommendations for Future RET Outcome Research

I would like to reiterate the comments made by

Kendall & Bemis (1983) quoted earlier. Future RET outcome research needs to employ: (a) actual clinical populations preferably with well defined clinical syndromes[4]; (b) experienced RET therapists who demonstrate high level skill in the conduct of therapy <u>in these studies</u>; (c) a variety of dependent measures - including self-report, behavioural and ratings by significant others and (d) long-term follow-up assessment.

It is only in this way that the outcome achieved by RET can be realistically compared with that achieved by other cognitive behavioural and behavioural therapies which traditionally have received more rigorous and systematic enquiry.

POSTSCRIPT

Since preparing the material for this final chapter, I have decided that in future I will concern myself with questions of RET evaluation rather than RET debate (Kendall, 1984a). Consequently this is likely to be my last discussion-orientated text on RET for the foreseeable future.

NOTES

1. It is my impression that the 'Journal of Rational-Emotive Therapy' has been publishing research articles of higher quality than were published by 'Rational Living', but still not in sufficient quantity to satisfy critics such as Philip Kendall (1982, 1984a, 1984b).

2. I have omitted the study by Rush et al.(1977) since this assessed the outcome of Beck's Cognitive Therapy rather than RET.

3. This study raises the interesting question concerning what is to be deemed RET for the purposes of research studies, since rational-emotive imagery and rational role reversal are methods regularly employed in RET rather than adjuncts to it (see also Chapter 4).

4. The study by Lipsky, Kassinove & Miller (1980) did not employ clients who had well-defined clinical problems but used those who were defined as either 'neurotic' or having 'adjustment reactions of adulthood'.

REFERENCES

Adler, A. (1927). Understanding human nature. New York: Garden City.

Anchin, J.C. & Kiesler, D.J. (Eds.).(1982). Handbook of interpersonal psychotherapy. New York: Pergamon.

Bandura, A. (1977). Social learning theory. Englewood Cliffs, NJ : Prentice-Hall.

Bard, J. (1980). Rational-emotive therapy in practice. Champaign, IL: Research Press.

Beck, A.T. (1976). Cognitive therapy and the emotional disorders. New York: International Universities Press.

Beck, A.T., Rush, A.J., Shaw, B.F., & Emery, G. (1979). Cognitive therapy of depression. New York: Guilford.

Beutler, L.E. (1983). Eclectic psychotherapy. A systematic approach. New York: Pergamon.

Bordin, E.S. (1979). The generalizability of the psychoanalytic concept of the working alliance. Psychotherapy: Theory, Research and Practice, 16, 252-260.

Bordin, E.S. (1983, February). Myths, realities, and alternatives to clinical trials. Paper presented at the International Conference on Psychotherapy, Bogota, Columbia.

Boutin, G.E., & Tosi, D.J. (1983). Modification of irrational ideas and test anxiety through rational stage directed hypnotherapy (RSDH). Journal of Clinical Psychology, 39, 382-391.

Burns, D.D. (1980). Feeling good: The new mood therapy. New York: Morrow.

Carmody, T.P. (1978). Rational-emotive, self-instructional, and behavioral assertion training: Facilitating maintenance. Cognitive Therapy and Research, 2, 241-253.

Church, V.A. (1974). Rational therapy in divorce practice. Rational Living, 9, 34-38.

Crawford, T. (1982, October). Communication and rational-emotive therapy. Workshop presented in Los Angeles.

Danysh, J. (1974). Stop without quitting. San Francisco: International Society for General Semantics.

DiGiuseppe, R. (1984). Thinking what to feel. British Journal of Cognitive Psychotherapy, 2(1), 27-33.

DiGiuseppe, R., Miller, N.J., & Trexler, L.D. (1979). A review of rational-emotive psychotherapy outcome studies. In A. Ellis & J.M. Whiteley (Eds.), Theoretical and empirical foundations

of rational-emotive therapy. Monterey, CA: Brooks/Cole.
Dorn, F.J. (1984). Counseling as applied social psychology: An introduction to the social influence model. Springfield, IL: Thomas.
Dryden, W. (1981). Some uses of audio-tape procedures in counselling: A personal view. Counselling, No. 36, 14-17.
Dryden, W. (1982). A guide for solving your emotional and behavioural problems by re-examining your self-defeating thoughts and attitudes. London: Institute for RET (U.K.).
Dryden, W. (1983). Audiotape supervision by mail: A rational-emotive approach. British Journal of Cognitive Psychotherapy, 1(1), 57-64.
Dryden, W. (1984a). Rational-emotive therapy. In W. Dryden (Ed.), Individual therapy in Britain. London: Harper & Row.
Dryden, W. (1984b). Issues in the eclectic practice of individual therapy. In W. Dryden (Ed.), Individual therapy in Britain. London: Harper & Row.
Dryden, W. (1984c). Rational-emotive therapy: Fundamentals and innovations. London: Croom Helm.
Dryden, W. (1984d). Therapeutic arenas. In W. Dryden (Ed.), Individual therapy in Britain. London: Harper & Row.
Dryden, W. (1985). Challenging but not overwhelming: A compromise in negotiating homework assignments. British Journal of Cognitive Psychotherapy, 3(1), 77-80.
Dryden, W. (1987). Counselling individuals: The rational-emotive approach. London: Taylor & Francis.
Dryden, W., & Hunt, P. (1985). Therapeutic alliances in marital therapy. II. Process issues. In W. Dryden (Ed.), Marital therapy in Britain. Volume 1: Context and therapeutic approaches. London: Harper & Row.
Dryden, W., Trower, P., & Casey, A. (1983). A comprehensive approach to social skills training II: Contributions from rational-emotive therapy. The Counsellor,3(7), 2-12.
Dunlap, K. (1932). Habits: Their making and unmaking. New York: Liveright.
Ellis, A. (1958). Neurotic interaction between marital partners. Journal of Counseling Psychology, 5, 24-28.
Ellis, A. (1957). How to live with a neurotic: At home and at work. New York: Crown.

Ellis, A. (1960). Marriage counseling with demasculinizing wives and demasculinized husbands. Marriage and Family Living, 22, 12-21.

Ellis, A. (1962). Reason and emotion in psychotherapy. Secaucus, NJ: Lyle Stuart.

Ellis, A. (speaker). (1971). How to stubbornly refuse to be ashamed of anything (cassette recording). New York: Institute for Rational-Emotive Therapy.

Ellis, A. (1972). Helping people get better: Rather than merely feel better. Rational Living, 7(2), 2-9.

Ellis, A. (1973). Humanistic psychotherapy: The rational-emotive approach. New York: McGraw-Hill.

Ellis, A. (1976a). The biological basis of human irrationality. Journal of Individual Psychology, 32, 145-168.

Ellis, A. (speaker). (1976b). Conquering low frustration tolerance (cassette recording). New York: Institute for Rational-Emotive Therapy.

Ellis, A. (1976c). Techniques of handling anger in marriage. Journal of Marriage and Family Counseling, 2, 305-316.

Ellis, A. (1977a). Intimacy in psychotherapy. Rational Living, 12(2), 13-19.

Ellis, A. (1977b). Fun as psychotherapy. Rational Living, 12(1), 2-6.

Ellis, A. (speaker). (1977c). A garland of rational humorous songs (cassette recording). New York: Institute for Rational-Emotive Therapy.

Ellis, A. (1977d). The basic clinical theory of rational-emotive therapy. In A. Ellis & R. Grieger (Eds.), Handbook of rational-emotive therapy. Volume 1. New York: Springer.

Ellis, A. (1977e). Skill training in counselling and psychotherapy. Canadian Counsellor, 12(1), 30-35.

Ellis, A. (1977f). Irrational ideas. In J. L. Wolfe & E. Brand (Eds.), Twenty years of rational therapy. New York: Institute for Rational-Emotive Therapy.

Ellis, A. (1979a). The theory of rational-emotive therapy. In A. Ellis & J. M. Whiteley (Eds.), Theoretical and empirical foundations of rational-emotive therapy. Monterey, CA: Brooks/Cole.

Ellis, A. (1979b). Discomfort anxiety: A new cognitive behavioral construct. Part 1. Rational Living, 14(2), 3-8.

Ellis, A. (1979c). The practice of rational-emotive

therapy. In A. Ellis & J. M. Whitely (Eds.), Theoretical and empirical foundations of rational-emotive therapy Monterey, CA: Brooks/Cole.

Ellis, A. (1979d). The issue of force and energy in behavioral change. Journal of Contemporary Psychotherapy, 10(2), 83-97.

Ellis, A. (1979e). Rejoinder: Elegant and inelegant RET. In A. Ellis & J. M. Whiteley (Eds.), Theoretical and empirical foundations of rational-emotive therapy. Monterey, CA: Brooks/Cole.

Ellis, A. (1979f). A note on the treatment of agoraphobics with cognitive modification versus prolonged exposure in vivo. Behaviour Research and Therapy, 17, 162-164.

Ellis, A. (1980a). Discomfort anxiety: A new cognitive behavioral construct. Part 2. Rational Living, 15(1), 25-30.

Ellis, A. (1980b). Rational-emotive therapy and cognitive behavior therapy: Similarities and differences. Cognitive Therapy and Research, 4, 325-340.

Ellis, A. (1980c). The value of efficiency in psychotherapy. Psychotherapy: Theory, Research and Practice, 17, 414-419.

Ellis, A. (1981a). The place of Immanuel Kant in cognitive psychotherapy. Rational Living, 16 (2), 13-16.

Ellis, A. (1981b). New developments in rational-emotive therapy. Address given at the First European Conference on Cognitive Behavioural Therapies, Lisbon, Portugal.

Ellis, A. (1981c). The use of rational humorous songs in psychotherapy. Voices, 16(4), 29-36.

Ellis, A. (1982a). Intimacy in rational-emotive therapy. In M. Fisher & G. Striker (Eds.), Intimacy. New York: Plenum.

Ellis, A. (1982b). Rational-emotive family therapy. In A. M. Horne & M. M. Ohlsen (Eds.), Family counseling and therapy. Itasca, IL: Peacock.

Ellis, A. (1983a). The case against religiosity. New York: Institute for Rational-Emotive Therapy.

Ellis, A. (1983b). How to deal with your most difficult client: You. Journal of Rational-Emotive Therapy, 1(1), 3-8.

Ellis, A. (1983c). The philosophic implications and dangers of some popular behavior therapy techniques. In M. Rosenbaum, C. M. Franks & Y. Jaffe (Eds.), Perspectives in behavior therapy

in the eighties. New York: Springer.
Ellis, A. (1983d). Rational-emotive therapy (RET) approaches to overcoming resistance 1: Common forms of resistance. British Journal of Cognitive Psychotherapy, 1(1), 28-38.
Ellis, A. (1983e). Failures in rational-emotive therapy. In E. B. Foa & P. M. G. Emmelkamp (Eds.), Failures in behavior therapy. New York: Wiley.
Ellis, A. (1984a). The essence of RET - 1984. Journal of Rational-Emotive Therapy, 2(1), 19-25.
Ellis, A. (1984b). Rational-emotive therapy. In R. J. Corsini (Ed.), Current psychotherapies. Third edition. Itasca, IL: Peacock.
Ellis, A. (1985a). Overcoming resistance. New York: Springer.
Ellis, A. (1985b). Expanding the ABCs of rational-emotive therapy. In M. J. Mahoney & A. Freeman (Eds.), Cognition and psychotherapy. New York: Plenum.
Ellis, A. (1986). Fanaticism that may lead to a nuclear holocaust: The contributions of scientific counseling and psychotherapy. Journal of Counseling and Development, 65, 146-151.
Ellis, A., & Abrahms, E. (1978). Brief psychotherapy in medical and health practice. New York: Springer.
Ellis, A., & Becker, I. (1982). A guide to personal happiness. North Hollywood, CA: Wilshire.
Ellis, A., & Dryden, W. (1987). The practice of rational-emotive therapy. New York: Springer.
Ellis, A., & Harper, R.A. (1961). A guide to successful marriage. North Hollywood, CA: Wilshire.
Ellis, A., & Harper, R.A. (1975). A new guide to rational living. North Hollywood, CA: Wilshire.
Ellis, A., & Knaus, W. (1977). Overcoming procrastination. New York: New American Library.
Ellis, A., & Whiteley, J. M. (Eds.), (1979). Theoretical and empirical foundations of rational-emotive therapy. Monterey, CA: Brooks/Cole.
Emmelkamp, P.M.G., Kuipers, A.C.M., & Eggeraat, J.B. (1978). Cognitive modification versus prolonged exposure in vivo: A comparison with agoraphobics as subjects. Behaviour Research and Therapy, 16, 33-41.
Eschenroeder, C. (1979). Different therapeutic styles in rational-emotive therapy. Rational Living, 14(1), 3-7.
Freud, A. (1937). The ego and the mechanics of defence. London: Hogarth.

References

Garcia, E. J. (1977). Working on the E in RET. In J. L. Wolfe & E. Brand (Eds.), Twenty years of rational therapy. New York: Institute for Rational-Emotive Therapy.

Gendlin, E.T. (1978). Focusing. New York: Everest House.

Golden, W.L. (1983). Rational-emotive hypnotherapy: Principles and practice. British Journal of Cognitive Psychotherapy, 1(1), 47-56.

Golden, W.L. (1985). An integration of Ericksonian and cognitive-behavioral hypnotherapy in the treatment of anxiety disorders. In E.T. Dowd & J. M. Healy (Eds.), Case studies in hypnotherapy. New York: Guilford.

Goldfried, M., & Davison, G. (1976). Clinical behavior therapy. New York: Holt, Rinehart & Winston.

Grieger, R. (Ed.). (1986). Rational-emotive couples therapy. Journal of Rational-Emotive Therapy, 4(1), 3-109.

Grieger, R., & Boyd, J. (1980). Rational-emotive therapy: A skills-based approach. New York: Van Nostrand Reinhold.

Grieger, R., & Grieger, I. (Eds.). (1982). Cognition and emotional disturbance. New York: Human Sciences Press.

Guerney, B. G., Jr. (1977). Relationship enhancement: Skill training programs for therapy, problem-prevention and enrichment. San Francisco: Jossey-Bass.

Harper, R.A. (1981). Limitations of Marriage and family therapy. Rational Living, 16(2), 3-6.

Hauck, P.A. (1972). Reason in pastoral counseling. Philadelphia: Westminster.

Hauck, P.A. (1977). Irrational parenting styles. In A. Ellis & R. Grieger (Eds.), Handbook of rational-emotive therapy. Volume 1. New York: Springer.

Hauck, P.A. (1981). Making marriage work. London: Sheldon Press.

Hauck, P.A. (1983a). How to love and be loved. London: Sheldon Press.

Hauck, P.A. (1983b). Working with parents. In A. Ellis & M. E. Bernard (Eds.), Rational-emotive approaches to the problems of childhood. New York: Plenum.

Heidegger, M. (1949). Existence and being. Chicago: Henry Regnery.

Hoehn-Saric, R. (1978). Emotional arousal, attitude change and psychotherapy. In J.D. Frank, R. Hoehn-Saric, S.D. Imber, B.L. Liberman & A.R.

Stone (Eds.), Effective ingredients of successful psychotherapy. New York: Brunner/Mazel.
Hollon, S., & Beck, A.T. (1986). Research on cognitive therapies. In S. L. Garfield & A. E. Bergin (Eds.), Handbook of psychotherapy and behavior change. 3rd edition. New York: Wiley.
Horney, K. (1950). Neurosis and human growth. New York: Norton.
Horwill, F. M. (1983). Thoughts towards a model for conciliation and conflict resolution in the Family Court of Australia. Australian Psychologist, 18(1), 39-53.
Janis, I.L. (1983). Short-term counseling. New Haven, CT: Yale University Press.
Jenni, M. A., & Wollersheim, J.P. (1979). Cognitive therapy, stress management training and the Type A behavior pattern. Cognitive Therapy and Research, 3, 61-73.
Jones, M.C. (1924). A laboratory study of fear: The case of Peter. Journal of Genetic Psychology, 31, 308-315.
Jones, R. (1968). A factored measure of Ellis' irrational belief system with personality and maladjustment correlates. Unpublished doctoral dissertation. Texas Technological University, Lubbock.
Jones, R.A. (1977). Self-fulfilling prophecies: Social, psychological and physiological effects of expectancies. Hillsdale, NJ: Lawrence Erlbaum.
Kadushin, A. (1968). Games people play in supervision. Social Work, 13, 23-32.
Kassinove, H. (1986). Self-reported affect and core irrational thinking: A preliminary analysis. Journal of Rational-Emotive Therapy, 4 (2), 119-130.
Kassinove, H., Miller, N.J., & Kalin, M. (1980). Effects of pretreatment with rational-emotive bibliotherapy and rational-emotive audiotherapy on clients waiting at a community mental health center. Psychological Reports, 46, 851-857.
Kelly, G. (1955). The psychology of personal constructs. New York: Norton.
Kendall, P.C. (1982). Cognitive processes and procedures in behavior therapy. In C. M. Franks, G. T. Wilson, P.C. Kendall & Brownell (Eds.), Annual review of behavior therapy. Volume 8. New York: Guilford.
Kendall, P.C. (1984a). Cognitive processes and procedures in behavior therapy. In G.T. Wilson,

C.M. Franks, K.D. Brownell & P.C. Kendall (Eds.), Annual review of behavior therapy. Volume 9. New York: Guilford.

Kendall, P.C. (1984b). Cognitive processes and procedures in behavior therapy. In C. M. Franks, G.T. Wilson, P.C. Kendall & K. D. Brownell (Eds.), Annual review of behavior therapy. Volume 10. New York: Guilford.

Kendall, P.C., & Bemis, K. M. (1983). Thought and action in psychotherapy: The cognitive-behavioral approaches. In M. Hersen, A. E. Kazdin & A. S. Bellack (Eds.), The clinical psychology handbook. New York: Pergamon.

Korzybski, A. (1933). Science and sanity. San Francisco: International Society of General Semantics.

Kwee, M.G.T., & Lazarus, A.A. (1986). Multimodal therapy: The cognitive behavioural tradition and beyond. In W. Dryden & W. L. Golden (Eds.), Cognitive-behavioural approaches to psychotherapy. London: Harper & Row.

Lazarus, A.A. (1981). The practice of multimodal therapy. New York: McGraw-Hill.

Lazarus, A. A. (1984). In the mind's eye. New York: Guilford.

Lazarus, A.A. (1985). Marital myths. San Luis Obispo, CA: Impact.

Lederer, W.J., & Jackson, D.D. (1968). The mirages of marriage. New York: Norton.

Lipsky, M.J., Kassinove, H. & Miller, N.J. (1980). Effects of rational-emotive therapy, rational role reversal, and rational-emotive imagery on the emotional adjustment of community mental health center patients. Journal of Consulting and Clinical Psychology, 48, 366-374.

Low, A.A. (1952). Mental health through will training. West Hanover, MA: Christopher.

Mackay, D. (1984). Behavioural psychotherapy. In W. Dryden (Ed.), Individual therapy in Britain. London: Harper & Row.

Mackay, D. (1985). Marital therapy: The behavioural approach. In W. Dryden (Ed.), Marital therapy in Britain. Volume 1: Context and therapeutic approaches. London: Harper & Row.

Madison, M. (1983). Defining levels of intervention in dispute resolution. Unpublished paper, Paramatta Registry, Family Court of Australia.

Maultsby, M.C. Jr. (1975). Help yourself to happiness: Through rational self-counseling. New York: Institute for Rational-Emotive Therapy.

Maultsby, M.C. Jr. (1984). Rational behavior ther-

apy. Englewood Cliffs, NJ: Prentice-Hall.
Maultsby, M.C., Jr., & Ellis, A. (1974). *Technique for using rational-emotive imagery*. New York: Institute for Rational-Emotive Therapy.
McClellan, T.A., & Stieper, D.R. (1973). A structural approach to group marriage counseling. *Rational Living, 8*(2), 13-18.
McGovern, T.E., & Silverman, M.S. (1984). A review of outcome studies of rational-emotive therapy from 1977 to 1982. *Journal of Rational Emotive Therapy, 2*(1), 7-18.
Meichenbaum, D. (1977). *Cognitive-behavior modification*. New York: Plenum.
Meichenbaum, D., & Gilmore, J.B. (1981). Resistance from a cognitive behavioral perspective. In P. L. Wachtel (Ed.), *Resistance*. New York: Plenum.
Moore, R.H. (1983). Inference as "A" in RET. *British Journal of Cognitive Psychotherapy, 1* (2), 17-23.
National Family Conciliation Council. (1984). Code of practice. *Family Law, 14*, 107-108.
Nelson-Jones, R. (1982). *The theory and practice of counselling psychology*. Eastbourne: Holt, Reinehart & Winston.
Parkinson, L. (1985). Conciliation in separation and divorce. In W. Dryden, (Ed.), *Marital therapy in Britain. Volume 2: Special areas*. London: Harper & Row.
Pinsof, W.M., & Catherall, D.R. (1986). The integrative psychotherapy alliance: Family, couple, and individual scales. *Journal of Marital and Family Therapy, 12*, 137-151.
Popper, K.R. (1963). *Conjectures and refutations*. New York: Harper & Bros.
Popper, K.R. (1959). *The logic of scientific discovery*. New York: Harper & Bros.
Powell, J. (1976). *Fully human, fully alive*. Niles, IL: Argus.
Preston, G., Ralph, S., & Madison, M. (1983). *The family assessment form*. Unpublished paper. Paramatta Registry, Family Court of Australia.
Reichenbach, J. (1953). *The rise of scientific philosophy*. Berkeley, CA: University of California Press.
Robinson, M., & Parkinson, L. (1985). A family systems to conciliation and divorce. *Journal of Family Therapy, 7*, 357-377.
Rogers, C.R. (1961). *On becoming a person*. Boston: Houghton Mifflin.
Rush, A.J., Beck, A.T., Kovacs, M., & Hollon, S.

(1977). Comparative efficacy of cognitive therapy and pharmacotherapy in the treatment of depressed outpatients. Cognitive Therapy and Research, 1, 17-38.

Russell, B. (1950). The conquest of happiness. New York: New American Library.

Russell, B. (1965). The basic writings of Bertrand Russell. New York: Simon & Schuster.

Safran, J.D. (1984). Assessing the cognitive-interpersonal circle. Cognitive Therapy and Research, 8, 333-347.

Sager, C.J. (1976). Marriage contracts and marital therapy. New York: Brunner/Mazel.

Saunders, J.B. (Ed.), (1969). Words and phrases legally defined. 2nd edition. London: Butterworth.

Saunders, J.B. (1977). Mozley and Whiteley's law dictionary. London: Butterworth.

Shorkey, C.T., & Whiteman, V.L. (1977). Development of the Rational Behavior Inventory: Initial validity and reliability. Educational and Psychological Measurement, 37, 527-534.

Sichel, J, & Ellis, A. (1984). RET self-help form. New York: Institute for Rational-Emotive Therapy.

Smith, T.W. (1982). Irrational beliefs in the cause and treatment of emotional distress: A critical review of the rational-emotive model. Clinical Psychology Review, 2, 505-522.

Smith, T.W., & Allred, K.D. (1986). Rationality revisited: A reassessment of the empirical support for the rational-emotive model. In P.C. Kendall (Ed.), Advances in cognitive-behavioral research and therapy. Volume 5. New York: Academic Press.

Strong, S.R., & Claiborn, C.D. (1982). Change through interaction. New York: Wiley-Interscience.

Stuart, R.B. (1980). Helping couples change: A social learning approach to marital therapy. New York: Guilford.

Tillich, P. (1977). The courage to be. New York: Fountain.

Vertes, R. (1971). The should: A critical analysis. Rational Living, 6(2), 22-25.

Wachtel, P.L. (1977). Psychoanalysis and behavior therapy: Toward an integration. New York: Basic Books.

Walen, S.R., DiGiuseppe, R., & Wessler, R.L., (1980). A practitioner's guide to rational-emotive

therapy. New York: Oxford University Press.
Watson, J.B., & Rayner, R. (1920). Conditioned emotional reactions. Journal of Experimental Psychology, 3, 1-14.
Weinrach, S.G. (1980). Unconventional therapist: Albert Ellis. Personnel and Guidance Journal, 59(2), 152-160.
Werner, E.E., & Smith, R.S. (1982). Vulnerable but not invincible: A study of resilient children. New York: McGraw-Hill.
Wessler, R.A. (1981). So you are angry: Now what's your problem? Rational Living, 16(1), 29-31.
Wessler, R.A., & Wessler, R.L. (1980). The principles and practice of rational-emotive therapy. San Francisco: Jossey-Bass.
Wessler, R.L. (1984). Alternative conceptions of rational-emotive therapy: Toward a philosophically neutral psychotherapy. In M.A. Reda & M.J. Mahoney (Eds.), Cognitive psychotherapies: Recent developments in theory, research and practice. Cambridge, MA: Ballinger.
Wessler, R.L., & Ellis, A. (1980). Supervision in rational-emotive therapy. In A.K. Hess (Ed.), Psychotherapy supervision. New York: Wiley.
Wessler, R.L., & Ellis, A. (1983). Supervision in counseling: Rational-emotive therapy. The Counseling Psychologist, 11(1), 43-49.
Wolfe, J.L., & Fodor, I.G. (1977). Modifying assertive behavior in women: A comparison of three approaches. Behavior Therapy, 8, 567-574.
Yalom, I.D. (1975). The theory and practice of group psychotherapy. 2nd edition. New York: Basic Books.
Young, H.S. (1974). A rational counseling primer. New York: Institute for Rational-Emotive Therapy.
Young, H.S. (1975). Rational thinkers and robots. Rational Living, 2(1), 3-7.
Young, H.S. (1977). Counseling strategies with working class adolescents. In J. L. Wolfe & E. Brand (Eds.), Twenty years of rational therapy. New York: Institute for Rational-Emotive Therapy.
Young, H.S. (1984a). Practising RET with lower-class clients. British Journal of Cognitive Psychotherapy, 2(2), 33-59.
Young, H.S. (1984b). Practising RET with bible-belt christians. British Journal of Cognitive Psychotherapy, 2(2), 60-76.
Young, H.S. (1984c). Teaching rational self-value

concepts to tough customers. British Journal of Cognitive Psychotherapy, 2(2), 77-97.

Zettle, R.D., & Hayes, S.C. (1980). Conceptual and empirical status of rational-emotive therapy. In M. Hersen, R.M. Eisler & P.M. Miller (Eds.), Progress in behavior modification. Volume 9. New York: Academic Press.

INDEX

ABC framework 5
absolutistic evaluations 8, 11, 16, 25, 47-8, 51-2, 89, 116-17, 120, 121
'acceptance' 13, 118
acceptance, unconditional by supervisor 181-2
  by therapist 21, 34 75
activating events, changing 81, 131, 132
active-directive approach 4, 34, 62
Adler, A. 3
agoraphobia 69
alcohol problems 93
alliance, therapeutic see therapeutic alliance
'all-or-nothing' thinking 176
anger 15, 78, 80-1, 114-15, 121, 149, 165
  meaning of 49-50
annoyance 15, 49-50
anti-procrastination exercises 35
anti-RET viewpoints 168-9
anxiety 13, 41-3, 135
  about anxiety 17
  about driving 41, 42
  about examinations 79-80
  about fate control 178, 179, 180-1, 184, 189-91
  about personal worth 178-80, 184, 185-9
  discomfort see discomfort disturbance
  ego see ego disturbance
  meaning of 47-8
  sexual 43, 44
  social 78-9, 84-5
  trainee counsellors' 172-81, 184-91
applications of RET, practical 20-41
approval, dire need for 22
assertion training 80-1, 199-200
assessment of problems 64-5
audience participation in RET 167-9
audiotape recordings of therapy sessions 28, 139, 171
  trainees' anxiety about 172-4
avoided techniques in RET 36-7
'awfulizing' 9, 12, 117-18

Beck, Aaron 121, 175, 176, 193, 198-9
behaviour therapy 4
behavioural techniques 35-6, 129

behaviourally-based change 79-81
beliefs see 'irrational' beliefs (IBs); 'rational' beliefs
Bemis, K.M. 198
Beutler, L.E. 62
bibliotherapy 28
biological basis of 'irrationality' 6-7, 15-16
blaming of others 130-1
bonds in therapy 59-63, 67, 89-90, 107
Bordin, Ed 59, 67, 82, 89, 108
Burns, D. D. 175-6

Carmody, T.P. 199-200
Catherall, D.R. 63
Center for Cognitive Therapy, Philadelphia 60, 69
'challenging but not overwhelming' 81-6, 91-2, 101, 102, 108-9, 111
change, therapeutic
  behaviourally-based 79-81
  client's views of 69-70
  goals for see goals, for change
  in couples therapy 132-3
  inferentially-based 78-9
  language of 54-5
  philosophic 19-20, 24, 72, 76, 77
  resistance to 50, 51, 57-8
  tactics for 65-6
  theory of 19-20, 69
children
  access to after divorce 147, 148-9, 150, 151
  involvement in conciliation 152
'cognitive distortions' 121; see also inferences, distorted
cognitive factors in functioning 5, 6
cognitive techniques 27-9, 127-8
cognitive therapy 193
cognitive-behaviour therapy 23, 72-3
  differences from RET 73-7
communication skills 149
compromises in RET 72-87
conceptualization of problems, shared 65
concern 13, 47-8
conciliation counselling, rational-emotive 140-53
  aims of conciliation process 141-2
  formulating agreed solutions 150-1
  goals of 146-7
  involvement of children in 152
  overcoming couple disturbance in 146, 147-9
  process of 147-52
  promoting constructive couple dialogue 146, 149-50
  reviewing 151-2
conclusions, jumping to 177
conditions, therapeutic 21-3
conferences on RET 196-7
confidentiality 152, 170, 172; see also secrets between client and therapist
conjoint therapy 123, 124, 126, 136-7, 148
contextual considerations 123-5
control, fear of los-

ing 103-4
couples therapy, rational-emotive 113-39
case example of 134-9
change process in 132-3
contextual considerations in 123-5
'enhancing couple satisfaction' phase 124, 127, 129, 136-7
'overcoming couple disturbance' phase 123-4, 126, 127-9, 135-6
practice of 123-34
problems encountered in 129-30
theory of 115-23
therapeutic alliance in 125-7
critical incidents in therapy 99-100, 101, 111-12

'damnation' 9, 13, 118
dance therapy 104, 107, 110
'debating' 27
defence mechanisms 18
'defining' 27
demonstration of RET, public 154-6, 167-70
depression 13-14, 43-5, 58, 80-1, 85, 134, 135, 167
meaning of 48-9
derivative language 53-4
derivatives
'irrational' 8-9, 11
'rational' 12-13
'desiring' 12, 177
'detecting' 27
dialogue
between divorced people 146, 149-50
between trainee and supervisor 185-91
with client 95, 97, 99-100, 101, 102-3, 157-67
'difficult customers' (DCs) 40-1
DiGiuseppe, R. 48, 50, 115
disappointment 14
discomfort disturbance 9, 15, 74, 84, 92, 179, 180-1
'discriminating' 27
disputing of 'irrational' beliefs 27-8, 34, 41-3, 74, 103, 128, 131, 135, 148, 156; see also dialogue
disqualifying positive experiences 176-7
dissatisfaction 117-18, 119-20, 135, 136-7
'disturbability', human 16
disturbance, psychological
acquisition of 15-16, 68-9
in interpersonal relationships 115-19, 120-3, 127-9, 131, 132-3, 135-6, 146, 147-9
nature of 8-12, 68
perpetuation of 16-19
see also discomfort disturbance; ego disturbance
divorce
conciliation after see conciliation counselling
'de-awfulizing' 136,139
dogmatism 169
Dryden, Windy 18, 26, 27, 30-1, 35, 60, 63, 88, 89, 171, 179, 192
dysfunctional behaviour 79-80, 121, 122

earthy language in RET 169-70
eclecticism, theoretically consistent 26, 88-112

ego disturbance 9, 15, 84, 179-80, 181
Ellis, Albert 1-4, 5, 6, 8, 9, 13, 15, 17, 18, 19-20, 21, 22, 27-8, 32-3, 39, 40, 49, 55, 70-1, 72, 74, 81-2,88, 92, 113, 114-15, 116, 131, 154-67, 168, 169, 170, 179-80, 192
embarrassment 14-15, 100, 111-12
emotional reasoning 177-8
emotions see feelings; negative emotions, 'rational' vs 'irrational'
emotive techniques 29, 34-5, 128-9
empathy from therapist 21-2, 99
'empty chair' technique 102-3, 107
end phase of therapy 104-5
Eschenroeder, C. 23
ethical humanism 3, 73
expectations
  client's 60-1, 90, 94
  unrealistic 114

failure, fear of 159-61
'failure' clients 40, 70-1
failures in RET 66-71
fallibility, human 7-8, 44, 49, 118
  meaning of 53-4
fate control, anxiety about 178, 179, 180-1, 184, 189-91
fears 136-7, 138; see also anxiety
feedback, from supervisor 183-4
feelings
  getting in touch with 99-100, 101-5, 107, 108-9
  language of 47-51
  repression of 93, 112
  see also negative emotions, 'rational' vs 'irrational'
filters, mental 176
fixed role therapy 35-6
flexibility in therapy 124-5, 133
focusing technique 98, 110
Fodor, I.G. 200
force/energy, use of in therapy 34-5, 75-6
'Friday night workshop' 154-70
'full-exposure' methods 82-3, 84

gains from therapy, client's account of 104-5, 110-12
gender identity 44, 45
Gendlin, E. T. 91, 98
'general' RET 23
genuineness of therapist 21
Gilmore, J. B. 65
goals
  basic 4-5
  for change 48, 63-4, 67, 90-1, 98, 107-8
  of couple therapy 125-6
Golden, W. L. 65
gradualism, psychotherapeutic 81-2
guilt 14, 42, 148-9
  meaning of 49

Harper, Robert 114, 125
health, psychological 12-13
Heidegger, M. 3
'hemmed in' feelings 42
hidden agenda in therapy 125, 126
historical development of RET 1-4, 192-3
Hoehn-Saric, R. 91
Hollon, S. 198-9
homework assignments 24-5, 26, 28, 55, 82-6, 103, 129

Horney, Karen 3
hostile interchanges in therapy 131
humanistic-existential outlook 3, 73
humour
from supervisor 183
from therapist 21, 34
Hunt, P. 63

'I-can't-stand-it-itis' 9, 12, 118
illogicalities in disturbance 9-11; _see also_ inferences, distorted
image of the person in RET 4-8
imagery techniques 29; _see also_ rational-emotive imagery (REI)
in vivo techniques 35
'inference chaining' 41
inferences, distorted 26, 74, 78-9, 168, 175-8
inferentially-based change 78-9
initial phase of therapy 94-9
Institute for Rational-Emotive Therapy, New York 154, 194, 196-7
intellectualization 94, 97, 98, 107-8, 109, 110-11; _see also_ rationalization
interactive/interdependent nature of intrapsychic processes 5-6
interpersonal issues 63-4; _see also_ conciliation counselling; couples therapy
'irrational' beliefs (IBs) 6-7, 8-11, 16-17, 20, 25-6, 29, 39, 40, 74 78-9, 89, 116-19, 127-8, 142, 143, 146, 148, 155, 156, 179-81; _see also_ disputing of 'irrational' beliefs
'Irrational Beliefs Test' 197

jealousy 50-1
Jenni, M. A. 199
Journal of Rational-Emotive Therapy 194-6, 201

Kadushin, A. 175
Kalin, M. 200
Kant, Immanuel 2
Kassinove, H. 197, 200, 201
Kelly, George 35-6, 57
Kendall, Philip 193, 198, 201

labelling 178
language and meaning in RET 46-58
change, language of 54-5
derivative language 53-4
earthy language 169-70
feeling, language of 47-51
premise language 51-3
shared meaning 56-8
unfamiliar words, using 56
Lazarus, A. A. 61, 94, 112
learning
explaining nature of 182-3
therapeutic 91-2
Life History Questionnaire 61
Lipsky, M. J. 200, 201
low frustration tolerance (LFT) 17, 22, 82, 129

McGovern, T. E. 199, 200
Mackay, D. 74

Madison, M. 141-2
magnification/minimization 177
marriages, disturbed 113; see also couples therapy; relationships
Maultsby, M. C. Jr. 17, 118
meaning see language and meaning in RET
measures of 'irrationality' 197-8
meditation, expressive 104, 107, 110
Meichenbaum, D. 65
metatherapy issues 63
middle phase of therapy 99-104
Miller, N. J. 200, 201
'mind-reading' 177
misunderstandings 46, 57; see also language and meaning in RET
model, 'rational', therapist as 34
'must', meaning of 51
'musturbation', 8, 116, 117, 120-1

National Family Conciliation Council 140, 141
negative emotions, 'rational' vs 'irrational' 12, 13-15, 47-51, 57, 75, 143, 144-5, 146-8
Nelson-Jones, R. 154
non-understanding by client 56

obstacles to client progress 37-41
  client obstacles 40-1
  relationship obstacles 37-8
  therapist obstacles 38-9
'operant conditioning' 156, 166; see also punishments/rewards
others, impact of behaviour on 168; see also interpersonal issues
outcome studies 198-201
overconcern for client, therapist's 172
overgeneralization 176

Parkinson, L. 140
passivity 62
pay-off from problems 18
persistence 55
'Personal Beliefs Test' 197-8
personal construct therapy 57-8
'personalization' 178
persuasion, psychotherapy as 62
philosophic change 19-20, 24, 72, 76, 77
philosophical influences on RET 2-3
Pinsof, W. M. 63
Popper, K. R. 2
prediction, negative 177
preferences 52
preferential RET 23-4
premise language 51-3
problems
  primary 25
  shared definition/conceptualization of 65
'problems about problems' 17-18 74-5
procrastination 157-8, 162-3
psychoanalysis 1-2, 113
psychological influences on RET 3-4
punishments/rewards 35, 76, 156, 166
purposelessness 93

qualities of effective therapists 133-4

'rating badness' 12, 117-18
'rational', meaning of 5, 46-7
'Rational Belief Inventory' 197
'rational' beliefs 52-3, 142-3
Rational Living 194, 195, 196, 201
rational-emotive couples therapy (RECT) *see* couples therapy, rational-emotive
rational-emotive imagery (REI) 29, 165-6, 167
rationalization 158
referenting techniques 29
regret 14, 49
Reichenbach, J. 2
Reichian therapy 68
reinforcement, social 76
relationships
  dialogue between divorced people 146, 149-50
  dissatisfaction in 117-18, 119-20, 135, 136-7
  disturbed 115-19, 120-3, 127-9, 131, 132-3, 135-6, 146, 147-9
  enhancing satisfaction in 129, 136-7
  hostile interchanges in therapy 131
  incompatibility in 119-20
  myths in 119, 129
  other-blaming in 130-1
  therapeutic *see* therapeutic relationship
repression, emotional 93, 112
research into RET 192-201
  and conferences on RET 196-7
  and *Journal of Rational-Emotive Therapy* 194-6
  at Institute for Rational-Emotive Therapy, New York 194
  on measures of 'irrationality' 197-8
  on outcome studies 198-201
resignation 54
'right', meaning of 52
risk-taking exercises 34-5
Rogers, C. R. 22
role expectations 137
role reversal, 'rational' 34
Russell, B. 2

sadness 13, 48-9, 58, 99-100, 101
Saunders, J. B. 141
Schopenhauer, Arthur 2
scientific method 2
secrets between client and therapist 130; *see also* confidentiality
self-acceptance 73
  meaning of 54
self-defeating thoughts/beliefs 30-1; *see also* 'irrational' beliefs (IBs)
self-disclosure
  by supervisor 182
  by therapist 21, 34
'self-fulfilling prophecies' 18-19
self-help form 32-3
self-rating 54
self-statements, 'rational' 28, 35
semantic confusion *see* language and meaning in RET
semantic techniques 29
sessions of RET, typical 24-6

shame 14-15
shame-attacking
exercises 34, 42-3, 103-4
'should', meaning of 51-2
Sichel, J. 32-3
Silverman, M. S. 199, 200
skill training methods 35, 80-1; see also assertion training; communication skills
Smith, Timothy 197
Spinoza, Baruch 2
'stay-in-there' activities 35
Stoicism 2, 113
strategies of treatment 23-6
structural profile 94, 95-7, 98, 106, 107, 111
structuring in therapy 64
style, therapeutic 23, 60-1, 62-3, 90, 91-2
supervision of counsellors 171-91
and trainee anxiety 172-81, 184-91
fostering a helpful climate in 181-5
systems theory 131, 133

tasks of therapy 64-6, 67-71, 82-3, 91
techniques of treatment 26-36
in couples therapy 127-31
theory of RET 4-20, 142-3, 146, 155
therapeutic alliance 59-71
and goals of therapy 63-4, 67, 90-1, 107-8
and tasks of therapy 64-6, 67-71, 82-3, 91
bonds in 59-63, 67, 89-90, 107
in couples therapy 125-7
repair of rifts in 108
therapeutic relationship 20-3, 37-8; see also therapeutic alliance
Tillich, P. 3
time projection 29
'tolerance' 12, 118
tragedies 53
trainee counsellors
anxieties of 172-81, 184
overcoming obstacles to learning by 181-91

unemployment 43

Vertes, R. 51
vivid methods of RET 128

Walen, S. R. 115
warmth, undue, from therapist 22-3, 70, 75
Wessler, R. A. 46
Wessler, R. L. 9, 46, 115
Wolfe, J. L. 200
Wollersheim, J. P. 199
women, independent 120, 136-7
worth, personal, anxiety about 178-80, 184, 185-9

Young, H. S. 46, 119

Index compiled by Peva Keane

For Product Safety Concerns and Information please contact our EU representative GPSR@taylorandfrancis.com
Taylor & Francis Verlag GmbH, Kaufingerstraße 24, 80331 München, Germany

www.ingramcontent.com/pod-product-compliance
Lightning Source LLC
LaVergne TN
LVHW011127300926
849160LV00008B/551

* 9 7 8 1 1 3 8 7 9 1 3 0 5 *